THE
ASIAN KITCHEN

THE
ASIAN KITCHEN

Consulting Editor
LILIAN WU

HERMES
HOUSE

This edition published by Hermes House
© Anness Publishing Limited 2001

Published in the USA by Hermes House, Anness Publishing Inc.
27 West 20th Street, New York, NY 10011

Hermes House is an imprint of Anness Publishing Inc.

Publisher: Joanna Lorenz
Senior Cookbook Editor: Linda Fraser
Project Editor: Sarah Duffin
Designers: Joyce Chester, Peter Laws, Lilian Lindblom,
Alan Marshall, Adrian Morris, Brian Weldon

1 3 5 7 9 10 8 6 4 2

NOTES

Standard spoon and cup measures are level.

Large eggs are used unless otherwise stated.

CONTENTS

INTRODUCTION

Much of Asian cooking is fast, healthy, nutritious and fun. There is an enormous variety of dishes, each with its own very distinctive character and flavor. Whether you want to cook one quick meal or prepare a feast from a selection of different Asian dishes, there are plenty of recipes in this collection to choose from.

Cooking techniques and equipment for stir-frying, steaming and preparation of fresh ingredients are clearly explained. The ingredients used in this book are generally available from large supermarkets and Asian markets. With the emphasis on quick cooking times, it's important to choose only the freshest ingredients. Fresh cuts of meat should be lean and tender and vegetables and herbs bright and fresh.

The book is broken down into chapters on Snacks and Appetizers, Soups, Fish and Shellfish, Meat and Poultry, Vegetable and Vegetarian Dishes, Noodle Dishes, Rice Dishes and Desserts. As well as popular recipes such as Crisp and Aromatic Duck, Pork Chow Mein and Mini Spring Rolls, *The Asian Kitchen* includes less familiar but equally delicious recipes such as Asian Scallops with Ginger Relish and Spicy Squid Salad.

With over 800 step-by-step color photographs to guide you through each stage of the recipes, and sumptuous pictures of the finished dish, *The Asian Kitchen* provides a comprehensive recipe sourcebook and wealth of information to make Asian cooking more accessible than ever before.

Fresh Produce

Almost any ingredient can be stir-fried, and, as the freshness and flavor of the produce will not be affected by cooking, it is important to choose the freshest, best quality ingredients you can.

Baby corn
These may be stir-fried whole or chopped.

Bean sprouts
These impart a lovely texture to vegetable and meat dishes. Do not keep for longer than a few days or they will wilt.

Bell peppers
Deseed and chop into strips before stir-frying.

Chinese greens
The crisp leaves are ideal for stir-frying. Shred or chop finely before using.

Coconut
Fresh coconut is infinitely better tasting than any other coconut product available. When selecting a coconut, choose one with plenty of milk inside.

Cress
This is usually added at the last moment, or as a garnish.

Cucumber
Cucumber can be chopped and sliced finely and stir-fried, or used in relishes.

Daikon
This has a very subtle flavor.

Fennel
Slice and stir-fry to impart an aniseed flavor.

Garlic
Crush or chop finely.

Leeks
Slice into very thin rings before stir-frying.

Lemons
Use the grated zest and juice in stir-fries and marinades, and lemon slices as a garnish.

Limes
Use the grated zest and juice in stir-fries and marinades, and lime slices as a garnish.

Lychees
Peel to use, remove the pit, and halve or slice.

Mango
Ripe mango should have a slightly soft flesh. Peel and remove the pit before use.

Onions
Every variety of onion makes a tasty addition to stir-fries.

Oyster mushrooms
Use as ordinary mushrooms, wiping clean with a damp cloth or paper towel.

Patty pan squash
These small squash taste similar to yellow squash.

Radishes
Slice finely, or use tiny baby radishes as a garnish.

Scallions
Chop finely before using, or cut into julienne strips.

Shiitake mushrooms
These tasty, firm-textured mushrooms may be treated as ordinary mushrooms. Only use half the amount if using the dried variety. Soak in boiling water for 20 minutes, and save the soaking water for a sauce.

Spinach
Remove the stalks before using and wash thoroughly in several changes of cold water to remove any grit.

Counter-clockwise from top left: *red bell peppers, coconuts, lychees, shiitake mushrooms, spinach, onions, bean sprouts, cress, Chinese greens, daikon, radishes, baby corn, scallions, leeks, oyster and shiitake mushrooms, yellow bell pepper, fennel, celery.* In center basket, from top left: *patty pan squash, mango, limes, garlic, lemons.*

Flavorings and Spices

Asian cooking is so popular that even small supermarkets tend to stock an extensive selection of flavoring ingredients.

Black bean sauce

This sauce is made from salted fermented soybeans that have been crushed and mixed to a thick paste with flavorings. Black bean sauce is highly concentrated and is usually added to hot oil at the start of cooking to release the flavor.

Yellow bean sauce

A purée of fermented yellow beans combined with salt, flour and sugar. This is a thick, sweetish, smooth sauce and is often used in marinades.

Chilies

A wide variety of these hot members of the capsicum family is available. They are most often used for flavoring, but plump ones can be stuffed and served as a vegetable, once the fiery seeds have been removed.

Chili oil

This reddish vegetable oil owes both its color and spicy flavor to the chilies that have been steeped or marinated in it. Use chili oil sparingly in cooking or as a peppery dipping sauce.

Dried shrimp

Dried, salty shrimp used as a flavoring and also as an ingredient. The shrimp are always soaked in warm water first to remove some of the salt.

They have a strong flavor, so should be used sparingly.

Five-spice powder

A finely ground mixture of fennel seeds, star anise, Szechuan peppercorns, cloves and cinnamon. It has a fairly strong licorice taste and a pungent spicy aroma and should be used sparingly. It can be used in both sweet and savory dishes.

Garlic

This small, aromatic vegetable is one of the most important flavoring ingredients in Asian cooking. The most common way of preparing garlic is to peel it, then chop it finely or grind it. However, garlic is sometimes simply bruised or peeled and sliced.

Above: Some typically piquant flavorings: dried shrimp, five-spice powder and licorice-tasting whole star anise.

Ginger

Fresh ginger root is an essential flavoring ingredient in Asian cooking. It is peeled, then sliced, shredded or ground before use. Dried ginger or ground ginger do not have the same fresh flavor and are not suitable as a substitute. Fresh ginger root freezes well. Keep a well-wrapped, peeled root in the freezer and grate it as required. It will thaw instantly.

Hoisin sauce

A thick, rich, dark sauce often used for flavoring meat and

Left: Chili oil, sesame oil and rice vinegar enliven savory dishes.

poultry before cooking. It is also sometimes used as one of the ingredients in a dipping sauce.

Lotus leaves

The dried leaves of the lotus plant are used as an aromatic wrapping for steamed dishes. Lotus leaves must be soaked in warm water for 30 minutes to soften them before use.

Oyster sauce

This thick, dark sauce is made from oyster juice, flour, salt and sugar. It is usually added to dishes at the end of cooking.

Rice vinegar

A colorless, slightly sweet vinegar used to add sharpness to sweet-and-sour dishes. If rice vinegar is not obtainable, white wine vinegar or cider vinegar sweetened with sugar can be used as a substitute.

Rock sugar

An aptly named ingredient that consists of irregular lumps of amber-colored sugar. Derived from sugar cane, rock sugar is mainly used in sweet dishes and has a caramelized flavor.

Sesame oil

This aromatic oil is made from roasted sesame seeds. Small quantities are used as an accent at the end of cooking to add flavor to a dish; in Asian cooking it is not used for frying.

Dark soy sauce

A rich, dark sauce that is used to add both color and flavor to many sauces and marinades. Dark soy sauce is quite salty and is often used instead of salt to season a dish.

Above (clockwise from top left): Yellow bean sauce, black bean sauce, oyster sauce, dark and light soy sauce and hoisin sauce.
Below left: Garlic, fresh ginger root and red and green, dried and fresh chilies are essential ingredients in any Asian kitchen.
Below far left: Aromatic dried lotus leaves are commonly soaked until soft and then used to make wrapped steamed dishes, such as Sticky Rice Parcels.

Light soy sauce

A thin, dark sauce used for flavoring many Asian dishes and also as a table condiment. The flavor is slightly lighter and fresher than dark soy sauce, but it is a little more salty.

Star anise

A strong licorice-tasting spice mainly used to flavor meat and poultry. The whole spice is frequently used in braised dishes so that the flavor can be released and absorbed slowly.

Seaweed, Rice and Wheat Products

All these ingredients keep well in the pantry or freezer, so it is worth stocking up next time you visit an Asian market.

Agar-agar

A setting agent made from seaweed and mainly used in sweet jellies. Unlike gelatin, agar-agar must be boiled if it is to dissolve completely, and will set firm without refrigeration.

Brown rice

This unpolished, long-grain rice has a delicious nutty flavor and slightly chewy texture. It is not normally used in traditional Asian cooking, but is included here because it has gained in popularity in recent years due to its nutritional value. Some enlightened restaurateurs now offer it either boiled or stir-fried (as in this book) as an alternative to white rice.

Above: Agar-agar, a setting agent made from seaweed. Right: Various types of noodles, thick and thin, fresh and dried.

Glutinous rice

This is a short-grain rice that sticks together when cooked. Glutinous rice is used in both savory and sweet dishes and is usually soaked in water for about 2 hours before being cooked over boiling water in a large steamer lined with clean muslin or cheesecloth.

Long-grain rice

Polished white rice that forms the basis of most Asian meals. The usual method of serving rice is simply boiled but sometimes, for variety and richness, boiled rice is fried with other flavoring ingredients, such as sliced scallions, chopped white or shiitake mushrooms, garlic, dried shrimp and eggs.

Egg noodles

Thick noodles made from flour, egg and water, these are sold fresh or dried. The noodles must be boiled before being used in fried or soup dishes, such as Seafood Soup Noodles.

Left: Rice in various forms. Although white rice (long-grain or the sticky glutinous type) is traditional, brown rice has become a tasty and nutritious option in Asian cooking.

available at most Asian markets. They should be thawed, then placed in a covered bamboo steamer or heatproof plate and steamed over boiling water in a large saucepan or wok for about 3 minutes before serving.

Wonton wrappers

Made from wheat flour, eggs and water, these small, square, wafer-thin wrappers are produced specifically for making wontons, which are essentially little ground pork dumplings encased in the wrappers and then gently poached in simmering water. Wonton wrappers are available either fresh or frozen at Asian markets.

Thin egg noodles

Made from the same ingredients as egg noodles, these are much thinner. Thin egg noodles must be precooked in boiling water according to the instructions on the package before being used in recipes, such as Toasted Noodles with Vegetables. In this recipe, the noodles are shallow-fried in a small frying pan until they stick together to form flat toasted noodle cakes, which are then used as a base for stir-fried mixed vegetables.

Rice noodles

Thin, white noodles made from rice flour, these are usually sold dried. The dried noodles cook very quickly and must simply be soaked in boiling water for about 5 minutes, until soft, before being added to stir-fries and other dishes.

Chinese crêpes

These thin, round, white crêpes, made from wheat flour and water, are best known for eating with Peking Duck. They are sold frozen and are

Right: Bamboo steamers with Chinese crêpes and wonton wrappers; both are used to wrap foods. Wonton wrappers are traditionally filled with a ground pork stuffing and then steamed or cooked in soup. Fish and shellfish can be substituted to make a low-fat version.

Vegetables and Mushrooms

Authentic ingredients make all the difference.
Look for these at Asian markets.

Bamboo shoots

Crunchy young shoots from the
bamboo plant, these have a delicate but distinctive flavor. They
are available in cans, either
whole, sliced or cut into thin,
matchstick-size shreds.

Chinese mushrooms

When fresh, these are sold as
shiitake mushrooms, but the
dried version is more widely
used in Asian cooking. Dried
Chinese mushrooms have a
more concentrated flavor. Soak
in hot water before use.

Cloud ears, wood ears

Dried edible fungi that have a
crunchy texture; cloud ears have
a more delicate flavor than
wood ears. Once reconstituted
in water they expand to many
times their original size.

Straw mushrooms

These are grown on rice straw
and have a slippery, meaty texture with little flavor. At present
these mushrooms are only available canned. In Asian cooking,
they are used mainly for their
texture.

Lotus root

A crunchy vegetable with natu-
rally occurring holes, lotus root
is occasionally sold fresh, but is
more frequently available dried
or frozen. When cut and pulled
apart, threadlike strands are
produced from the cut surfaces.
Also known as renkon.

Taro

A starchy tuber used in both
savory and sweet dishes. It
looks like a hairy rutabaga with
white flesh slightly marked
by purplish dots. The flavor
and texture resemble those of
a potato.

Water chestnuts

Once peeled, these black-
skinned bulbs reveal a white,
crunchy interior with a sweet
flavor. Canned, peeled water
chestnuts are available in most
supermarkets, but the fresh,
unpeeled bulb can sometimes
be bought in Asian markets.

*Above, from top left: Fresh shi-
itake mushrooms, canned
straw mushrooms, dried cloud
ears and Chinese mushrooms.
Left, from top left: Bamboo
shoots, the large tuber known
as taro, lotus root with its nat-
urally occurring holes and
water chestnuts.*

Beans and Bean Products

Packed with protein, these are essential staple ingredients that no self-respecting Asian cook should be without.

Adzuki beans

Small red beans used mainly in sweet dishes. As with most dried beans, adzuki beans must be soaked in water before use. They should be boiled rapidly for 10 minutes at the start of cooking, then simmered until soft before use.

Bean curd (tofu)

As its name suggests, this is a cheeselike product made from soybeans. Fresh bean curd is sold covered in water. It has very little flavor of its own, but readily absorbs flavorings. Bean curd is used extensively in Asian cooking and is a good source of protein. There are several different types, including "silken" tofu and smoked tofu, but the firm variety is the one normally used by the Chinese.

Dried bean curd (tofu) sticks

These are sheets of bean curd that have been formed into sticks and dried. They are an important ingredient in Asian vegetarian dishes. They must be soaked in hot water before being used. Bean curd sticks are usually available only in Asian markets.

Right, from bottom left: Aduki beans, fresh bean curd (tofu) and dried bean curd (tofu) sticks, protein-rich components of many Asian recipes.

Equipment

You will not need any special equipment to cook the recipes in this book. There are, however, one or two inexpensive items, such as bamboo steamers or a trivet, that are well worth buying if you don't already possess them.

Bamboo steamers

These are available in a range of sizes at Asian markets and all are quite inexpensive. Steamers of the same size will stack on top of each other and offer a novel way of presenting individual portions of steamed food. Be sure to buy the steamer lid as well, to prevent water from dripping onto the food that is being cooked.

Bamboo strainer (skimmer)

This is made from twisted thin wire and is wide and flat in shape with a long bamboo handle. Useful for lifting food from stock or boiling water, they come in various sizes.

Food processor

Not a traditional Asian utensil, but nonetheless a very useful piece of equipment that saves a lot of preparation time and effort. If you do not have one, don't worry—with patience and a sharp knife, you can often achieve the desired result. Cooked foods that require puréeing can be passed through a fine sieve if necessary.

Muslin or cheesecloth

Muslin and cheesecloth are useful for straining stock. Muslin can be washed and used over and over again; scald the muslin by pouring boiling water over it in a large, heatproof bowl.

Nonstick pan

A deep-sided nonstick frying pan is essential for low-fat cooking, as the special coating will help to prevent the food

Above: Wooden spoons and spatulas and wire strainers or skimmers with bamboo handles are ideal for stirring, turning or lifting food during cooking.

from sticking to the pan without the need to add lots of oil.

Roasting pan and meat rack

A small roasting pan with a metal rack is useful for roasting or broiling meats, as it allows the meat to cook dry rather than in a pool of juice. This also cuts the fat content, since the fat drips away.

Sharp knives

Sharp knives are vital in Asian cooking, as many ingredients are cut or chopped into bite-size pieces. A cook's knife is necessary for chopping and cutting and a small paring knife for peeling or cutting small items. It is not necessary to buy a cleaver, as this utensil can be

Left: Useful pans for stir-frying include a nonstick frying pan with deep sides and single-handled woks. Save two-handled woks for steaming

heavy and needs getting used to if it is to be used effectively.

Trivet

A round metal trivet is very useful in the kitchen. When steaming in a wok or saucepan, stand the trivet in the pan to raise a plate or bamboo steamer above the water level.

Woks

Nonstick woks are available but tend to be fairly expensive. Unless you already have a nonstick wok, use a deep-sided nonstick frying pan for stir-frying and save your iron wok for steaming. When buying a wok, give some thought to its use. Two-handled woks are used for steaming and braising, while those with a single long handle are normally used for stir-frying (the wok is lifted and shaken with one hand while the other hand stirs the food inside).

Wok lid

The domed lid that is provided with the wok is extremely useful for steaming. It provides ample space for the steam to circulate and also allows the condensed water to slip down the sides without falling onto the food.

Wooden spoons and spatulas

When using a nonstick pan it is important to use a wooden spoon or spatula to stir the food so that the nonstick coating is neither scratched nor damaged.

Right: Bamboo steamers in different sizes, with tight-fitting lids. Several steamers can be stacked and used at once.

Cooking Techniques

STIR-FRYING

This quick technique retains the fresh flavor, color and texture of ingredients and its success depends upon having all the required ingredients prepared before cooking.

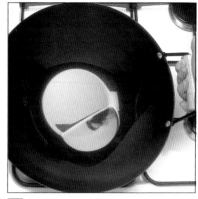

1 Heat an empty wok over high heat. This prevents food sticking and will ensure an even heat. Add the oil and swirl it around so that it coats the bottom and halfway up the sides of the wok. It is important that the oil is hot enough so that when food is added it will start to cook immediately, but it should not be so hot that it is smoking.

2 Ingredients should then be added in a specific order, usually aromatics first (garlic, ginger, scallions). If this is the case, do not wait for the oil to get so hot that it is almost smoking or they will burn and become bitter. Toss them in the oil for a few seconds. Now add the main ingredients which require longer cooking, such as dense vegetables or meat, followed by the faster-cooking items. Toss and turn the ingredients from the center of the wok to the sides.

DEEP FRYING

A wok is ideal for deep-frying as it uses far less oil than a deep-fat fryer. Make sure, however, that it is fully secure on its stand before adding the oil and never leave the wok unattended.

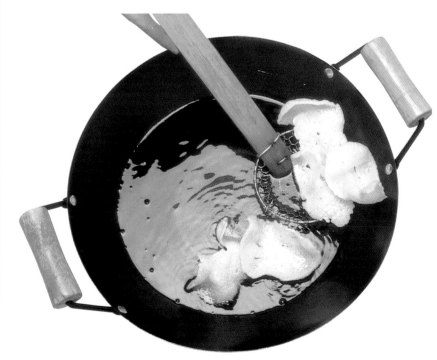

1 Put the wok on a stand and half-fill with oil. Heat until the required temperature registers on a thermometer. Alternatively, test it by dropping in a small piece of food; if bubbles form all over the surface of the food, the oil is ready.

2 Carefully add the food to the oil using long wooden chopsticks or tongs and move it around to prevent it sticking together. Using a bamboo strainer or slotted spoon, carefully remove the food and drain on paper towels before serving.

STEAMING

Steamed foods are cooked by a gentle moist heat which must circulate freely in order for the food to cook. Increasingly popular with health conscious cooks, steaming preserves flavor and nutrients. It is perfect for vegetables, meat, poultry and especially fish. The easiest way to steam in a wok is with a bamboo steamer but you can do without.

USING A BAMBOO STEAMER IN A WOK

1 Put the wok on a stand. Pour about 2 in water into the wok and bring to simmering point. Put the bamboo steamer containing the food into the wok, where it will rest on the sloping sides.

2 Cover the steamer with its matching lid and steam for the recommended time. Check the water level occasionally and add with boiling water as necessary.

USING A WOK AS A STEAMER

1 Place a trivet in the wok, then place the wok on its stand on the burner. Pour in enough boiling water to come just below the trivet, then carefully place the plate holding whatever is to be steamed on the trivet.

2 Cover the wok with its lid, bring to a boil, then lower the heat to a gentle simmer. Steam for the recommended time, checking the water level occasionally and adding with boiling water as necessary.

Preparing Shrimp

While not harmful, the black threadlike vein may spoil the flavor of shrimp if not removed.

1 Holding the shrimp firmly in one hand, pull off the legs with the fingers of the other hand. Pull off the head.

2 Peel the shell away from the body. When you reach the tail, hold the body and firmly pull away the tail; the shell will come off with it.

3 Make a shallow cut down the center of the curved back of the shrimp. Using the knife tip, pull out and discard the black vein that runs along the length of the body.

Preparing Squid

Large or small squid are easy to prepare once you know how, and there is very little waste.

1 Holding the body of the squid in one hand, gently pull away the head and tentacles. Discard the head, then trim and reserve the tentacles.

2 Remove the transparent "quill" from inside the body of the squid, then peel off the purple skin. Rub a little salt into the squid and wash well.

3 Cut the body of the squid into rings or slit it open lengthwise, score crisscross patterns on the inside and cut it into pieces.

Five Ways of Cutting Scallions

In Asian cooking, the appearance of a dish is almost as important as its taste.

1 Trim off the roots and remove any wilted ends or leaves.

2 Rings: Gather the scallions and cut straight across into fine rings.

3 Diagonal cuts: Thickly slice the scallions, holding the knife at an angle of about 60° to give uniform diamond-shaped pieces.

4 Shreds: Cut the scallions into 2-inch lengths, then slice each piece in half lengthwise. Finally, cut the scallions lengthwise into fine shreds.

5 Chunks: Cut the scallions into uniform 1-inch pieces.

6 Tassels: Cut the white part only into 2½-inch lengths. Shred one end of each piece, keeping the other end of the piece intact. Place in ice water for about 30 minutes, until the shreds curl.

Cutting Carrots and Similar Vegetables

Use these techniques for other firm vegetables, such as zucchini.

1 Peel the carrots using a vegetable peeler and trim off both ends.

2 Rounds: Hold the carrot with one hand and cut straight across to give thin, uniform-size rounds.

3 Diagonal cuts: Holding the knife with the blade at an angle of about 60°, cut the carrot into thin, even diagonal slices.

4 Matchsticks: Cut the carrot into thin diagonal slices (see step 3 above). Stack two or three of the slices at a time and cut them into matchsticks.

5 Roll cuts: Holding one end of the carrot firmly, cut the other end off diagonally in a fairly thick slice. Roll the carrot through 180° and make another diagonal slice to make a triangular wedge. Roll and slice the rest of the carrot in the same way.

Preparing Fresh Ginger Root

Always use a very sharp knife to ensure that the pieces are an even size.

Preparing Dried Chinese Mushrooms or Cloud Ears

Dried wood ears are prepared in the same way as the cloud ears pictured at bottom.

1 Bruising: Lay the washed but unpeeled ginger on a board. Using the side of a large knife, a cleaver or a rolling pin, bang down hard on the ginger.

2 any of the knobbly pieces. Using a vegetable peeler or a small sharp knife, peel off the skin.

1 Soak mushrooms or cloud ears in hot water for 30 minutes, or until softened. Rinse thoroughly.

2 Remove and discard the stalks from the soaked mushrooms and use the caps whole, sliced or chopped.

3 Slicing: Holding the ginger firmly with one hand, cut diagonally in thin slices.

4 Shredding: Stack several thin slices of ginger on top of each other and cut carefully into fine shreds.

5 Chopping: Gather the shreds together and cut across to give fine pieces, then chop repeatedly until the ginger is finely ground.

3 Cut soaked cloud ears into small pieces, discarding the tough base.

Preparing Chilies

The strong taste of chili is a wonderful flavoring, but fresh chilies must be handled with care. Always work in a well ventilated area, and do not let the chili touch your skin. Do not rub your eyes after handling.

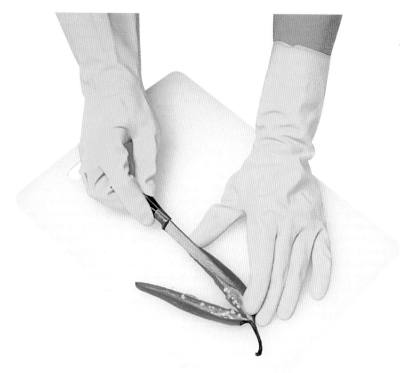

1 Slice the chilies, and remove the seeds. You may want to wear rubber gloves to protect your skin.

2 Finely chop and use as required.

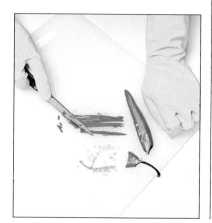

Shredding Cabbage

Delicious stir-fried, this method means the cabbage will cook evenly.

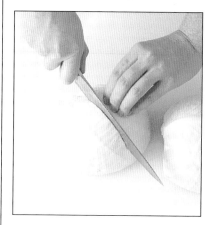 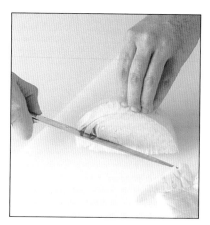

1 Use a large knife to cut the cabbage into quarters.

2 Cut the core from each quarter.

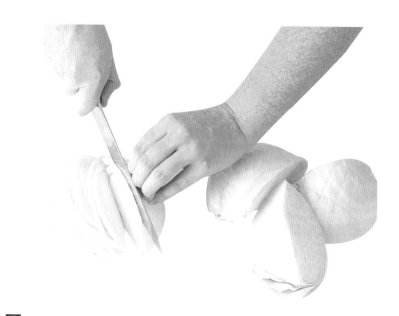

3 Slice across each quarter to form fine shreds.

Preparing Coconut Flakes

Although many convenient coconut products are available—canned milk and dried coconut flakes—nothing beats fresh coconut for flavor in cooking.

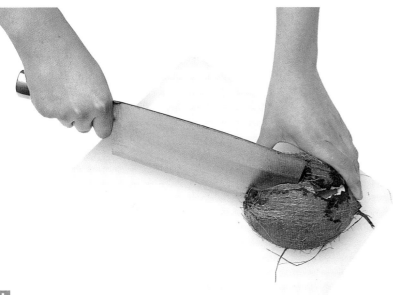

1 Cut the coconut in two using a heavy cleaver, and pour out the milk.

2 Peel the flesh away from the shell using a vegetable peeler.

Preparing Daikon

This giant white radish is appreciated in stir-fries for its crisp texture.

1 Peel the daikon and cut into 3-inch long sticks for stir-frying.

2 To use as a relish, grate with a lemon zester. If you don't have a zester, chop the daikon very finely.

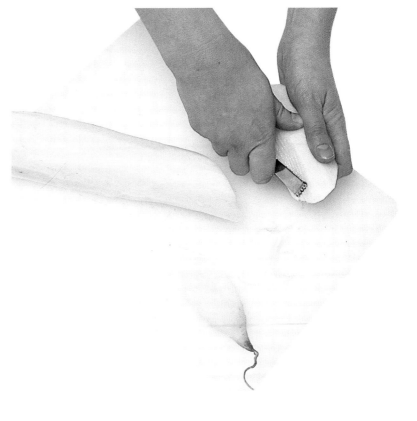

Slicing Onions

Stir-fry onion slices with the main vegetables. Ensure they are all cut to the same size for even cooking.

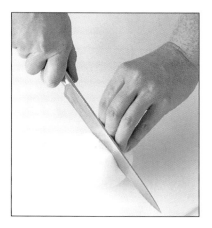

1 Peel the onion. Cut in half with a large knife and set it cut-side down on to a chopping board.

2 Cut out a triangular piece of the core from each half.

3 Cut across each half in vertical slices.

Chopping Onions

Diced onions can be used to flavor oil before stir-frying the main ingredients.

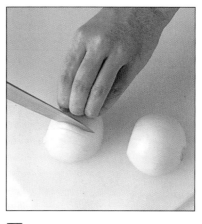

1 Peel the onion. Cut in half with a knife and set it cut-side down on a board. Make lengthwise vertical cuts along the onion, cutting almost through to the root.

2 Make 2 horizontal cuts from the stalk and toward the root, but not through it.

3 Cut the onion crosswise to form small dice.

Garnishes

Many Asian dishes rely on garnishes to add a colorful finishing decorative touch. The garnishes can be simple, such as chopped cilantro, fresh herb sprigs, or finely shredded scallions or chili, or more elaborate, such as cucumber fans, scallion brushes and chili flowers.

CHILI FLOWER

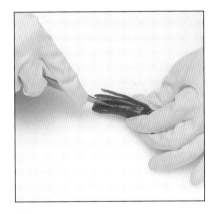

1 Make several lengthwise cuts through a chili from below the stalk to the tip. Remove and discard any seeds.

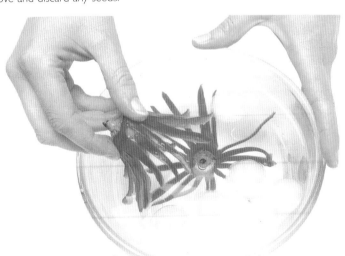

2 Soak the chili in iced water until the ends curl to form a "flower". Pat dry with paper towels before use.

CUCUMBER FAN

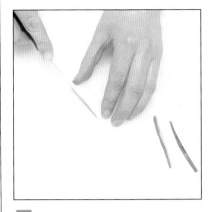

1 Cut a slice of cucumber lengthwise, about 3 in long, avoiding the seeds. Remove any skin and cut into strips to within ½ in from the end. Remove alternate strips.

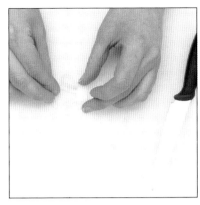

2 Carefully bend the strips towards the uncut end, tucking them in so that they stay securely in place. Allow to soak in iced water until required and pat dry before use.

SCALLION BRUSH

1 Trim the green part of a scallion and remove the base of the bulb – you should then be left with a piece about 3 in long. Then make a lengthwise cut approximately 1 in long at one end of the scallion.

2 Roll the scallion through 90° and cut again. Repeat this process at the other end. Place in iced water until the shreds open out and curl. Pat dry with paper towels before use.

Vegetable Stock

Use this light but flavorful stock for cooking rice and noodles, as well as for soup.

Makes about 5 cups

INGREDIENTS
3 carrots
2 zucchini
2 leeks
1 celery rib
1 large onion
10 black peppercorns
5 cups cold water

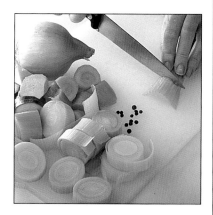

1 Cut the carrot into chunks. Slice the zucchini, leeks, celery and onion.

2 Place all the vegetables in a large saucepan with the peppercorns and water. Bring to a boil, lower the heat, cover and simmer for 15 minutes.

3 Allow the stock to cool before straining through a sieve lined with muslin or cheesecloth. The stock can be stored in the refrigerator for up to 3 days or frozen for about 3 weeks.

Fish Stock

Make shellfish stock in the same way, using an equivalent amount of shrimp shells and heads.

Makes about 7½ cups

INGREDIENTS
1 onion
2 leeks
2 carrots
3–3½ pounds fish heads and bones
5 black peppercorns
7½ cups cold water

1 Cut the onion into quarters, slice the leeks and cut the carrots into chunks.

2 Place all the vegetables and the fish heads and bones in a large saucepan with the peppercorns and water. Bring to a boil. Skim off any scum that rises to the surface, then lower the heat, cover and simmer for 15 minutes.

3 Allow the stock to cool completely. Strain through a sieve lined with muslin or cheesecloth before use. The stock can be stored in the refrigerator for 2–3 days or frozen for 2–3 weeks.

Chicken Stock

This versatile stock is an essential ingredient in every Asian kitchen.

Makes about 6¼ cups

INGREDIENTS
3 chicken carcasses
2 onions, quartered
3 carrots, cut into large chunks
2-inch piece of fresh ginger
    root, bruised
10 black peppercorns
7½ cups cold water

1 Using a pair of poultry shears, cut the chicken carcasses into small pieces. Place them in a large saucepan. Add the onions, carrots, ginger, peppercorns and water and bring to a boil.

2 Boil for 5 minutes, skimming off any scum that rises to the surface. Lower the heat, cover and simmer for 1 hour.

3 Allow the stock to cool. Strain through a sieve lined with muslin or cheesecloth. The stock can be stored in the refrigerator for 2–3 days or frozen for 2–3 weeks. Skim off any hardened fat from the surface of the stock before use.

Beef Stock

Browning the beef bones in the oven first creates a richly flavored stock.

Makes about 5 cups

INGREDIENTS
5 pounds beef shin bones, broken
    into small pieces
4 carrots, cut into large chunks
2 onions, quartered
2 celery ribs, cut into large pieces
5 garlic cloves, crushed
10 black peppercorns
7½ cups cold water

1 Preheat the oven to 375°F. Spread out the beef bones in a large roasting pan. Add the prepared carrots, onions, celery and garlic and roast for about 25 minutes.

2 Using a slotted spoon or tongs, transfer the bones and vegetables to a large saucepan, leaving behind any fat in the roasting pan. Add the peppercorns.

3 Pour in the water and bring to a boil. Boil for 5 minutes, skimming off any scum that rises to the surface of the liquid, then lower the heat, cover and simmer for 2 hours. The stock can be stored in the refrigerator for 2–3 days or frozen for 2–3 weeks. Skim off any hardened fat from the surface of the stock before use.

SNACKS AND APPETIZERS

Many of the recipes in this section can be served separately as snacks or at the table before the main course. Balance and contrast play an important part in an Asian meal, so consider how each dish complements another when planning the menu.

Crisp "Seaweed" with Sliced Almonds

This popular appetizer in Chinese restaurants is in fact usually made not with seaweed but collard greens or Swiss chard! It is easy to make at home.

Serves 4-6

INGREDIENTS
1 lb spring greens
peanut oil, for deep-frying
¼ tsp sea salt flakes
1 tsp sugar
½ cup sliced almonds, toasted

greens

almonds

peanut oil

sea salt

sugar

COOK'S TIP
It is important to dry the greens thoroughly before deep-frying them, otherwise it will be difficult to achieve the desired crispness without destroying their vivid color.

1 Wash the greens under cold running water and then pat well with paper towels to dry thoroughly. Remove and discard the thick white stalks from the greens.

2 Lay several leaves on top of one another, roll up tightly and, using a sharp knife, slice as finely as possible into thread-like strips.

3 Half-fill a wok with oil and heat to 350°F. Deep-fry the greens in batches for about 1 minute until they darken and crisp. Remove each batch from the wok as soon as it is ready and drain on paper towels.

4 Transfer the "seaweed" to a serving dish, sprinkle with the salt and sugar, then mix well. Garnish with the toasted sliced almonds sprinkled over.

Shrimp Toasts with Sesame Seeds

This healthy version of the ever-popular appetizer has lost none of its classic crunch and taste.

Serves 4–6

INGREDIENTS
6 slices white bread, crusts removed
8 oz raw tiger shrimp, shelled
   and deveined
⅓ cup drained, canned water
   chestnuts
1 egg white
1 tsp sesame oil
½ tsp salt
2 scallions, finely chopped
2 tsp dry sherry
1 tbsp sesame seeds, toasted
   (see Cook's Tip)
shredded scallion, to garnish

sherry

bread

shrimp

water chestnuts

egg

sesame seeds

sesame oil

scallions

COOK'S TIP
To toast sesame seeds, put them in a dry frying pan and place over medium heat until the seeds change color. Shake the pan constantly to prevent them from burning.

1 Preheat the oven to 250°F. Cut each slice of bread into four triangles. Spread out on a baking sheet and bake for 25 minutes, or until crisp.

2 Meanwhile, put the shrimp in a food processor with the water chestnuts, egg white, sesame oil and salt. Process until a coarse purée is formed.

3 Scrape the mixture into a bowl, stir in the chopped scallions and sherry and marinate for 10 minutes.

4 Remove the toast from the oven and raise the temperature to 400°F. Spread the shrimp mixture on the toast, sprinkle with sesame seeds and bake for 12 minutes. Garnish with scallion and serve hot or warm.

Mini Spring Rolls

Eat these light crispy parcels with your fingers. If you like slightly spicier food, sprinkle them with a little cayenne pepper before serving.

Makes 20

INGREDIENTS
1 green chili
½ cup vegetable oil
1 small onion, finely chopped
1 clove garlic, crushed
3 oz cooked chicken breast portion
1 small carrot, cut into fine matchsticks
1 scallion, finely sliced
1 small red bell pepper, seeded and cut into fine matchsticks
1 oz bean sprouts
1 tsp sesame oil
4 large sheets filo pastry
1 medium egg white, lightly beaten
long chives, to garnish (optional)
3 tbsp light soy sauce, to serve

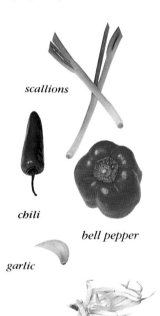

scallions

chili

bell pepper

garlic

bean sprouts

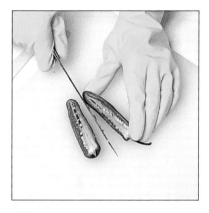

1 Carefully remove the seeds from the chili and chop finely, wearing rubber gloves to protect your hands, if necessary.

2 Heat the wok, then add 2 tbsp of the vegetable oil. When hot, add the onion, garlic and chili. Stir-fry for 1 minute.

3 Slice the chicken thinly, then add to the wok and fry over a high heat, stirring constantly until browned.

COOK'S TIP
Be careful to avoid touching your face or eyes when deseeding and chopping chilies because they are very potent and may cause burning and irritation to the skin. Try preparing chilies under running water.

4 Add the carrot, scallion and red bell pepper and stir-fry for 2 minutes. Add the bean sprouts, stir in the sesame oil and leave to cool.

COOK'S TIP
Always keep filo pastry sheets covered with a dry, clean cloth until needed, to prevent them drying out.

5 Cut each sheet of filo into 5 short strips. Place a small amount of filling at one end of each strip, then fold in the long sides and roll up the pastry. Seal and glaze the parcels with the egg white, then chill uncovered for 15 minutes before frying.

6 Wipe out the wok with paper towels, heat it, and add the remaining vegetable oil. When the oil is hot, fry the rolls in batches until crisp and golden brown. Drain on paper towels and serve dipped in light soy sauce.

Chinese Spiced Salt Spareribs

Fragrant with spices, this authentic Chinese dish makes a great beginning to an informal meal. Don't forget the finger bowls!

Serves 4

INGREDIENTS
1½–2 lb meaty pork spareribs
1½ tbsp cornstarch
peanut oil, for deep frying
cilantro sprigs, to garnish

FOR THE SPICED SALT
1 tsp Szechuan peppercorns
2 tbsp coarse sea salt
½ tsp Chinese five-
    spice powder

FOR THE MARINADE
2 tbsp light soy sauce
1 tsp sugar
1 tbsp Chinese rice wine
ground black pepper

Chinese rice wine

pork spareribs

Szechuan peppercorns

Chinese five-spice powder

cilantro

light soy sauce

peanut oil

sea salt

1 Using a heavy sharp cleaver, chop the spareribs into pieces about 2 in long or ask your butcher to do this, then place them in a shallow dish.

2 To make the spiced salt, heat a wok to medium heat. Add the Szechuan peppercorns and salt and dry-fry for about 3 minutes, stirring constantly, until the mixture colors slightly. Remove from the heat and stir in the five-spice powder. Allow to cool.

3 Using a mortar and pestle or an electric coffee grinder, grind the spiced salt to a fine powder.

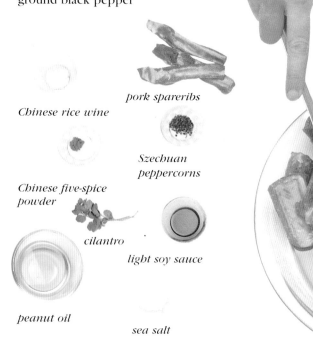

4 Sprinkle 1 tsp of the spiced salt over the spareribs and rub in well with your hands. Add the soy sauce, sugar, rice wine or sherry and some freshly ground black pepper, then toss the ribs in the marinade until well coated. Cover and allow to marinate in the refrigerator for about 2 hours, turning the spareribs occasionally.

COOK'S TIP

Any leftover spiced salt can be kept for several months in a screw-top jar. Use to rub on the flesh of duck, chicken or pork before cooking.

5 Pour off any excess marinade from the spareribs. Sprinkle the pieces with cornstarch and mix well to coat evenly.

6 Half-fill a wok with oil and heat to 350°F. Deep-fry the spareribs in batches for 3 minutes, until pale golden. Remove and set aside. Reheat the oil to the same temperature. Return the spareribs to the oil and deep-fry for a second time for 1–2 minutes, until crisp and thoroughly cooked. Drain on paper towels. Transfer the ribs to a warmed serving platter and sprinkle over 1–1½ tsp spiced salt. Garnish with cilantro sprigs.

Steamed Spiced Pork and Water Chestnut Wontons

Ginger and Chinese five-spice powder flavor this version of steamed open dumplings—a favorite snack in many teahouses.

Makes about 36

INGREDIENTS
2 large Chinese cabbage leaves, plus extra for lining the steamer
2 scallions, finely chopped
½-in piece fresh ginger root, finely chopped
2 oz canned water chestnuts (drained weight), rinsed and finely chopped
8oz ground pork
½ tsp Chinese five-spice powder
1 tbsp cornstarch
1 tbsp light soy sauce
1 tbsp Chinese rice wine
2 tsp sesame oil
generous pinch of sugar
about 36 wonton wrappers, each 3 in square
light soy sauce and hot chili oil, for dipping

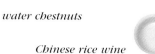
caster sugar

Chinese cabbage

scallions

cornstarch

water chestnuts

pork

Chinese rice wine

ginger root

light soy sauce

sesame oil

wonton wrappers

Chinese five-spice powder

VARIATION
These can also be deep-fried, in which case fold the edges over the filling to enclose it completely. Press well to seal. Deep-fry in batches in hot oil for about 2 minutes.

1 Place the Chinese cabbage leaves one on top of another. Cut them lengthwise into quarters and then across into thin shreds.

2 Place the shredded Chinese cabbage leaves in a bowl. Add the scallions, ginger, water chestnuts, pork, five-spice powder, cornstarch, soy sauce, rice wine, sesame oil and sugar; mix well.

3 Set one wonton wrapper on a work surface. Place a heaped teaspoon of the filling in the center of the wrapper, then lightly dampen the edges with water.

4 Lift the wrapper up around the filling, gathering to form a purse. Squeeze the wrapper firmly around the middle, then tap on the bottom to make a flat base. The top should be open. Place the wonton on a tray and cover with a damp dish towel.

5 Line the steamer with cabbage leaves and steam the dumplings for 12–15 minutes or until tender. Remove each batch from the steamer as soon as they are cooked, cover with foil and keep warm. Serve hot with soy sauce and chili oil for dipping.

Chicken Cigars

These small crisp rolls can be served warm as canapés with a drink before a meal, or as a first course with a crisp, colorful salad.

Serves 4

INGREDIENTS
1 x 10 oz package of phyllo pastry
3 tbsp olive oil
fresh parsley, to garnish

FOR THE FILLING
12 oz ground raw chicken
salt and freshly ground black pepper
1 egg, beaten
½ tsp ground cinnamon
½ tsp ground ginger
2 tbsp raisins
1 tbsp olive oil
1 small onion, finely chopped

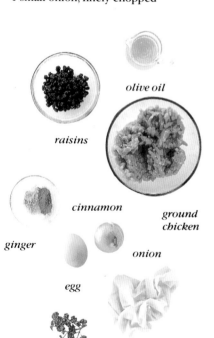

olive oil

raisins

cinnamon

ground chicken

ginger

onion

egg

parsley

phyllo pastry

1 Mix all the filling ingredients, except the oil and onion, together in a bowl. Heat the oil in a large frying pan and cook the onion until tender. Leave to cool, then add the remaining mixed ingredients.

2 Preheat the oven to 350°F. Once the filo pastry package has been opened, keep the pastry completely covered at all times with a damp dish towel. Work fast, as the pastry dries out very quickly when exposed to the air. Unravel the pastry and cut into even 10 × 4 in strips.

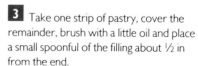

3 Take one strip of pastry, cover the remainder, brush with a little oil and place a small spoonful of the filling about ½ in from the end.

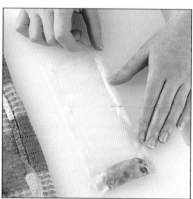

4 To encase the filling, fold the sides inwards to a width of 2 in and roll into a cigar shape. Place on a greased baking sheet and brush with oil. Bake for about 20–25 minutes until golden brown and crisp. Garnish with fresh parsley.

Fried Vegetables in Wonton Cups

These crispy cups are an ideal way to serve stir-fried vegetables; use your imagination to vary the fillings.

Makes 24

INGREDIENTS

2 tbsp vegetable oil, plus extra
  for greasing
24 small wonton wrappers
½ cup hoisin sauce or plum sauce
  (optional)
1 tsp sesame oil
1 garlic clove, finely chopped
½-in piece fresh ginger root, finely
  chopped
2-in piece of lemongrass, crushed
6 to 8 asparagus spears, cut into
  1¼-in pieces
**8 to 10 ears baby corn, cut in half
  lengthwise**
1 small red bell pepper, seeded and
  cut into short slivers
1 to 2 tbsp sugar
2 tbsp soy sauce
juice of 1 lime
1 to 2 tsp Chinese-style chili sauce
  (or to taste)
1 tsp *huac nam* or Thai or other fish
  sauce

lemongrass

hoisin sauce

red bell pepper

wonton wrappers

baby corn

vegetable oil

asparagus

sesame oil

soy sauce

garlic

lime

3 Add the sugar, soy sauce, lime juice, chili sauce, and fish sauce and toss well to coat. Stir-fry for 30 seconds longer.

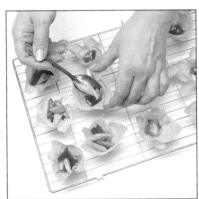

4 Spoon an equal amount of vegetable mixture into each of the prepared wonton cups and serve hot.

1 Preheat the oven to 350°F. Lightly grease twenty-four 1½-inch muffin cups. Press one wonton wrapper into each cup, turning the edges up to form a cup shape. Bake for 8 to 10 minutes until crisp and golden. Carefully remove to a wire rack to cool. If you like, brush each cup with a little hoisin or plum sauce (this will help keep the cups crisp if preparing them in advance).

2 In a wok or large skillet, heat 2 tablespoons vegetable oil and the sesame oil until very hot. Add the garlic, ginger, and lemongrass and stir-fry for 15 seconds until fragrant. Add the asparagus, corn, and red bell pepper pieces and stir-fry for 2 minutes until tender crisp.

Quick-fried Shrimp with Hot Spices

These spicy shrimp that cook in moments make a wonderful appetizer. Don't forget to provide your guests with finger bowls.

Serves 4

INGREDIENTS
1 lb large raw shrimp
1-in piece ginger root, grated
2 garlic cloves, crushed
1 tsp cayenne pepper
1 tsp ground turmeric
2 tsp black mustard seeds
seeds from 4 green cardamom pods, crushed
4 tbsp ghee or butter
½ cup coconut milk
2–3 tbsp chopped fresh cilantro
salt and ground black pepper
nan bread, to serve

shrimp

cilantro

coconut milk

cayenne

ghee

black mustard seeds

turmeric

ginger root

garlic

cardamom pods

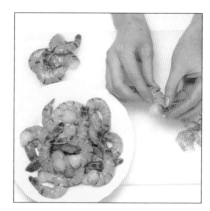

1 Shell the shrimp carefully, leaving the tails attached.

2 Using a small sharp knife, make a slit along the back of each shrimp and remove the dark vein. Rinse under cold running water, drain and pat dry.

3 Put the ginger, garlic, cayenne pepper, turmeric, mustard seeds and cardamom seeds in a bowl. Add the shrimp and toss to coat with the spices.

4 Heat a karahi or wok until hot. Add the ghee or butter and swirl it around until foaming.

5 Add the marinated shrimp and stir-fry for 1–1½ minutes, until they are just turning pink.

6 Stir in the coconut milk and simmer for 3–4 minutes, until the shrimp are cooked through. Season with salt and pepper. Sprinkle over the cilantro and serve immediately with nan bread.

Sesame Seed Chicken Bites

Best eaten warm, these crunchy bites are delicious served with a glass of chilled dry white wine.

Makes 20

INGREDIENTS
6 oz raw chicken breast
2 cloves garlic, crushed
1 in piece ginger root, peeled
    and grated
1 medium egg white
1 tsp cornstarch
¼ cup shelled pistachio nuts,
    roughly chopped
4 tbsp sesame seeds
2 tbsp grapeseed oil
salt and freshly ground black pepper

FOR THE SAUCE
¼ cup hoisin sauce
1 tbsp sweet chili sauce

TO GARNISH
ginger root, finely shredded
pistachio nuts, roughly chopped
fresh dill sprigs

sesame seeds

egg

pistachio nuts

garlic

ginger

1 Place the chicken, garlic, grated ginger, egg white and cornstarch into the food processor and process them to a smooth paste.

2 Stir in the pistachio nuts and season well with salt and pepper.

3 Roll into 20 balls and coat with sesame seeds. Heat the wok and add the oil. When the oil is hot, stir-fry the chicken bites in batches, turning regularly until golden. Drain on paper towels.

4 Make the sauce by mixing together the hoisin and chili sauces in a bowl. Garnish the bites with shredded ginger, pistachio nuts and dill, then serve hot, with a dish of sauce for dipping.

Mixed Spiced Nuts

These make an excellent accompaniment to drinks. They will store for up to a month in an air-tight container if they are not mixed together.

Serves 4–6

INGREDIENTS

3 oz dried unsweetened
   shredded coconut
5 tbsp peanut oil
½ tsp chili powder
1 tsp ground paprika
1 tsp tomato paste
2 cups unsalted cashews
2 cups whole blanched almonds
4 tbsp superfine sugar
1 tsp ground cumin
½ tsp salt
freshly ground black pepper
cress, to garnish

cashews

paprika

chili powder

cumin

almonds

1 Heat the wok, add the coconut and dry-fry until golden. Leave to cool.

2 Heat the wok and add 3 tbsp of the peanut oil. When the oil is hot, add the chili, paprika and tomato paste. Gently stir-fry the cashews in the spicy mix until well coated. Drain well and season. Leave to cool.

3 Wipe out the wok with paper towels, heat it, then add the remaining oil. When the oil is hot, add the almonds and sprinkle in the sugar. Stir-fry gently until the almonds are golden brown and the sugar is caramelized. Place the cumin and salt in a bowl. Add the almonds, toss well, then leave to cool.

4 Mix the cashews, almonds and coconut together, garnish with cress and serve with drinks.

Butterfly Shrimp

Use raw shrimp if you can because the flavor will be better, but if you substitute cooked shrimp, cut down the stir-fry cooking time by one third.

Serves 4

INGREDIENTS
1 in piece ginger root
12 oz raw shrimp, thawed
    if frozen
½ cup raw peanuts, roughly
    chopped
3 tbsp vegetable oil
1 clove garlic, crushed
1 red chili, finely chopped
3 tbsp smooth peanut butter
1 tbsp fresh cilantro, chopped
fresh cilantro sprigs, to garnish

FOR THE DRESSING
⅔ cup plain low-fat yogurt
2 in piece cucumber, diced
salt and freshly ground black pepper

1 To make the dressing, mix together the yogurt, cucumber and seasoning in a bowl, then leave to chill while preparing and cooking the shrimp.

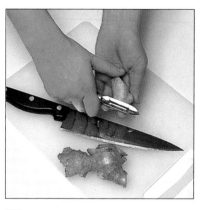

2 Peel the ginger, and chop it finely.

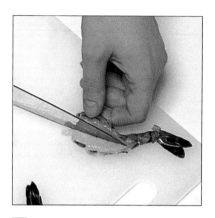

3 Prepare the shrimp by peeling off the shells, leaving the tails intact. Make a slit down the back of each shrimp and remove the black vein, then slit the shrimp completely down the back and open it out to make a "butterfly."

diced cucumber

peanuts

cilantro

shrimp

chili

4 Heat the wok and dry-fry the peanuts, stirring constantly until golden brown. Leave to cool. Wipe out the wok with paper towels.

5 Heat the wok, add the oil and when hot add the ginger, garlic and chili. Stir-fry for 2–3 minutes until the garlic is softened but not brown.

6 Add the shrimp, then increase the heat and stir-fry for 1–2 minutes until the shrimp turn pink. Stir in the peanut butter and stir-fry for 2 minutes. Add the chopped cilantro, then scatter in the peanuts. Garnish with cilantro sprigs and serve with the cucumber dressing.

Lettuce-wrapped Garlic Lamb

This tasty first course lamb is stir-fried with garlic, ginger and spices, then served in crisp lettuce leaves with yogurt, a dab of lime pickle and mint leaves—the contrast of hot and spicy and cool and crisp is excellent.

Serves 4

INGREDIENTS
1 lb lamb, shoulder cutlet
½ tsp cayenne pepper
2 tsp ground coriander
1 tsp ground cumin
½ tsp ground turmeric
2 tbsp peanut oil
3–4 garlic cloves,
　chopped
1 tbsp grated fresh ginger root
⅔ cup lamb stock or
　water
4–6 scallions, sliced
2 tbsp chopped fresh
　cilantro
1 tbsp lemon juice
lettuce leaves, yogurt, lime pickle
　and mint leaves, to serve

cilantro

stock

garlic

lamb

ginger

peanut oil

scallions

VARIATION
Vegetables, such as cooked diced potatoes or peas, can be added to the ground lamb mixture.

1 Trim the lamb cutlet of any fat and cube into small pieces, then grind in a blender or food processor, taking care not to over-process.

2 In a bowl mix together the cayenne pepper, ground coriander, cumin and turmeric. Add the lamb and rub the spice mixture into the meat. Cover and let marinate for about 1 hour.

3 Heat a wok until hot. Add the oil and swirl it around. When hot, add the garlic and ginger and allow to sizzle for a few seconds.

4 Add the lamb and continue to stir-fry for 2–3 minutes.

5 Pour in the stock and continue to stir-fry until all the stock has been absorbed and the lamb is tender, adding more stock if necessary.

6 Add the scallions, fresh cilantro and lemon juice, then stir-fry for another 30–45 seconds. Serve immediately with the lettuce leaves, yogurt, pickle and mint leaves.

Thai Fish Cakes

Bursting with the flavors of chilies, lime and lemongrass, these little fish cakes make a wonderful appetizer.

Serves 4

INGREDIENTS
1 lb white fish fillets, such as
    cod or haddock
3 scallions, sliced
2 tbsp chopped fresh cilantro
2 tbsp Thai red curry paste
1 fresh green chili,
    seeded and chopped
2 tsp grated lime zest
1 tbsp lime juice
2 tbsp peanut oil
salt, to taste
crisp lettuce leaves,
    shredded scallions,
    fresh red chili slices,
    cilantro sprigs and
    lime wedges, to serve

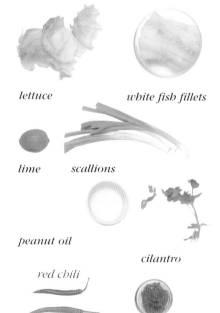

lettuce   *white fish fillets*

lime   *scallions*

peanut oil

cilantro

red chili

green chili   *Thai red curry paste*

1 Cut the fish into chunks, then place in a blender or food processor.

2 Add the scallions, cilantro, red curry paste, green chili, lime zest and juice to the fish. Season with salt. Process until finely ground.

3 Using lightly floured hands, divide the mixture into 16 pieces and shape each one into a small cake about 1½ in across. Place the fish cakes on a plate, cover with plastic wrap and chill for about 2 hours, until firm. Heat the wok over high heat until hot. Add the oil and swirl it around.

4 Fry the fish cakes, a few at a time, for 6–8 minutes, turning them carefully until evenly browned. Drain each batch on paper towels and keep hot while cooking the remainder. Serve on a bed of crisp lettuce leaves with shredded scallions, red chili slices, cilantro sprigs and lime wedges.

Stuffed Chilies

This pretty dish is not as fiery as you might expect. Do give it a try.

Serves 4–6

INGREDIENTS

10 fat fresh green chilies
4 oz lean pork, roughly chopped
3 oz raw tiger shrimp, shelled
   and deveined
½ cup cilantro leaves
1 tsp cornstarch
2 tsp dry sherry
2 tsp soy sauce
1 tsp sesame oil
½ tsp salt
1 tbsp cold water
1 fresh red and 1 fresh green chili,
   seeded and sliced into rings, and
   cooked peas, to garnish

shrimp

chilies

pork

cilantro

sherry

sesame oil

soy sauce

cornstarch

1 Cut the chilies in half lengthwise, keeping the stalk. Scrape out and discard the seeds and set the chilies aside.

2 Mix together the pork, shrimp and cilantro leaves in a food processor. Process until smooth. Scrape into a bowl and mix in the cornstarch, sherry, soy sauce, sesame oil, salt and water; cover and let marinate for 10 minutes.

COOK'S TIP
If you prefer a slightly hotter taste, stuff fresh hot red chilies as well as the green ones.

3 Fill each half chili with some of the meat mixture. Have ready a steamer or a heatproof plate and a pan with about 2 inches boiling water.

4 Place the stuffed chilies in the steamer or on a plate, meat side up, and cover with a lid or foil. Steam for 15 minutes, or until the meat filling is cooked. Serve immediately, garnished with the chili rings and peas.

Pork Saté with Crisp Noodle Cake

Crisp noodles are a popular and tasty accompaniment to saté, and are particularly good with the spicy saté sauce.

Serves 4–6

INGREDIENTS
1 lb lean pork
3 garlic cloves, finely chopped
1 tbsp Thai curry powder
1 tsp ground cumin
1 tsp sugar
1 tbsp fish sauce
6 tbsp oil
12 oz thin egg noodles
cilantro leaves, to garnish

FOR THE SATÉ SAUCE
2 tbsp oil
2 garlic cloves, finely chopped
1 small onion, finely chopped
½ tsp hot chili powder
1 tsp Thai curry powder
1 cup coconut milk
1 tbsp fish sauce
2 tbsp sugar
juice of ½ lemon
½ cup plus 2 tbsp crunchy
   peanut butter

pork
garlic
Thai curry powder
onion
ground cumin
sugar
fish sauce
cilantro
thin egg noodles
hot chili powder
coconut milk
lemon
crunchy peanut butter

1 Cut the pork into thin 2-inch-long strips. Mix the garlic, curry powder, cumin, sugar and fish sauce in a bowl. Stir in about 2 tablespoons of the oil. Add the meat to the bowl, toss to coat and let marinate in a cool place for at least 2 hours. Meanwhile, cook the noodles in a large saucepan of boiling water until just tender. Drain thoroughly.

2 Make the saté sauce. Heat the oil in a saucepan and sauté the garlic and onion with the chili powder and curry powder for 2–3 minutes. Stir in the coconut milk, fish sauce, sugar, lemon juice and peanut butter. Mix well. Reduce the heat and cook, stirring frequently, for about 20 minutes, or until the sauce thickens. Be careful not to let the sauce stick to the bottom of the pan or it will burn.

3 Heat about 1 tablespoon of the remaining oil in a frying pan. Spread the noodles evenly over the pan and fry for 4–5 minutes, until crisp and golden. Turn the noodle cake over carefully and cook the other side until crisp. Keep hot.

4 Drain the meat and thread it onto soaked, drained bamboo skewers. Cook under a hot broiler for 8–10 minutes, until cooked, turning occasionally and brushing with the remaining oil. Serve with wedges of noodle cake, accompanied by the saté sauce. Garnish with cilantro leaves.

Chinese-style Cabbage and Noodle Parcels

The noodles and Chinese mushrooms give a delightful Asian flavor to these traditional cabbage rolls. Serve with rice for a tasty meal.

Serves 4–6

INGREDIENTS
4 dried Chinese mushrooms, soaked
   in hot water until soft
2 oz cellophane noodles,
   soaked in hot water until soft
1 lb ground pork
8 scallions, 2 finely chopped
2 garlic cloves, finely chopped
2 tbsp fish sauce
12 large outer green cabbage leaves
salt and freshly ground black pepper

FOR THE SAUCE
2 tbsp oil
1 small onion, finely chopped
2 garlic cloves, crushed
14-ounce can chopped plum
   tomatoes
pinch of sugar

Chinese
mushrooms   *scallions*

cellophane   *ground pork*
noodles

garlic   *fish sauce*   *onion*

chopped plum
tomatoes

1 Drain the mushrooms, remove and discard the stems and coarsely chop the caps. Put them in a bowl. Next, drain the noodles and cut them into short lengths. Add the noodles to the bowl with the pork, chopped scallions and garlic. Season with the fish sauce and pepper.

2 Blanch the cabbage leaves a few at a time in a saucepan of salted boiling water for about 1 minute. Remove the leaves from the pan and refresh under cold water. Drain and dry on paper towels. Blanch the remaining scallions in the same fashion. Drain well. Fill one of the cabbage leaves with a generous spoonful of the pork and noodle filling. Taking hold of the corner closest to you, roll up the leaf sufficiently to enclose the filling, then tuck in the sides and continue rolling the leaf to make a tight parcel. Make more parcels in the same way.

5 Season the tomato mixture with salt, pepper and a pinch of sugar, then bring to the simmering point. Add the cabbage parcels. Cover and cook gently for 20–25 minutes, or until the filling is cooked. Taste the sauce to check the seasoning and serve immediately.

3 Split each scallion lengthwise by cutting through the bulb and then tearing upward. Tie each of the cabbage parcels with a length of scallion.

4 To make the sauce, heat the oil in a large frying pan and add the onion and garlic. Sauté for 2 minutes, until soft. Pour the plum tomatoes into a bowl. Mash with a fork, then add to the onion mixture.

COOK'S TIP

If at any time the tomato sauce looks a little dry, add some water or vegetable stock to the pan and stir thoroughly.

Deep-fried Wonton Cushions with Sambal Kecap

These delicious, golden packages, called *pansit goreng*, are popular in Indonesia as party fare or for a quick snack.

Makes 40

INGREDIENTS
4 oz pork fillet, trimmed and sliced
8 oz cooked shelled shrimp
2–3 garlic cloves, crushed
2 scallions, roughly chopped
1 tbsp cornstarch
about 40 wonton wrappers
oil, for deep-frying
salt and freshly ground black pepper

FOR THE SAMBAL KECAP
1–2 red chilies, seeded and sliced
1–2 garlic cloves, crushed
3 tbsp dark soy sauce
3–4 tbsp lemon or lime juice

cornstarch
oil

pork fillet

cooked
shrimp

garlic

scallions

wonton
wrappers

red
chilies

lemon
juice

dark soy
sauce

1 Grind the slices of pork finely in a food processor. Add the shrimp, garlic, scallions and cornstarch. Season and then process briefly.

2 Place a little of the prepared filling onto each wonton wrapper, just off center, with the wrapper positioned like a diamond in front of you. Dampen all the edges, except for the uppermost corner of the diamond.

3 Lift the corner nearest you toward the filling and then roll up the wrapper to cover the filling. Turn over. Bring the two extreme corners together, sealing one on top of the other. Squeeze lightly to plump up the filling. Repeat the process until all the wrappers and the filling are used up. The prepared "cushions" and any leftover wonton wrappers can be frozen at this stage.

4 Meanwhile, prepare the sambal. Mix the chilies and garlic together and then stir in the dark soy sauce, lemon or lime juice and 1–2 tablespoons water. Pour into a serving bowl and set aside.

5 Deep-fry the wonton cushions in hot oil, a few at a time, for 2–3 minutes, or until cooked through, crisp and golden brown. Serve on a large platter together with the sambal kecap.

Fried Monkfish Coated with Rice Noodles

These marinated medallions of fish are coated in rice vermicelli and deep-fried—they taste as good as they look.

Serves 4

INGREDIENTS

1 lb monkfish
1 tsp grated fresh ginger root
1 garlic clove, finely chopped
2 tbsp light soy sauce
6 oz rice vermicelli noodles
2 oz cornstarch
2 eggs, beaten
oil, for deep-frying
banana leaves, to serve (optional)

FOR THE DIPPING SAUCE

2 tbsp light soy sauce
2 tbsp rice vinegar
1 tbsp sugar
salt and freshly ground black pepper
2 red chilies, seeded and thinly
    sliced
1 scallion, thinly sliced

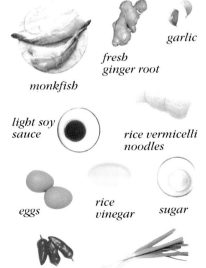

monkfish *fresh ginger root* *garlic* *light soy sauce* *rice vermicelli noodles* *eggs* *rice vinegar* *sugar* *red chilies* *scallions*

1 Cut the monkfish into 1-inch-thick medallions. Place in a dish and add the ginger, garlic and soy sauce. Let marinate for 10 minutes. For the dipping sauce, heat the soy sauce, vinegar and sugar in a saucepan until boiling. Add the salt and pepper. Remove from the heat and add the chilies and scallion.

2 Using kitchen scissors, cut the noodles into 1½-inch lengths. Spread them out in a shallow bowl.

3 Coat the fish medallions in cornstarch, dip in beaten egg and cover with noodles, pressing them onto the fish so that they stick.

4 Deep-fry the coated fish in hot oil, 2–3 pieces at a time, until the noodle coating is crisp and golden brown. Drain and serve hot on banana leaves if you like, accompanied by the dipping sauce.

Baby Ginger Rösti with Chili Bouquets

Chilies make a wonderfully versatile garnish— even a single chili placed on the side of a plate can set off a dish.

Makes 20–24

INGREDIENTS
1 lb potatoes
2 tbsp grated fresh ginger root
1 tbsp all-purpose flour
oil, for frying
salt and freshly ground black
   pepper

FOR THE GARNISH
2 large red chilies
raffia, for tying
large sprigs of parsley or
   cilantro (optional)

raffia

potatoes

all-purpose flour

oil

red chilies

fresh ginger root

parsley

1 Preheat the oven to 275°F. Line a baking sheet with paper towels. Peel the potatoes and grate them coarsely into a bowl. Stir in the fresh ginger. Add the flour, salt and pepper, then mix together well.

3 Fry the rösti for 2–3 minutes on each side until golden brown.

2 Heat a little oil in a non-stick frying pan, then gently drop in a few small spoonfuls of the coarsely grated potato mixture.

4 Place on the prepared baking sheet and keep warm in the oven. Make more rösti in the same way.

5 To make the garnish, tie the stems of the chilies together with a small piece of raffia. For an interesting color contrast, add a large sprig of parsley or cilantro. Arrange the rösti on a plate, set the chilies on the rim and serve.

Vegetable Tempura

These deep-fried fritters are based on Kaki-age, a Japanese dish that often incorporates fish and shrimp as well as vegetables.

Makes 8

INGREDIENTS
2 medium zucchini
½ medium eggplant
1 large carrot
½ small Spanish onion
1 egg
½ cup ice water
1 cup all-purpose flour
salt and ground black pepper
vegetable oil,
    for deep-frying
sea salt flakes, lemon slices and
    Japanese soy sauce (*shoyu*),
    to serve

zucchini

carrot   *eggplant*

Spanish onion

all-purpose flour

egg   *vegetable oil*

COOK'S TIP
Paring strips of peel from the zucchini and eggplant will avoid too much tough skin in the finished dish.

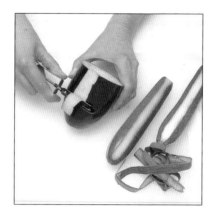

1 Using a vegetable peeler, pare strips of peel from the zucchini and eggplant to give a striped effect.

2 Cut the zucchini, eggplant and carrot into strips about 3–4 in long and ⅛ in wide.

3 Put the zucchini, eggplant and carrot in a colander and sprinkle liberally with salt. Let stand for about 30 minutes, then rinse thoroughly under cold running water. Drain well.

4 Thinly slice the onion from top to base, discarding the plump pieces in the middle. Separate the layers so that there are lots of fine long strips. Mix all the vegetables together and season with salt and pepper.

5 Make the batter immediately before frying: mix the egg and iced water in a bowl, then sift in the flour. Mix very briefly using a fork or chopsticks. Do not overmix—the batter should remain lumpy. Add the vegetables to the batter and mix to combine.

6 Meanwhile, half-fill a wok with oil and heat to 350°F. Scoop up one heaped tablespoon of the mixture at a time and carefully lower into the oil. Deep-fry in batches for about 3 minutes, until golden brown and crisp. Drain on paper towels. Serve each diner with salt, lemon slices and a tiny bowl of Japanese soy sauce for dipping.

Thai Red Curry Sauce

Serve this with mini spring rolls or spicy Indonesian crackers, or toss it into freshly cooked rice noodles for a delicious main-meal accompaniment.

Serves 4

INGREDIENTS
scant 1 cup coconut cream
2–3 tsp Thai red curry paste
4 scallions, plus extra, to garnish
2 tbsp chopped fresh
    cilantro
1 red chili, seeded and thinly sliced
    into rings
1 tsp soy sauce
juice of 1 lime
sugar, to taste
¼ cup dry-roasted peanuts
salt and pepper

coconut cream

scallions

Thai red curry paste

soy sauce

cilantro

red chili

lime juice

sugar

dry-roasted peanuts

1 Pour the coconut cream into a small bowl and stir in the curry paste.

2 Trim and finely slice the scallions diagonally. Stir into the coconut cream with the cilantro and chili.

COOK'S TIP
The dip may be prepared in advance up to the end of step 3. Sprinkle the peanuts on top just before serving.

3 Stir in the soy sauce, lime juice, sugar, salt and pepper to taste. Pour the sauce into a small serving bowl.

4 Finely chop the dry-roasted peanuts and sprinkle them over the sauce. Serve immediately. Garnish with scallions sliced lengthwise.

Asian Hoisin Dip

This speedy Asian dip needs no cooking and can be made in just a few minutes—it tastes great with mini spring rolls or shrimp crackers.

Serves 4

INGREDIENTS
4 scallions
1½-in piece ginger root
2 red chilies
2 garlic cloves
¼ cup hoisin sauce
½ cup bottled strained tomatoes
1 tsp sesame oil (optional)

scallions

ginger root

garlic

red chilies

sesame oil

hoisin sauce

bottled strained tomatoes

1 Trim off and discard the green ends of the scallions. Slice the remainder very thinly.

2 Peel the ginger with a swivel-bladed vegetable peeler, then chop it finely.

3 Halve the chilies lengthwise and remove their seeds. Finely slice the flesh horizontally into tiny strips. Finely chop the garlic.

4 Stir together the hoisin sauce, bottled strained tomatoes, scallions, ginger, chili, garlic and sesame oil, if using, and serve within 1 hour.

COOK'S TIP

Hoisin sauce makes an excellent base for full-flavor dips, especially when combining crunchy vegetables and other Asian seasonings.

Crisp Turkey Balls

Turkey is not traditionally used in Chinese cooking, but it makes a good alternative to chicken.

Serves 4–6

INGREDIENTS

4 thin slices white bread, crusts removed
1 tsp olive oil
8 oz skinless, boneless turkey meat, roughly chopped
⅓ cup drained, canned water chestnuts
2 fresh red chilies, seeded and roughly chopped
1 egg white
¼ cup cilantro leaves
1 tsp cornstarch
½ tsp salt
¼ tsp ground white pepper
2 tbsp light soy sauce
1 tsp sugar
2 tbsp rice vinegar
½ tsp chili oil
shredded red chilies and cilantro sprigs, to garnish

bread

turkey

chilies

water chestnuts

cornstarch chili oil sugar

egg soy sauce rice vinegar

1 Preheat the oven to 250°F. Brush the bread slices lightly with olive oil and cut them into ¼-inch cubes. Spread over a baking sheet and bake for 15 minutes until, dry and crisp.

4 Remove the toasted bread cubes from the oven and set them aside. Raise the oven temperature to 400°F. With dampened hands, divide the turkey mixture into 12 portions and form into balls.

2 Meanwhile, mix together the turkey meat, water chestnuts and chilies in a food processor. Process until a coarse paste is formed.

5 Roughly crush the toasted bread cubes, then transfer to a plate. Roll each ball in turn in the toasted crumbs until coated. Place on a baking sheet and bake for about 20 minutes, or until the coating is brown and the turkey filling has cooked through.

3 Add the egg white, cilantro leaves, cornstarch, salt and pepper. Pour in half the soy sauce and process for about 30 seconds. Scrape into a bowl, cover and let sit in a cool place for 20 minutes.

6 In a small bowl, mix the remaining soy sauce with the sugar, rice vinegar and chili oil. Serve the sauce with the turkey balls, garnished with shredded chilies and cilantro sprigs.

Smoked Duck Wontons with Spicy Mango Sauce

These Chinese-style wontons are easy to make using cooked smoked duck or chicken, or even left-over meat from Sunday lunch.

Makes about 40

INGREDIENTS
1 tbsp light soy sauce
1 tsp sesame oil
2 green onions, finely chopped
grated peel of ½ orange
1 tsp brown sugar
1½ cups chopped smoked duck
about 40 small wonton wrappers
1 tbsp vegetable oil

FOR THE SPICY MANGO SAUCE
2 tbsp vegetable oil
1 tsp ground cumin
½ tsp ground cardamom
¼ tsp ground cinnamon
1 cup mango purée (about 1 large mango)
1 tbsp honey
½ tsp Chinese chili sauce (or to taste)
1 tbsp cider vinegar
chopped fresh chives, to garnish (optional)

mango

green onions

wonton wrappers

soy sauce

brown sugar

smoked duck

cardamom

cumin

cinnamon

sesame oil

chili sauce

cider vinegar

1 Prepare the sauce. In a medium-size saucepan, heat the oil over medium-low heat. Add the spices and cook for about 3 minutes, stirring constantly.

2 Stir in the mango purée, honey, chili sauce, and vinegar. Remove from the heat and cool. Pour into a bowl and cover until ready to serve.

3 Prepare the wonton filling. In a large bowl, mix together the soy sauce, sesame oil, green onions, orange peel, and brown sugar until well blended. Add the duck and toss to coat well.

4 Place a teaspoonful of the duck mixture in the center of each wonton wrapper. Brush the edges lightly with water and then draw them up to the center, twisting to seal and forming a pouch shape.

5 Preheat the oven to 375°C. Line a large cookie sheet with foil and brush lightly with oil. Arrange the wontons on the cookie sheet and bake for 10 to 12 minutes until crisp and golden. Serve with the Spicy Mango Sauce. If you wish, tie each wonton with a fresh chive.

Spicy Crab and Coconut

This spicy dish makes a delicious and exotic starter. Serve by itself or with warm bread.

Serves 4

INGREDIENTS
1½ oz dried unsweetened shredded
   coconut
2 cloves garlic
2 in piece ginger root, peeled
   and grated
½ tsp cumin seeds
1 small stick cinnamon
½ tsp ground turmeric
2 dried red chilies
1 tbsp coriander seeds
½ tsp poppy seeds
1 tbsp vegetable oil
1 medium onion, sliced
1 small green bell pepper, cut
   into strips
16 crab claws
fresh cilantro sprigs, crushed,
   to garnish
⅔ cup plain low-fat yogurt, to serve

bell pepper

cumin seeds

cinnamon

crab claw

1 Place the shredded coconut, garlic, ginger, cumin seeds, cinnamon, turmeric, red chilies, cilantro and poppy seeds. into a food processor and process until well blended.

2 Heat the oil in the wok and fry the onion until soft, but not colored.

3 Stir in the green bell pepper and stir-fry for 1 minute.

4 Remove the vegetables with a slotted spoon and heat the wok. Add the crab claws, stir-fry for 2 minutes, then briefly return all the spiced vegetables to the wok. Garnish with fresh cilantro sprigs and serve with the cooling yogurt.

Saté Sauce

There are many versions of this tasty peanut sauce. This one is very speedy and tastes delicious drizzled over broiled or grilled chicken skewers. For parties, spear chunks of chicken with toothpicks and arrange around a bowl of warm sauce.

Serves 4

INGREDIENTS
scant 1 cup coconut cream
¼ cup crunchy peanut butter
1 tsp Worcestershire sauce
red Tabasco sauce, to taste
fresh coconut, to garnish (optional)

coconut cream

peanut butter

Worcestershire sauce

red Tabasco sauce

coconut

COOK'S TIP
Thick coconut milk can be substituted for coconut cream; coconut milk is usually packed in 14-oz cans, but be sure to buy an unsweetened variety for this recipe.

1 Pour the coconut cream into a small saucepan and heat it gently over low heat for about 2 minutes.

2 Add the peanut butter and stir vigorously until it is blended into the coconut cream. Continue to heat until the mixture is warm but not boiling.

3 Add the Worcestershire sauce and a dash of Tabasco to taste. Pour into a serving bowl.

4 Use a vegetable peeler to shave thin strips from a piece of fresh coconut, if using. Scatter the coconut over the sauce and serve immediately.

Chicken and Vegetable Bundles

This popular and delicious dim sum is extremely easy to prepare in your own kitchen.

Serves 4

INGREDIENTS

4 skinless, boneless chicken thighs
1 tsp cornstarch
2 tsp dry sherry
2 tbsp light soy sauce
½ tsp salt
large pinch of ground white pepper
4 fresh shiitake mushrooms
½ cup sliced drained canned
    bamboo shoots
1 small carrot
1 small zucchini
1 leek, trimmed
¼ tsp sesame oil

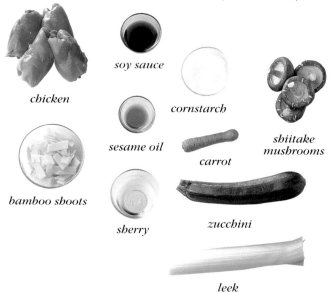

chicken

soy sauce

cornstarch

shiitake mushrooms

sesame oil

carrot

bamboo shoots

sherry

zucchini

leek

1 Remove any fat from the chicken thighs and cut each lengthwise into eight strips. Place the strips in a bowl.

2 Add the cornstarch, sherry and half the soy sauce to the chicken. Stir in the salt and pepper and mix well. Cover and marinate for 10 minutes.

3 Remove and discard the mushroom stalks, then cut each mushroom cap in half (or in slices if very large). Cut the carrot and zucchini into eight sticks, each about 2 inches long, then mix the mushroom halves and bamboo shoots together.

4 Bring a small saucepan of water to the boil. Add the leek and blanch until soft. Drain thoroughly, then slit the leek down its length. Separate each layer to give eight long strips.

5 Divide the marinated chicken into eight portions. Do the same with the vegetables. Wrap each strip of leek around a portion of chicken and vegetables to make eight neat bundles. Have ready a saucepan with about 2 inches boiling water and a steamer or a heatproof plate that will fit inside it on a metal trivet.

6 Place the chicken and vegetable bundles in the steamer or on the plate. Place in the pan, cover and steam over high heat for 12–15 minutes, or until the filling is cooked. Meanwhile, mix the remaining soy sauce with the sesame oil; use as a sauce for the bundles.

Thai Pork Spring Rolls

Crunchy spring rolls are as popular in Thai cuisine as they are in Chinese. In this version they are filled with noodles, garlic and pork.

Makes about 24

INGREDIENTS
4–6 dried Chinese mushrooms,
   soaked in hot water until soft
2 oz cellophane noodles
2 tbsp oil
2 garlic cloves, chopped
2 red chilies, seeded and chopped
8 oz ground pork
2 oz cooked shelled shrimp,
   chopped
2 tbsp fish sauce
1 tsp sugar
freshly ground black pepper
1 carrot, very finely sliced
2 oz bamboo shoots, chopped
¼ cup bean sprouts
2 scallions, chopped
1 tbsp chopped cilantro
2 tbsp all-purpose flour
24 × 6-in square spring roll
   wrappers
oil, for deep-frying
Thai sweet chili sauce, to serve
   (optional)

Chinese mushrooms

cellophane noodles

garlic

ground pork

cooked shrimp

fish sauce

cilantro

bean sprouts

spring roll wrappers

1 Drain and finely chop the Chinese mushrooms. Remove and discard the stems. Soak the noodles in hot water until soft, then drain. Cut into short lengths, about 2 inches.

2 Heat the oil in a wok or large frying pan, add the garlic and chilies and fry for 30 seconds. Add the pork and stir-fry for a few minutes, until the meat is browned. Add the noodles, mushrooms and shrimp. Season with fish sauce, sugar and pepper. Pour into a bowl. Add the carrot, bamboo shoots, bean sprouts, scallions and cilantro and stir well to mix.

3 Put the flour in a small bowl and blend with a little water to make a paste. Place a spoonful of filling in the center of a spring roll wrapper.

4 Turn the bottom edge over to cover the filling, then fold in the left and right sides. Roll the wrapper up almost to the top edge. Brush the top edge with flour paste and seal. Repeat with the rest of the wrappers.

5 Heat the oil in a wok or deep-fat fryer. Slide in the spring rolls a few at a time and fry until crisp and golden brown. Remove with a slotted spoon and drain on paper towels. Serve with Thai sweet chili sauce to dip them into, if you like.

Chili Shrimp in Cucumber Cups on a Herb-rimmed Plate

Try garnishing the rim of the plate rather than the food itself—a very simple but stunning idea.

Makes 20– 24

INGREDIENTS
4 small red chilies, seeded and
  finely diced
2 tsp finely grated
  fresh ginger root
1 large garlic clove, crushed
3 tbsp light soy sauce
8 oz cooked shrimp,
  shelled and deveined
2 cucumbers

FOR THE GARNISH
1 tbsp butter, softened
2 tbsp chopped fresh chives

shrimp

garlic

chives

butter   red chilies

cucumber

soy sauce   fresh ginger root

COOK'S TIP
Use any type of chopped herb or, for a more colorful edge, dust with chili powder or ground turmeric.

1 Combine the chilies, ginger, garlic and soy sauce in a bowl. Add the shrimp and toss them in the marinade. Cover and chill for 2– 4 hours.

2 Trim both ends of the cucumbers, then cut them into ¾-inch lengths. Use a 1¼-inch round aspic cutter to stamp out rounds, and discard the skin.

3 Using a melon baller, scoop out the cucumber seeds to make little cups. Place upside-down on paper towels to drain for 20–30 minutes.

4 Brush the butter around the rim of the plate. Sprinkle the chives over the butter to form a decorative edge. Tip the plate and shake lightly to remove any loose chives. Arrange the cucumber cups in the center of the plate and fill each with 2–3 marinated shrimp.

Egg and Tomato Tartlets with a Quail Egg Nest

Quail eggs make a delightful garnish with their pretty shells left on. Hard-cook a few to use as an edible garnish, but shell before eating.

Makes 24

INGREDIENTS
24 cooked tartlet cases
24 quail eggs
6 cherry tomatoes
24 parsley sprigs
salt and freshly ground
  black pepper

FOR THE GARNISH
12 quail eggs
2 leeks, trimmed

quail eggs

cherry tomatoes

parsley

tartlet cases

leek

1 Preheat the oven to 350°F. Season the tartlet shells and place them on baking sheets. Carefully break the quail eggs into a bowl, taking care to keep the yolks intact. Cut the cherry tomatoes into quarters.

2 Spoon a yolk into each tartlet. Add a small amount of egg white to each, but do not overfill. Place a tomato quarter in each tartlet. Cover with foil and bake for 10–12 minutes until just set. Top each one with a parsley sprig.

3 Make the garnish. Place the quail's eggs in a saucepan of cold water, bring to a boil, cover and remove from the heat. Let sit for 6–8 minutes. Drain the eggs and refresh under cold running water until they are cool. Drain and pat the shells dry.

4 Shred the leeks finely by hand, or with a food processor fitted with a fine shredding plate. Form the shredded leeks into a nest on a large platter, with the hard-cooked quail eggs nestled on top. Add the warm egg and tomato tartlets and serve.

Fiery Citrus Salsa

This very unusual salsa makes a great marinade for shellfish and it is also delicious drizzled over grilled meat.

Serves 4

INGREDIENTS
1 orange
1 green apple
2 fresh red chilies
1 garlic clove
8 fresh mint leaves
juice of 1 lemon
salt and pepper

orange   *apple*

red chilies   *garlic*

mint   *lemon juice*

1 Slice the bottom off the orange so that it will stand upright on a cutting board. Using a sharp knife, remove the peel by slicing from the top to the bottom of the orange.

2 Hold the orange in one hand over a bowl. Slice toward the middle of the fruit, to one side of a segment, and then gently twist the knife to ease the segment away from the membrane and out of the orange. Repeat to remove all the segments. Squeeze any juice from the remaining membrane into the bowl.

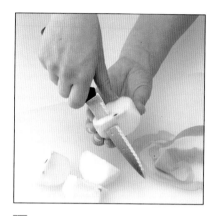

3 Peel the apple, slice it into wedges and remove the core.

4 Halve the chilies and remove their seeds, then place them in a blender or food processor with the orange segments and juice, apple wedges, garlic and fresh mint.

5 Process until smooth. Then, with the motor running, pour in the lemon juice.

6 Season to taste with a little salt and pepper. Pour into a bowl or small pitcher and serve immediately.

VARIATION
If you're feeling really fiery, don't seed the chilies! They will make the salsa particularly hot and zesty.

Mini Phoenix Rolls

These rolls are ideal as an easy appetizer and can be served hot or cold.

Serves 4

INGREDIENTS
2 large eggs, plus 1 egg white
5 tbsp cold water
1 tsp vegetable oil
6 oz lean pork, diced
½ cup drained canned water
    chestnuts
2-in piece fresh ginger root,
    grated
4 dried Chinese mushrooms, soaked
    in hot water until soft
1 tbsp dry sherry
¼ tsp salt
large pinch of ground white pepper
2 tbsp rice vinegar
½ tsp sugar
cilantro or flat-leaf parsley, to
    garnish

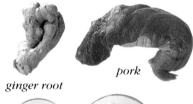

ginger root

pork

dry sherry

water chestnuts

rice vinegar

sugar

vegetable oil

eggs

*dried Chinese
mushrooms*

1 Lightly beat the 2 whole eggs with 3 tablespoons of the water. Heat an 8-inch nonstick omelet pan and brush with a little of the oil. Pour in a quarter of the egg mixture, swirling the pan to coat the bottom lightly. Cook the omelet until the top is set. Slide it onto a plate and make three more omelets in the same way.

2 Mix the pork and water chestnuts in a food processor. Add 1 teaspoon of the ginger root. Drain the mushrooms, chop the caps roughly and add them to the mixture. Process until smooth.

3 Scrape the pork paste into a bowl. Stir in the egg white, sherry, remaining water, salt and pepper. Mix thoroughly, cover and let sit in cool place for about 15 minutes.

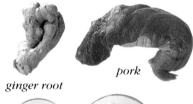

4 Have ready a saucepan with about 2 inches boiling water and a large heat-proof plate that will fit inside it on a metal trivet. Divide the pork mixture among the omelets and spread into a large square shape in the center of each one.

5 Bring the sides of each omelet over the filling and roll up from the bottom to the top. Arrange the rolls on the plate. Cover the plate tightly with foil and place it in the pan on the trivet. Steam over high heat for 15 minutes.

COOK'S TIP
These rolls can be prepared a day in advance and steamed just before serving.

6 Make a dipping sauce by mixing the remaining ginger with the rice vinegar and sugar in a small dish. Cut the rolls diagonally into ½-inch slices, garnish with the cilantro or flat-leaf parsley leaves and serve with the sauce.

SOUPS

In Asia, soup is often served alongside the rest of the meal rather than as a separate course. Familiar favorites include Hot-and-Sour Soup, Seafood Wonton Soup and Corn and Chicken Soup.

Corn and Chicken Soup

This popular classic Chinese soup is delicious, and very easy to make.

Serves 4-6

INGREDIENTS
1 chicken breast fillet,
   about 4 oz, cubed
2 tsp light soy sauce
1 tbsp Chinese rice wine
1 tsp cornstarch
4 tbsp cold water
1 tsp sesame oil
2 tbsp peanut oil
1 tsp fresh ginger root,
   finely grated
4 cups chicken stock, or
   bouillon cube and water
15-oz can cream-style corn
8-oz can corn kernels
2 eggs, beaten
2-3 scallions, green parts only,
   cut into tiny rounds
salt and ground black pepper

cornstarch

chicken stock

cream-style corn

chicken

corn kernels

Chinese rice wine

egg

sesame oil

ginger root

1 Grind the chicken in a food processor, taking care not to over-process. Transfer the chicken to a bowl and stir in the soy sauce, rice wine, cornstarch, water, sesame oil and seasoning. Cover and leave for about 15 minutes to absorb the flavors.

2 Heat a wok over medium heat. Add the peanut oil and swirl it around. Add the ginger and stir-fry for a few seconds. Add the stock, creamed corn and corn kernels. Bring to just below boiling point.

3 Spoon about 6 tbsp of the hot liquid into the chicken mixture and stir until it forms a smooth paste. Return this to the wok. Slowly bring to a boil, stirring constantly, then simmer for 2–3 minutes until the chicken is cooked.

4 Pour the beaten eggs into the soup in a slow steady stream, using a fork or chopsticks to stir the top of the soup in a figure-eight pattern. The egg should set in lacy shreds. Serve immediately with the scallions sprinkled over.

Hot-and-Sour Shrimp Soup

How hot this soup is depends upon the type of chili used. Try tiny Thai chilies, if you really want to "go for the burn."

Serves 6

INGREDIENTS

8 oz raw shrimp, in their shells
2 lemongrass stalks
6¼ cups vegetable stock
4 kaffir lime leaves
2 slices peeled fresh ginger root
4 tbsp Thai fish sauce
4 tbsp fresh lime juice
2 garlic cloves, crushed
6 scallions, chopped
1 fresh red chili, seeded and cut
    into thin strips
4 oz oyster mushrooms, sliced
cilantro leaves and kaffir lime slices,
    to garnish

1 Shell the shrimp and set them aside. Put the shells in a large saucepan.

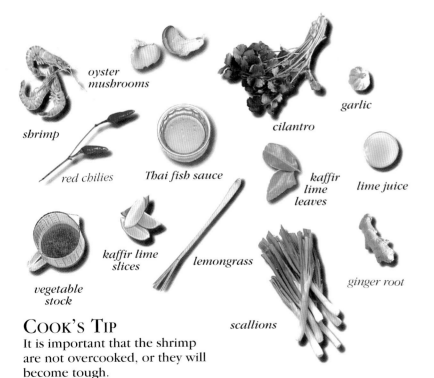

oyster mushrooms

garlic

cilantro

shrimp

red chilies   Thai fish sauce

kaffir lime leaves

lime juice

vegetable stock

kaffir lime slices

lemongrass

ginger root

scallions

COOK'S TIP
It is important that the shrimp are not overcooked, or they will become tough.

2 Lightly crush the lemongrass and add to the pan with the stock, lime leaves and ginger. Bring to a boil, lower the heat and simmer for 20 minutes.

3 Strain the stock into a clean pan, discarding the shrimp shells and aromatics. Add the fish sauce, lime juice, garlic, scallions, chili and mushrooms. Bring to a boil, lower the heat and simmer for 5 minutes. Add the shelled shrimp and cook for 2–3 minutes. Serve, garnished with cilantro leaves and kaffir lime slices.

Hanoi Beef and Noodle Soup

Millions of North Vietnamese eat this fragrant noodle soup every day for breakfast.

Serves 4–6

INGREDIENTS
1 onion
3–3½ lb stewing beef
1-in piece fresh ginger root, peeled
1 star anise
1 bay leaf
2 whole cloves
½ tsp fennel seeds
1 piece cassia or cinnamon stick
fish sauce, to taste
juice of 1 lime
5 oz beef tenderloin
1 lb fresh flat rice noodles
salt and freshly ground black pepper
handful of cilantro leaves and lime
    wedges, to garnish

FOR THE ACCOMPANIMENTS
1 small red onion, sliced into rings
½ cup bean sprouts
2 red chilies, seeded and sliced
2 scallions, finely sliced

stewing beef · fresh ginger root · star anise · bay leaf · whole cloves · fennel seeds · cassia · fish sauce · lime · beef tenderloin · rice noodles · cilantro · onion · bean sprouts · red chilies · scallions

1 Cut the onion in half. Broil under high heat, cut side up, until the exposed sides are caramelized and deep brown.

3 Add 12½ cups water, bring to a boil, reduce the heat and simmer gently for 2–3 hours, skimming off the fat and scum from time to time.

2 Cut the stewing beef into large chunks and then place in a large saucepan or stockpot. Add the caramelized onion with the ginger, star anise, bay leaf, cloves, fennel seeds and cassia or cinnamon stick.

4 Using a slotted spoon, remove the meat from the stock; when cool enough to handle, cut into small pieces. Strain the stock and return to the pan or stockpot together with the meat. Bring back to a boil and season with the fish sauce, lime juice and salt and pepper to taste.

5 Slice the tenderloin very thinly and then chill until required. Cook the noodles in a large pan of boiling water until just tender. Drain and divide among individual serving bowls. Arrange the thinly sliced tenderloin over the noodles, pour the hot stock on top and garnish with cilantro and lime wedges. Serve, offering the accompaniments in separate bowls.

Seafood Wonton Soup

This is a variation on the popular wonton soup that is traditionally prepared using pork.

Serves 4

INGREDIENTS

2 oz raw tiger shrimp
2 oz scallops
3 oz skinless cod fillet,
    roughly chopped
1 tbsp finely chopped chives
1 tsp dry sherry
1 small egg white, lightly beaten
½ tsp sesame oil
¼ tsp salt
large pinch of ground white pepper
3¾ cups fish stock
20 wonton wrappers
2 romaine lettuce leaves, shredded
cilantro leaves and garlic chives, to
    garnish

cod fillet

wonton wrappers

romaine lettuce

cilantro *sherry* *shrimp*

sesame oil

egg

scallops *chives*

fish stock

COOK'S TIP
The filled wonton wrappers can be made ahead, then frozen for several weeks and cooked straight from the freezer.

1 Shell and devein the shrimp. Rinse them well, pat them dry on paper towels and cut them into small pieces.

2 Rinse the scallops. Pat them dry, using paper towels. Chop them into small pieces the same size as the shrimp.

3 Place the cod in a food processor and process until a paste is formed. Scrape into a bowl and stir in the shrimp, scallops, chives, sherry, egg white, sesame oil, salt and pepper. Mix thoroughly, cover and let sit in a cool place to marinate for 20 minutes.

4 Heat the fish stock gently in a saucepan. Make the wontons. Place a teaspoonful of the seafood filling in the center of a wonton wrapper, then bring the corners together to meet at the top. Twist them together to enclose the filling. Fill the remaining wonton wrappers in the same way.

5 Bring a large saucepan of water to a boil. Drop in the wontons. When the water returns to a boil, lower the heat and simmer gently for 5 minutes, or until the wontons float to the surface. Drain the wontons and divide them among four heated soup bowls.

6 Add a portion of lettuce to each bowl. Bring the fish stock to a boil. Ladle it into each bowl, garnish each portion with cilantro leaves and garlic chives and serve immediately.

Beef Noodle Soup

This rich, satisfying soup is packed with all sorts of flavors and textures, brought together with delicious egg noodles.

Serves 4

INGREDIENTS

¼ oz dried porcini mushrooms
6 scallions
4 oz carrots
12 oz sirloin steak
about 2 tbsp oil
1 garlic clove, crushed
1-in piece fresh ginger root,
    finely chopped
5 cups beef stock
3 tbsp light soy sauce
4 tbsp dry sherry
3 oz thin egg noodles
3 oz spinach, shredded
salt and freshly ground black pepper

dried porcini mushrooms   scallions

carrots   sirloin steak

garlic

fresh ginger root   beef stock   dry sherry

egg noodles   light soy sauce   spinach

1 Break the mushrooms into small pieces, place in a bowl, pour ⅔ cup boiling water over and let soak for 15 minutes. Strain the mushrooms, squeezing as much liquid from them as possible. Reserve the liquid.

2 Meanwhile, cut the scallions and carrots into fine 2-inch-long strips. Trim any fat from the meat and slice into thin strips.

3 Heat the oil in a large saucepan and cook the beef in batches until browned, adding a little more oil if necessary. Remove the beef with a slotted spoon and drain on paper towels.

4 Add the garlic, ginger, scallions and carrots to the pan and stir-fry for 3 minutes.

5 Add the beef stock, the mushrooms and their soaking liquid, the soy sauce, sherry and plenty of seasoning. Bring to a boil and simmer, covered, for 10 minutes.

6 Break up the noodles slightly and add to the pan, with the spinach. Simmer gently for 5 minutes, or until the beef is tender. Adjust the seasoning before serving.

Thai Vichyssoise with Chive Braids

Give a classic French recipe an Asian slant and serve it topped with edible braids of chives.

Serves 6

INGREDIENTS

4 tbsp butter
**4 leeks, trimmed and thinly
sliced**
2 onions, thinly sliced
**2 tbsp Thai green
curry paste**
2 kaffir lime leaves
**12 oz floury potatoes,
peeled and diced**
4 cups vegetable stock
**2 × 14-oz cans unsweetened
coconut milk**
1 tbsp fish sauce
**30–60 thick chives, about 8 in
long, to garnish**

onion

coconut milk

fish sauce

butter

Thai green curry paste

leek

chives

potato

kaffir lime leaves

1 Melt the butter in a large saucepan. Add the leeks, onions, curry paste and lime leaves. Stir to mix, then cover and cook for 15 minutes until the onions are tender but not colored.

2 Add the potatoes, stock and coconut milk. Bring to a boil, lower the heat, cover and simmer for about 25–30 minutes or until the potatoes are tender. Remove the lime leaves.

3 Purée the mixture in batches in a blender or pass through a food mill. Return to the clean pan and season with the fish sauce. Set aside.

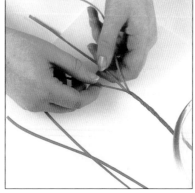

4 Make the garnish. Pick out three of the thickest chives and two that are slightly thinner. Align the thicker chives on a work surface with a small bowl on one end to hold them still. Carefully braid the chives together to within 1 inch of the end.

5 Tie one of the thinner chives around the exposed end of the braid, then remove the bowl or board and tie the other end in the same way. Trim the ends of the ties and braids neatly with kitchen shears. Make five to eleven more braids in the same way.

6 Place the braids in a bowl and pour boiling water over them. Let stand for 20–30 seconds then drain and refresh under cold water. Drain again. Reheat the soup or serve it chilled, with one or two of the chive braids floating on the top.

Mock Shark's Fin Soup

Shark's fin soup is a renowned delicacy. In this vegetarian version, cellophane noodles mimic shark's fin needles.

Serves 4–6

INGREDIENTS

4 dried Chinese mushrooms
1½ tbsp dried wood ears
4 oz cellophane noodles
2 tbsp oil
2 carrots, cut into fine strips
4 oz canned bamboo shoots,
    rinsed, drained and cut into
    fine strips
4 cups vegetable stock
1 tbsp light soy sauce
1 tbsp arrowroot or
    potato flour
1 egg white, beaten (optional)
1 tsp sesame oil
salt and freshly ground black pepper
2 scallions, finely chopped, to
    garnish
Chinese red vinegar, to serve
    (optional)

dried Chinese mushrooms

dried wood ears

cellophane noodles

carrots

bamboo shoots

vegetable stock

light soy sauce

egg

sesame oil

scallions

1 Soak the mushrooms and wood ears separately in warm water for 20 minutes. Drain. Remove the mushroom stems and slice the caps thinly. Cut the wood ears into fine strips, discarding any hard bits. Soak the noodles in hot water until soft. Drain and cut into short lengths.

2 Heat the oil in a large saucepan. Add the mushrooms and stir-fry for 2 minutes. Add the wood ears, stir-fry for 2 minutes, then stir in the carrots, bamboo shoots and noodles.

3 Add the stock to the pan. Bring to a boil, then simmer for 15–20 minutes.

4 Season with salt, pepper and soy sauce. Blend the arrowroot or potato flour with about 2 tablespoons water. Pour into the soup, stirring all the time to prevent lumps from forming as the soup continues to simmer.

5 Remove the pan from the heat. Stir in the egg white, if using, so that it sets to form small threads in the hot soup. Stir in the sesame oil, then pour the soup into individual bowls. Sprinkle each portion with chopped scallions and offer the Chinese red vinegar separately, if using.

Pork and Pickled Mustard Greens Soup

The pickled mustard greens give the flavor while the cellophane noodles bring texture to this traditional Thai soup.

Serves 4–6

INGREDIENTS
8 oz pickled mustard greens, soaked
2 oz cellophane noodles, soaked
1 tbsp oil
4 garlic cloves, finely sliced
4 cups chicken stock
1 lb pork ribs, cut into large chunks
2 tbsp fish sauce
pinch of sugar
freshly ground black pepper
2 red chilies, seeded and finely sliced, to garnish

cellophane noodles

garlic

chicken stock

fish sauce

pork ribs

red chilies

1 Drain the pickled mustard greens and cut them into bite-size pieces. Taste to check that the seasoning is to your liking. If they are too salty, soak them in water for a little bit longer.

2 Drain the cellophane noodles and cut them into short lengths.

3 Heat the oil in a small frying pan, add the garlic and stir-fry until golden, taking care not to let it burn. Transfer the mixture to a bowl and set aside.

4 Put the stock in a saucepan, bring to a boil, then add the pork and simmer gently for 10–15 minutes. Add the pickled mustard greens and cellophane noodles. Bring back to a boil. Season to taste with fish sauce, sugar and freshly ground black pepper. Serve hot, topped with the fried garlic and red chilies.

Malaysian Spicy Shrimp and Noodle Soup

This is a Malaysian version of Hanoi Beef and Noodle Soup using fish and shrimp instead of beef. If laksa noodles aren't available, flat rice noodles can be used instead.

Serves 4–6

INGREDIENTS

1 oz unsalted cashew nuts
3 shallots, or 1 medium onion, sliced
2-in piece lemongrass, shredded
2 cloves garlic, crushed
2 tbsp oil
½-in cube shrimp paste or 1 tbsp fish sauce
1 tbsp mild curry paste
1¾ cups coconut milk
½ chicken bouillon cube
3 curry leaves (optional)
1 lb white fish fillets, e.g. cod, haddock or whiting
8 oz shrimp, fresh or cooked
5 oz laksa noodles, soaked for 10 minutes before cooking
1 small head romaine lettuce, shredded
½ cup bean sprouts
3 scallions, cut into lengths
½ cucumber, thinly sliced
shrimp crackers, to serve

1 Grind the cashew nuts using a mortar and pestle and then spoon into a food processor and process with the shallots or onion, lemongrass and garlic.

2 Heat the oil in a large wok or saucepan, add the cashew and onion mixture and fry for 1–2 minutes, until the mixture begins to brown.

3 Add the shrimp paste or fish sauce and curry paste, followed by the coconut milk, bouillon cube and curry leaves, if using. Simmer for 10 minutes.

cashew nuts (unsalted)

garlic   *shrimp paste*

curry paste

coconut milk

curry leaves

white fish fillets

shrimp

laksa noodles

lemongrass

bean sprouts

shallots

scallions

cucumber

4 Cut the fish into bite-size pieces. Add the fish and shrimp to the coconut stock, immersing them with a frying basket or a slotted spoon. Cook for 3–4 minutes, until the fish is tender. Cook the noodles according to the instructions on the package.

Hot-and-Sour Soup

This spicy, warming soup really whets the appetite and is the perfect introduction to a simple Chinese meal.

Serves 4

INGREDIENTS
¼ oz dried cloud ears
8 fresh shiitake mushrooms
3 oz bean curd (tofu)
½ cup sliced drained canned
    bamboo shoots
3¾ cups vegetable stock
1 tbsp sugar
3 tbsp rice vinegar
1 tbsp light soy sauce
¼ tsp chili oil
½ tsp salt
large pinch of ground white pepper
1 tbsp cornstarch
1 tbsp cold water
1 egg white
1 tsp sesame oil
2 scallions, cut into fine rings

1 Soak the cloud ears in hot water for 30 minutes, or until soft. Drain, trim off and discard the hard base from each and chop the cloud ears roughly.

2 Remove and discard the stalks from the shiitake mushrooms. Cut the caps into thin strips. Cut the bean curd into ½-inch cubes and shred the bamboo shoots finely.

sugar

egg

bamboo shoots

soy sauce

sesame oil

bean curd

shiitake mushrooms

cloud ears

scallions

vegetable stock

cornstarch

chili oil

rice vinegar

3 Place the stock, mushrooms, bean curd, bamboo shoots and cloud ears in a large saucepan. Bring the stock to a boil, lower the heat and simmer for about 5 minutes.

4 Stir in the sugar, vinegar, soy sauce, chili oil, salt and pepper. Mix the cornstarch to a paste with the water. Add the mixture to the soup, stirring constantly until it thickens slightly.

COOK'S TIP
To transform this tasty soup into a nutritious light meal, simply add extra mushrooms, bean curd and bamboo shoots.

5 Lightly beat the egg white, then pour it slowly into the soup in a steady stream, stirring constantly. Cook, stirring, until the egg white changes color.

6 Add the sesame oil just before serving. Ladle into heated bowls and top each portion with scallion rings.

Noodles in Soup

In China, noodles in soup (*tang mein*) are far more popular than fried noodles (*chow mein*). This is a basic recipe, which you can adapt by using different ingredients for the dressing.

Serves 4

INGREDIENTS
8 oz chicken breast fillet, pork
   tenderloin, or cooked meat
3–4 Chinese dried mushrooms,
   soaked
4 oz sliced bamboo shoots,
   drained
4 oz spinach leaves, lettuce center
   leaves, or napa cabbage
2 scallions
12 oz dried egg noodles
2½ cups chicken stock
2 tbsp vegetable oil
1 tsp oil
½ tsp light brown sugar
1 tbsp light soy sauce
2 tsp Chinese rice wine or dry
   sherry
few drops sesame oil

spinach leaves

chicken

bamboo shoots

noodles

mushrooms

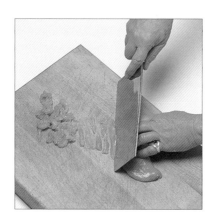

1 Thinly slice the meat. Squeeze the mushrooms dry and discard the hard stalks. Thinly shred the mushrooms, bamboo shoots, spinach/lettuce center leaves or cabbage and scallions.

2 Cook the noodles in boiling water according to the instructions on the package, then drain and rinse under cold water. Place in a serving bowl.

3 Bring the stock to a boil and pour it over the noodles; keep warm.

4 Heat the oil in a preheated wok over high heat, add about half of the scallions and the meat, and stir-fry for about 1 minute.

5 Add the mushrooms, bamboo shoots and greens and stir-fry for 1 minute. Add the remaining ingredients and blend well.

6 Pour the "dressing" over the noodles, garnish with the remaining scallions and serve.

Thai-style Chicken Soup

A fragrant blend of coconut milk, lemongrass, ginger and lime makes a delicious soup, with just a hint of chili.

Serves 4

INGREDIENTS

1 tsp oil
1–2 fresh red chilies,
    seeded and chopped
2 garlic cloves, crushed
1 large leek, thinly sliced
2½ cups chicken stock
1⅔ cups coconut milk
boneless, skinless chicken thighs,
    (1 lb) cut into bite-sized pieces
2 tbsp Thai fish sauce
1 lemongrass stalk, split
1-in piece fresh ginger root, peeled
    and finely chopped
1 tsp sugar
4 kaffir lime leaves (optional)
¾ cup frozen peas, thawed
3 tbsp chopped fresh cilantro

peas

chicken
stock

chicken
thighs

oil

sugar

fresh
cilantro

fresh
ginger root

garlic

Thai fish
sauce

coconut
milk

red
chilies

lemon-
grass

leek

kaffir
lime
leaves

1 Heat the oil in a large saucepan and cook the chilies and garlic for about 2 minutes. Add the leek and cook for 2 more minutes.

2 Stir in the stock and coconut milk and bring to a boil.

3 Add the chicken, with the fish sauce, lemongrass, ginger, sugar and lime leaves, if using. Simmer, covered, for 15 minutes or until the chicken is tender, stirring occasionally.

4 Add the peas and cook for 3 more minutes. Remove the lemongrass and stir in the cilantro just before serving.

Tomato and Beef Soup

Fresh tomatoes and scallions give this light beef broth a superb flavor.

Serves 4

INGREDIENTS
3 oz sirloin steak, trimmed of fat
3¼ cups beef stock
2 tbsp tomato paste
6 tomatoes, halved, seeded
   and chopped
2 tsp sugar
1 tbsp cornstarch
1 tbsp cold water
1 egg white
½ tsp sesame oil
2 scallions, finely shredded
salt and ground black pepper

steak

tomato paste

sugar

beef stock

egg

tomatoes

cornstarch

sesame oil

scallions

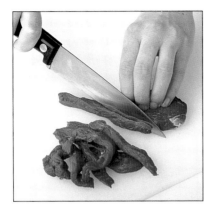

1 Cut the beef into thin strips and place it in a saucepan. Pour in boiling water to cover. Cook for 2 minutes, then drain thoroughly and set aside.

2 Bring the stock to a boil in a clean pan. Stir in the tomato paste, then the tomatoes and sugar. Add the beef strips, allow the stock to boil again, then lower the heat and simmer for 2 minutes.

COOK'S TIP
Try the soup topped with thin strips of fresh basil instead of scallions for a more Mediterranean taste.

3 Mix the cornstarch to a paste with the water. Add the mixture to the soup, stirring constantly until it thickens slightly. Lightly beat the egg white in a cup.

4 Pour the egg white into the soup in a steady stream, stirring all the time. As soon as the egg white changes color, add salt and pepper, stir the soup and pour it into heated bowls. Drizzle each portion with a few drops of sesame oil, sprinkle with the scallions and serve.

Seafood Soup Noodles

Audible sounds of enjoyment are a compliment to the Chinese cook, so slurping this superb soup is not only permissible, but positively desirable.

Serves 6

INGREDIENTS

6 oz tiger shrimp, shelled
   and deveined
8-oz monkfish fillet, cut
   into chunks
8-oz salmon fillet, cut
   into chunks
1 tsp vegetable oil
1 tbsp dry white wine
8 oz (2 cups) dried thin Chinese
   egg noodles
5 cups fish stock
1 carrot, thinly sliced
8 oz asparagus, cut into 2-in lengths
2 tbsp dark soy sauce
1 tsp sesame oil
salt and ground black pepper
2 scallions, cut into thin rings,
   to garnish

1 Mix the shrimp and fish in a bowl. Add the vegetable oil and wine with ¼ teaspoon salt and a little pepper. Mix lightly, cover and marinate in a cool place for 15 minutes.

2 Bring a large saucepan of water to a boil and cook the noodles for 4 minutes, until just tender, or according to the instructions on the package. Drain the noodles thoroughly and divide among four serving bowls. Keep hot.

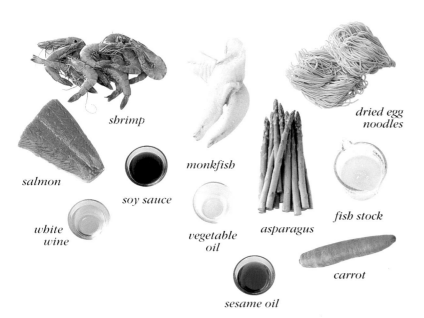

shrimp

salmon

monkfish

soy sauce

white wine

vegetable oil

asparagus

sesame oil

fish stock

dried egg noodles

carrot

3 Bring the fish stock to a boil in a separate pan. Add the shrimp and monkfish and cook for 1 minute. Add the salmon and cook for 2 minutes more.

4 Using a slotted spoon, lift the fish and shrimp out of the stock, add to the noodles in the bowls and keep hot.

VARIATION
Try this simple recipe using rice noodles for a slightly different texture and taste.

5 Strain the stock through a sieve lined with muslin or cheesecloth into a clean pan. Bring to a boil and cook the carrot and asparagus for 2 minutes, then add the soy sauce and sesame oil with salt to taste. Stir well.

6 Pour the stock and vegetables over the noodles and seafood, garnish with the scallions and serve.

Crab and Egg Noodle Broth

This delicious broth is an ideal solution when you are hungry and time is short, and you need something fast, nutritious and filling.

Serves 4

INGREDIENTS
3 oz fine egg noodles
2 tbsp sweet butter
1 small bunch scallions, chopped
1 celery stick, sliced
1 medium carrot, peeled and cut
  into sticks
5 cups chicken stock
4 tbsp dry sherry
4 oz white crabmeat, fresh
  or frozen
pinch of celery salt
pinch of cayenne pepper
2 tsp lemon juice
1 small bunch cilantro or flat-leaf
  parsley, to garnish

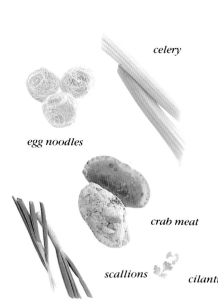

celery

egg noodles

crab meat

scallions   *cilantro*

1 Bring a large saucepan of salted water to a boil. Toss in the egg noodles and cook according to the instructions on the package. Cool under cold running water and leave immersed in water until required.

2 Heat the butter in another large pan, add the scallions, celery and carrot, cover and soften the vegetables over a gentle heat for 3–4 minutes.

3 Add the chicken stock and sherry, bring to a boil and simmer for a further 5 minutes.

4 Flake the crabmeat between your fingers onto a plate and remove any stray pieces of shell.

5 Drain the noodles and add to the broth together with the crabmeat. Season to taste with celery salt and cayenne pepper, and sharpen with the lemon juice. Return to a simmer.

6 Ladle the broth into shallow soup plates, scatter with roughly chopped cilantro or parsley and serve.

Beef Soup with Noodles and Meatballs

Egg noodles and spicy meatballs make this a really sustaining main soup-dish. In Asia, it is often served from street stalls.

Serves 6

INGREDIENTS

1 lb dried medium egg noodles
3 tbsp sunflower oil
1 large onion, finely sliced
2 garlic cloves, crushed
1-in piece fresh ginger root, cut into thin matchsticks
5 cups beef stock
2 tbsp dark soy sauce
2 celery ribs, finely sliced, leaves reserved
6 bok choy leaves, cut into bite-size pieces
1 handful snow peas, cut into strips
salt and freshly ground black pepper

FOR THE MEATBALLS

1 large onion, roughly chopped
1–2 red chilies, seeded and chopped
2 garlic cloves, crushed
½-in cube shrimp paste
1 lb lean ground beef
1 tbsp ground coriander
1 tsp ground cumin
2 tsp dark soy sauce
1 tsp dark brown sugar
juice of ½ lemon
a little beaten egg

dark soy sauce

dark brown sugar

lemon juice

snow peas

chilies

garlic

ground beef

ground coriander

ground cumin

onion

bok choy

celery

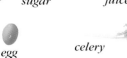
egg

fresh ginger root

dried egg noodles

beef stock

1 For the meatballs, put the onion, chilies, garlic and shrimp paste in a food processor. Process in short bursts, taking care not to overchop the onion.

2 Put the meat in a large bowl. Stir in the onion mixture. Add the ground coriander and cumin, soy sauce, brown sugar, lemon juice and seasoning.

4 Cook the noodles in a large pan of boiling salted water for 3–4 minutes, or until al dente. Drain in a colander and rinse with plenty of cold water. Set aside. Heat the oil in a wide pan and sauté the onion, garlic and ginger until soft but not browned. Add the stock and soy sauce and bring to a boil.

Shrimp paste, or *terasi*, has a strong, salty, distinctive flavor and smell. Use sparingly if unsure of its flavor.

3 Bind the mixture with a little beaten egg and shape into small balls.

5 Add the meatballs, half-cover and simmer until they are cooked, 5–8 minutes. Just before serving, add the sliced celery and, after 2 minutes, the bok choy and snow peas. Adjust the seasoning. Divide the noodles among soup bowls, pour the soup on top and garnish with the reserved celery leaves.

Chicken and Asparagus Soup

This is a very delicate and delicious soup. When fresh asparagus is not in season, canned white asparagus is an acceptable substitute.

Serves 4

INGREDIENTS

5 oz chicken breast fillet
pinch of salt
1 tsp egg white
1 tsp cornstarch paste
4 oz asparagus
3 cups chicken stock
salt and pepper, to taste
cilantro leaves, to garnish

asparagus

chicken

1 Cut the chicken meat into thin slices. Rub the meat with a pinch of salt, then add the egg white, and finally the cornstarch paste.

2 Discard the tough stems of the asparagus, and diagonally cut the tender spears into short lengths.

3 In a wok or saucepan, bring the stock to a rolling boil, add the asparagus and bring back to a boil, cooking for 2 minutes. (This is not necessary if using canned asparagus.)

4 Add the chicken, stir to separate and bring back to a boil once more, until the chicken is cooked through. Adjust the seasonings. Serve hot, garnished with cilantro leaves.

Wonton Soup

In China, wonton soup is served as a snack or dim sum during a large meal as well as being a separate soup course.

Serves 4

INGREDIENTS

6 oz pork, not too lean, coarsely
   chopped
2 oz shelled shrimp, finely
   chopped
1 tsp light brown sugar
1 tbsp Chinese rice wine or
   dry sherry
1 tbsp light soy sauce
1 tsp finely chopped scallions
1 tsp finely chopped fresh ginger
   root
24 wonton skins
3 cups chicken or fish stock
1 tbsp light soy sauce
finely chopped scallions, to garnish

1 In a bowl, mix the pork and shrimp with the sugar, wine or sherry, soy sauce, scallions and ginger. Blend well and let stand in a cool place for 25–30 minutes.

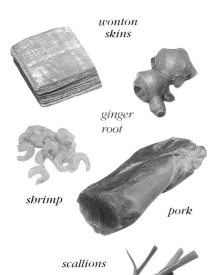

wonton skins

ginger root

shrimp

pork

scallions

2 Place about 1 teaspoon of the filling at the center of each wonton skin.

3 Wet and join the edges of each wonton, pressing down with your fingers to seal together, then fold each wonton over.

4 To cook, bring the stock to a rolling boil in a wok or saucepan, add the wontons and cook for 4–5 minutes. Season with the soy sauce and garnish with the scallions. Serve.

FISH AND SHELLFISH

There is an abundance of delicious seafood cuisine from Asia. This chapter contains classic Cantonese fish dishes along with Thai, Malaysian and Indonesian dishes.

Monkfish and Scallop Skewers

Using lemongrass stalks as skewers imbues the seafood with a subtle citrus flavor.

Serves 4

INGREDIENTS

1 lb monkfish fillet
8 lemongrass stalks
2 tbsp fresh lemon juice
1 tbsp olive oil
1 tbsp finely chopped cilantro
½ tsp salt
large pinch of ground black pepper
12 large scallops, halved crosswise
cilantro leaves, to garnish rice,
    to serve

lemongrass

olive oil

monkfish

scallops

cilantro

lemon

1 Remove any membrane from the monkfish, then cut into 16 large chunks.

2 Remove the outer leaves from the lemongrass to leave thin, rigid stalks. Chop the tender parts of the lemongrass leaves finely and place in a bowl. Stir in the lemon juice, oil, chopped cilantro, salt and pepper.

VARIATION

Raw tiger shrimp and salmon make an excellent alternative ingredient for the skewers, with or without the monkfish.

3 Thread the fish and scallop chunks alternately on the eight lemongrass stalks. Arrange the skewers of fish and shellfish in a shallow dish and pour the marinade over them.

4 Cover and leave in a cool place for 1 hour, turning occasionally. Transfer the skewers to a heatproof dish or bamboo steamer, cover and steam over boiling water for 10 minutes until just cooked. Garnish with cilantro and serve with rice and the cooking juice poured over.

Stir-fried Five-spice Squid with Black Bean Sauce

Squid is perfect for stir-frying, as it should be cooked quickly. The spicy sauce makes the ideal accompaniment.

Serves 6

INGREDIENTS

1 lb small cleaned squid
3 tbsp oil
1-in piece fresh ginger root, grated
1 garlic clove, crushed
8 scallions, cut diagonally into 1-in lengths
1 red bell pepper, seeded and cut into strips
1 fresh green chili, seeded and thinly sliced
6 mushrooms, sliced
1 tsp five-spice powder
2 tbsp black bean sauce
2 tbsp soy sauce
1 tsp sugar
1 tbsp rice wine or dry sherry

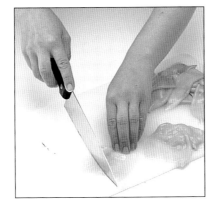

1 Rinse the squid and pull away the outer skin. Dry on paper towels. Using a sharp knife, slit the squid open and score the outside of the flesh into diamonds with a sharp knife. Cut the squid into strips.

green chili
sugar
oil
fresh ginger root
mushrooms
garlic
scallions
squid
five-spice powder
red bell pepper
soy sauce
black bean sauce
rice wine
dry sherry

COOK'S TIP

As with all stir-fried dishes, it is important to have every ingredient cut or prepared before you start to cook.

2 Heat the wok briefly and add the oil. When it is hot, stir-fry the squid for 2–3 minutes, then transfer to a plate with a slotted spoon. Add the ginger, garlic, scallions, pepper, chili and mushrooms and stir-fry for 2 minutes.

3 Return the squid to the wok and stir in the five-spice powder together with the black bean sauce, soy sauce, sugar and rice wine or sherry. Bring to a boil and cook, stirring, for 1 minute. Serve immediately.

Spiced Salmon Stir-fry

Marinating the salmon allows all the flavors to develop, and the lime tenderizes the fish beautifully, so it needs very little stir-frying—be careful not to overcook it.

Serves 4

INGREDIENTS
4 salmon steaks, about 8 oz each
4 whole star anise
2 stalks lemongrass, sliced
juice of 3 limes
zest of 3 limes, finely grated
2 tbsp honey
2 tbsp grapeseed oil
salt and freshly ground black pepper
lime wedges, to garnish

1 Remove the middle bone from each steak, using a very sharp filleting knife, to make two strips from each steak.

2 Remove the skin by inserting the knife at the thin end of each piece of salmon. Sprinkle 1 tsp salt on the cutting board to prevent the fish slipping while you remove the skin. Slice into pieces using diagonal cuts.

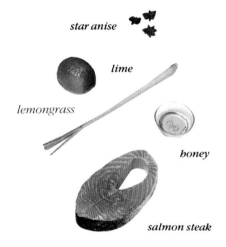

star anise

lime

lemongrass

honey

salmon steak

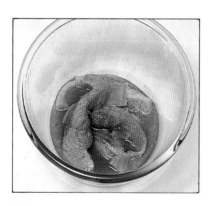

3 Coarsely crush the star anise in a mortar and pestle. Marinate the salmon in a non-metallic dish, with the star anise, lemongrass, lime juice and zest and honey. Season well with salt and pepper, cover and chill overnight.

4 Carefully drain the salmon from the marinade, pat dry on paper towels, and reserve the marinade.

5 Heat the wok, then add the oil. When the oil is hot, add the salmon and stir-fry, stirring constantly until cooked. Increase the heat, pour over the marinade and bring to a boil. Garnish with lime wedges and serve.

COOK'S TIP

Always dry off any marinade from meat, fish or vegetables to ensure that the hot oil does not splutter when you add them to the wok.

Fish Balls with Chinese Greens

These tasty fish balls are easy to make using a food processor. Here they are partnered with a selection of green vegetables—bok choy is available at most Asian stores.

Serves 4

INGREDIENTS

FOR THE FISH BALLS

1 lb white fish fillets, skinned, boned and cubed
3 scallions, chopped
1 slice Canadian bacon, rinded and chopped
1 tbsp Chinese rice wine
2 tbsp light soy sauce
1 egg white

FOR THE VEGETABLES

1 small head bok choy
1 tsp cornstarch
1 tbsp light soy sauce
⅔ cup fish stock
2 tbsp peanut oil
2 garlic cloves, sliced
1-in piece fresh ginger root, cut into thin shreds
3 oz green beans
6 oz snow peas
3 scallions, sliced diagonally into 2–3-in lengths
salt and ground black pepper

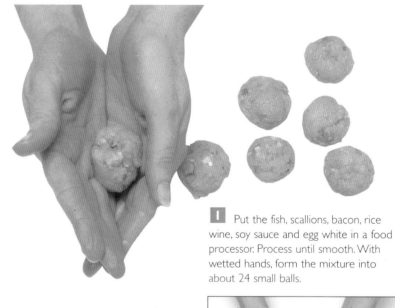

garlic   *ginger*

bacon

scallions

light soy sauce

bok choy

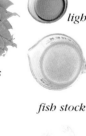

snow peas

green beans   *fish stock*

fish fillets

Chinese rice wine   *peanut oil*

1 Put the fish, scallions, bacon, rice wine, soy sauce and egg white in a food processor. Process until smooth. With wetted hands, form the mixture into about 24 small balls.

2 Steam the fish balls in batches in a lightly greased bamboo steamer in a wok for 5–10 minutes until firm. Remove from the steamer and keep warm.

3 Meanwhile, trim the bok choy, removing any discolored leaves or damaged stems, then tear into manageable pieces.

4 In a small bowl blend together the cornstarch, soy sauce and stock.

VARIATION
Replace the snow peas and green beans with broccoli florets. Blanch them before stir-frying.

5 Heat a wok until hot, add the oil and swirl it around. Add the garlic and ginger and stir-fry for 1 minute. Add the beans and stir-fry for 2–3 minutes, then add the snow peas, scallions and bok choy. Stir-fry for 2–3 minutes.

6 Add the sauce to the wok and cook, stirring, until it has thickened and the vegetables are tender but crisp. Taste and adjust the seasoning, if necessary. Serve immediately with the fish balls.

Squid with Peppers in Black Bean Sauce

Salted black beans add a traditionally Chinese flavor to this tasty stir-fry.

Serves 4

INGREDIENTS

2 tbsp salted black beans
2 tbsp medium-dry sherry
1 tbsp light soy sauce
1 tsp cornstarch
½ tsp sugar
2 tbsp water
3 tbsp peanut oil
1 lb cleaned squid, scored and
  cut into thick strips
1 tsp finely chopped fresh
  ginger root
1 garlic clove, finely chopped
1 fresh green chili,
  seeded and sliced
6–8 scallions, cut diagonally
  into 1-in lengths
½ red and ½ green bell pepper,
  cored, seeded and cut into
  1-in diamonds
3 oz shiitake mushrooms,
  thickly sliced

scallions

shiitake mushrooms

medium-dry sherry

light soy sauce

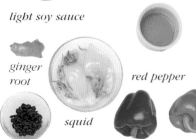

ginger root

red pepper

squid

salted black beans   *green pepper*   *green chili*

1 Rinse and finely chop the black beans. Place them in a bowl with the sherry, soy sauce, cornstarch, sugar and water; mix well.

2 Heat a wok until hot, add the oil and swirl it around. When the oil is very hot, add the squid and stir-fry for 1–1½ minutes, until opaque and curled at the edges. Remove with a slotted spoon and set aside.

3 Add the ginger, garlic and chili to the wok and stir-fry for a few seconds. Then add the scallions, peppers and mushrooms, then stir-fry for 2 minutes.

4 Return the squid to the wok with the sauce. Cook, stirring, for about 1 minute, until thickened. Serve at once.

Shrimp and Snow Pea Stir-fry

It's a good idea to keep some frozen shrimp in stock, as they are always handy for a quick stir-fry like this one. Serve with plain boiled rice or chapatis.

Serves 4

INGREDIENTS
1 tbsp corn oil
2 medium onions, diced
1 tbsp tomato paste
1 tsp Tabasco sauce
1 tsp lemon juice
1 tsp ginger pulp
1 tsp garlic pulp
1 tsp chili powder
1 tsp salt
1 tbsp chopped cilantro
6 oz frozen cooked shelled
    shrimp, thawed
12 snow peas, halved

Tabasco sauce
shrimp
onions
ginger pulp
salt
cilantro
garlic pulp
snow peas
tomato paste
chili powder

1 Heat the oil in a nonstick wok or frying pan and stir-fry the onions over low heat for about 2 minutes, or until they are golden brown.

2 Meanwhile, mix the tomato paste with 2 tablespoons water in a bowl, then stir in the Tabasco sauce, lemon juice, ginger pulp, garlic pulp, chili powder and salt and blend to a sauce.

3 Lower the heat, pour the sauce over the onions and stir-fry.

4 Add the cilantro, shrimp and snow peas and stir-fry for 5–7 minutes, or until the sauce is thick. Serve hot.

Fragrant Swordfish with Ginger and Lemongrass

Swordfish is a meaty fish which cooks well in a wok if it has been marinated as a steak rather than in strips. If you cannot get swordfish, use tuna.

Serves 4

INGREDIENTS

1 kaffir lime leaf
3 tbsp kosher salt
5 tbsp brown sugar
4 swordfish steaks, about 8 oz each
1 stalk lemongrass, sliced
1 in piece ginger root, cut into
    matchsticks
1 lime
1 tbsp grapeseed oil
1 large ripe avocado, peeled and
    pitted
salt and freshly ground black pepper

avocado

ginger

lemon grass

lime

lime leaf

swordfish steak

1 Bruise the lime leaf by crushing slightly, to release the flavor.

2 To make the marinade, process the kosher salt, brown sugar and lime leaf together in a food processor until thoroughly blended.

3 Place the swordfish steaks in a bowl. Sprinkle the marinade over them and add the lemongrass and ginger. Let stand for 3–4 hours to marinate.

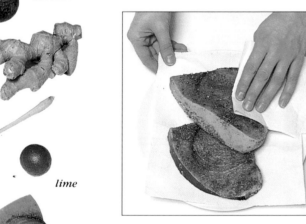

4 Rinse off the marinade and pat dry with paper towels.

5 Peel the lime. Remove any excess pith from the peel, then cut into very thin strips.

6 Heat the wok, then add the oil. When the oil is hot, add the lime zest and then the fish steaks, and stir-fry for 3–4 minutes. Add the juice of the lime. Remove from the heat, slice the avocado and add to the fish. Season and serve.

Stir-fried Squid with Black Bean Sauce

If you cannot buy fresh squid you will certainly find small or baby frozen squid, skinned, boned and with heads removed, at your local fishmonger.

Serves 4

INGREDIENTS
½ lb fresh or frozen squid
1 red chili
2 tsp peanut oil
1 clove garlic, crushed
2 tbsp black bean sauce
4 tbsp water
fresh parsley sprigs, to garnish
steamed rice, to serve

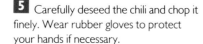
black bean sauce

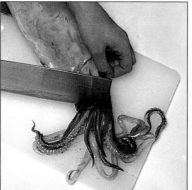
garlic

squid

chilies

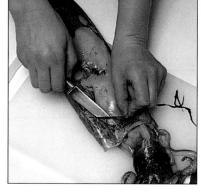

1 Carefully remove the skin from the squid and discard.

2 Cut off the head of each squid just below the eye, and discard.

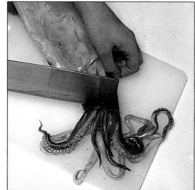

3 Remove the bone from the squid and discard.

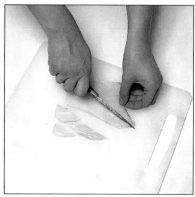

4 Cut the squid into bite-size pieces and score the flesh in a criss-cross pattern with a sharp knife.

5 Carefully deseed the chili and chop it finely. Wear rubber gloves to protect your hands if necessary.

6 Heat the wok, then add the oil. When the oil is hot, add the garlic and cook until it starts to sizzle but does not color. Stir in the squid and fry until the flesh starts to stiffen and turn white. Quickly stir in the black bean sauce, water and chili. Continue stirring until the squid is cooked and tender (not more than a minute). Garnish with parsley sprigs and the tentacles and serve with steamed rice.

Mussels in Black Bean Sauce

Large green-lipped mussels are perfect for this delicious dish. Buy the cooked mussels on the half shell.

Serves 4

INGREDIENTS

1 tbsp vegetable oil
1-in piece of fresh ginger root, finely chopped
2 garlic cloves, finely chopped
1 fresh red chili, seeded and chopped
1 tbsp black bean sauce
1 tbsp dry sherry
1 tsp sugar
1 tsp sesame oil
2 tsp dark soy sauce
20 cooked large green-lipped mussels
2 scallions, 1 shredded and 1 cut into fine rings

garlic

ginger

chili

mussels

black bean sauce

sherry

sugar

soy sauce

sesame oil

vegetable oil

scallions

1 Heat the vegetable oil in a small frying pan. Fry the ginger, garlic and chili with the black bean sauce for a few seconds, then add the sherry and sugar and cook for 30 seconds more.

2 Remove the sauce from the heat and stir in the sesame oil and soy sauce. Mix thoroughly.

COOK'S TIP
Large scallops in their shells can be cooked in the same way. Do not overcook the shellfish.

3 Have ready a saucepan with about 2 inches of boiling water and a heatproof plate that will fit neatly inside it. Place the mussels in a single layer on the plate. Spoon the sauce over them.

4 Sprinkle the scallions over the mussels, cover the plate tightly with foil and place it in the pan on a metal trivet. Steam over high heat for about 10 minutes, or until the mussels have heated through. Serve immediately.

Spiced Scallops in their Shells

Scallops are excellent steamed. When served with this spicy sauce, they make a delicious yet simple appetizer. Each person spoons sauce onto the scallops before eating them.

Serves 4

INGREDIENTS

8 scallops, shelled (the shells are available in cooking ware stores and some good fish markets)
2 slices fresh ginger root, finely shredded
½ garlic clove, shredded
2 scallions, green parts only, shredded
salt and pepper

FOR THE SAUCE

1 garlic clove, crushed
1 tbsp fresh ginger root, finely grated
2 scallions, white parts only, chopped
1-2 fresh green chilies, seeded and finely chopped
1 tbsp light soy sauce
1 tbsp dark soy sauce
2 tsp sesame oil

scallops

ginger root

scallions

garlic

light soy sauce

green chili

dark soy sauce

sesame oil

1 Remove the dark beard-like fringe and tough muscle from the scallops.

2 Place 2 scallops in each shell. Season lightly with salt and pepper, then sprinkle the ginger, garlic and scallions on top. Place the shells in a bamboo steamer and steam for about 6 minutes, until the scallops look opaque (you may have to do this in batches).

3 Meanwhile, mix together all the sauce ingredients and pour into a small serving bowl.

4 Carefully remove each shell from the steamer, taking care not to spill the juices, and arrange them on a serving plate with the sauce bowl in the center. Serve immediately.

Spicy Squid Salad

This tasty, colorful salad is a refreshing way of serving succulent squid.

Serves 4

INGREDIENTS

1-lb squid

1¼ cups fish stock

6 oz green beans, trimmed and halved

3 tbsp cilantro leaves

2 tsp sugar

2 tbsp rice vinegar

1 tsp sesame oil

1 tbsp light soy sauce

1 tbsp vegetable oil

2 garlic cloves, finely chopped

2 tbsp finely chopped fresh ginger root

1 fresh chili, seeded and chopped

salt

fish stock

green beans

cilantro

squid

rice vinegar

sugar

sesame oil

vegetable oil

soy sauce

garlic

chili

ginger root

COOK'S TIP

If you hold your knife at an angle when scoring the squid there is less of a risk of cutting right through it.

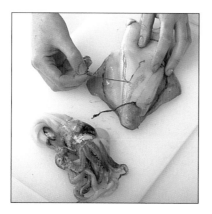

1 Prepare the squid. Holding the body in one hand, gently pull away the head and tentacles. Discard the head; trim and reserve the tentacles. Remove the transparent "quill" from inside the body of the squid and peel off the purplish skin on the outside.

2 Cut the body of the squid open lengthwise and wash thoroughly. Score crisscross patterns on the inside, taking care not to cut through the squid, then cut into 3 x 2-inch pieces.

3 Bring the fish stock to a boil in a wok or saucepan. Add all the squid pieces, then lower the heat and cook for about 2 minutes, until they are tender and have curled. Drain.

4 In a separate pan of lightly salted boiling water, cook the beans until crisp-tender. Drain, refresh under cold water, then drain again. Mix the squid and beans in a serving bowl.

5 In a bowl or measuring cup, mix the cilantro leaves, sugar, rice vinegar, sesame oil and soy sauce. Pour the mixture over the squid and beans.

6 Heat the vegetable oil in a wok or small pan until very hot. Stir-fry the garlic, ginger and chili for a few seconds, then pour the dressing over the squid mixture. Toss gently and let sit for at least 5 minutes. Add salt to taste and serve warm or cold.

Shrimp and Vegetable Balti

A simple and delicious accompaniment to many other Balti dishes.

Serves 4

INGREDIENTS
6 oz frozen cooked, shelled shrimp
2 tbsp corn oil
¼ tsp onion seeds
4–6 curry leaves
4 oz frozen peas
4 oz frozen corn
1 large zucchini, sliced
1 medium red bell pepper, seeded and roughly diced
1 tsp crushed coriander seeds
1 tsp crushed dried red chilies
1 tbsp lemon juice
salt
1 tbsp cilantro leaves, to garnish

shrimp   peas   corn

red bell pepper   curry leaves   zucchini

cilantro

onion seeds   dried red chilies   coriander seeds

lemon juice

COOK'S TIP
The best way to crush whole seeds is to use an electric spice grinder or a small marble mortar and pestle.

1 Thaw the shrimp and drain them of any excess liquid.

2 Heat the oil with the onion seeds and curry leaves in a nonstick wok or frying pan.

3 Add the shrimp to the wok and stir-fry until the liquid has evaporated.

4 Next add the peas, corn, zucchini and bell pepper. Continue to stir for 3–5 minutes.

5 Finally, add the coriander seeds, chilies, salt to taste and lemon juice.

6 Serve immediately, garnished with cilantro leaves.

Sea Bass with Chinese Chives

Chinese chives are widely available in Oriental supermarkets but if you are unable to buy them, use half a large Spanish onion, finely sliced, instead.

Serves 4

INGREDIENTS
4 sea bass fillets, about 1 lb in all
1 tsp cornstarch
3 tbsp vegetable oil
6 oz/2 cups Chinese chives
1 tbsp rice wine
1 tsp superfine sugar
salt and freshly ground black pepper
Chinese chives with flowerheads,
    to garnish
mixed lettuce salad, to serve

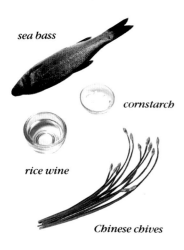

sea bass

cornstarch

rice wine

Chinese chives

1 Remove the scales from the bass by scraping the fillets with the back of a knife, working from tail end to head end.

2 Cut the fillets into large chunks and dust them lightly with cornstarch, salt and pepper.

3 Heat the wok, then add 2 tbsp of the oil. When the oil is hot, toss the chunks of fish in the wok briefly to seal, then set aside. Wipe out the wok with paper towels.

4 Cut the Chinese chives into 2 in lengths and discard the flowers. Heat the wok and add the remaining oil, then stir-fry the Chinese chives for 30 seconds. Add the fish and rice wine, then bring to the boil and stir in the sugar. Serve hot, garnished with some flowering Chinese chives, and with a side dish of crisp mixed green salad.

Mixed Seafood Stir-fry

This is a substantial dish: it is best served with chunks of fresh crusty white bread, for mopping up all the delicious, spicy juices.

Serves 4

INGREDIENTS
1½ lb mixed seafood (for example, red snapper, cod, raw shrimp), filleted and skinned
1¼ cups coconut milk
1 tbsp vegetable oil
salt and freshly ground black pepper

FOR THE SAUCE
2 large red chilies
1 onion, roughly chopped
2 in piece ginger root, peeled and sliced
2 in piece lemongrass, outer leaf discarded, roughly sliced
2 in piece galangal, peeled and sliced
6 blanched almonds, chopped
½ tsp turmeric
½ tsp salt

chili

onion

ginger root

shrimp

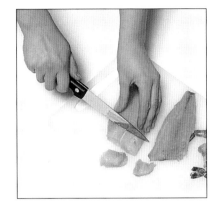

1 Cut the filleted fish into large chunks. Shell the shrimp, keeping their tails intact.

2 Carefully remove the seeds from the chilies and chop roughly, wearing rubber gloves to protect your hands if necessary. Then, make the sauce by putting the chilies and the other sauce ingredients in the food processor with 3 tbsp of the coconut milk. Blend until smooth.

3 Heat the wok, then add the oil. When the oil is hot, stir-fry the seafood for 2–3 minutes, then remove.

4 Add the sauce and the remaining coconut milk to the wok, then return the seafood. Bring to the boil, season well and serve with crusty bread.

Red Snapper with Ginger and Scallions

This is a classic Chinese way of cooking fish. Pouring the oil slowly over the scallions and ginger allows it to partially cook them, enhancing their flavor.

Serves 2-3

INGREDIENTS
1 red snapper, about
 1½-2 lb, cleaned and scaled
 with head left on
1 bunch scallions, cut into thin
 shreds
1-in piece fresh ginger root, cut
 into thin shreds
¼ tsp salt
¼ tsp sugar
3 tbsp peanut oil
1 tsp sesame oil
2-3 tbsp light soy sauce
scallion brushes, to garnish

scallions

ginger root

peanut oil

sesame oil

red snapper

light soy sauce

sugar

COOK'S TIP
If the fish is too big to fit inside the steamer, cut off the head and place it alongside the body, which can then be reassembled after it is cooked for serving.

1 Rinse the fish, then pat dry with paper towels. Slash the flesh diagonally, three times on each side. Set the fish on a heatproof oval plate that will fit inside your bamboo steamer.

2 Tuck about one-third of the scallions and ginger inside the body cavity. Place the plate inside the steamer, cover with its lid, then place in a wok.

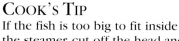

3 Steam over medium heat for 10–15 minutes, until the fish flakes easily when tested with the tip of a knife.

4 Carefully remove the plate from the steamer. Sprinkle over the salt, sugar and remaining scallions and ginger.

5 Heat the oils in a small pan until very hot, then slowly pour over the fish.

6 Drizzle over the soy sauce and serve at once, garnished with scallion brushes.

Three Sea Flavors Stir-Fry

This delectable seafood combination is enhanced by the use of fresh ginger root and scallions.

Serves 4

INGREDIENTS
4 large scallops, preferably with
    the corals
8 oz firm white fish fillet, such as
    monkfish or cod
4 oz raw tiger shrimp
1¼ cups fish stock
1 tbsp vegetable oil
2 garlic cloves, coarsely chopped
2-in piece of fresh ginger root,
    thinly sliced
8 scallions, cut into 1½-in pieces
2 tbsp dry white wine
1 tsp cornstarch
1 tbsp cold water
salt and ground white pepper
noodles or rice, to serve

fish stock
wine
garlic
shrimp
ginger root
vegetable oil
fish fillet
cornstarch
scallops
scallions

COOK'S TIP
Do not overcook the seafood, or it will become rubbery.

1 Separate the corals, if using, and slice each scallop in half horizontally. Cut the fish fillet into bite-size chunks. Shell and devein the shrimp.

2 Bring the fish stock to a boil in a saucepan. Add the seafood, lower the heat and poach gently for 1–2 minutes, until the fish, scallops and corals are just firm and the shrimp have turned pink. Drain the seafood, reserving about 4 tablespoons of the stock.

3 Heat the oil in a nonstick frying pan or wok over high heat until very hot. Stir-fry the garlic, ginger and scallions for a few seconds.

4 Add the seafood and wine. Stir-fry for 1 minute, then add the reserved stock and simmer for 2 minutes.

5 Mix the cornstarch to a paste with the water. Add the mixture to the pan or wok and cook, stirring gently, just until the sauce thickens.

6 Season the stir-fry with salt and pepper to taste. Serve at once, with noodles or rice.

Thai Seafood Salad

This seafood salad with chili, lemongrass and fish sauce is light and refreshing.

Serves 4

INGREDIENTS
8 oz cleaned squid
8 oz raw large shrimp
8 sea scallops, whole
8 oz firm white fish
2–3 tbsp olive oil
small mixed lettuce leaves and
   cilantro sprigs, to serve

FOR THE DRESSING
2 small fresh red chilies, seeded
   and finely chopped
2-in piece lemongrass,
   finely chopped
2 fresh kaffir lime leaves,
   shredded
2 tbsp Thai fish sauce
   (*nam pla*)
2 shallots, thinly sliced
2 tbsp lime juice
2 tbsp rice vinegar
2 tsp sugar

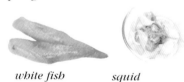

white fish   *squid*

scallops

large shrimp

lemongrass

Thai fish sauce

shallots   *kaffir lime leaves*

1 Prepare the seafood: slit open the squid bodies, score the flesh with a sharp knife, then cut into square pieces. Halve the tentacles, if necessary. Shell and devein the shrimp. Cut the sea scallops in half (if using bay scallops, leave whole). Cube the white fish.

2 Heat a wok until hot. Add the oil and swirl it around, then add the shrimp and stir-fry for 2–3 minutes until pink. Transfer to a large bowl. Stir-fry the squid and scallops for 1–2 minutes, until opaque. Remove and add to the shrimp. Stir-fry the white fish for 2–3 minutes. Remove and add to the cooked seafood. Reserve any juices.

3 Put all the dressing ingredients in a small bowl with the reserved juices from the wok; mix well.

4 Pour the dressing over the seafood and toss gently. Arrange the salad leaves and cilantro sprigs on four individual plates, then spoon the seafood on top. Serve at once.

Spicy Fish Fritters

These crispy, spicy fritters are based on a dish from Baltistan, India.

Serves 4

INGREDIENTS

2 tsp cumin seeds
2 tsp coriander seeds
1–2 dried red chilies
2 tbsp vegetable oil
1½ cups gram flour
1 tsp salt
2 tsp garam masala
1 cup water
peanut oil, for deep-frying
1½ lb fish fillets, such as cod,
    skinned, boned and cut into
    thick strips
mint sprigs and lime halves,
    to garnish

fish fillets

peanut oil

gram flour

red chilies

vegetable oil

coriander *garam masala*

1 Crush the cumin, coriander and chili(es), using a mortar and pestle. Heat the vegetable oil in a kadhai or wok and stir-fry the spices for 1–2 minutes.

2 Put the gram flour, salt, spice mixture and garam masala in a bowl. Gradually stir in enough water to make a thick batter. Cover and allow to rest for 30 minutes.

3 Half-fill a kadhai or wok with peanut oil and heat to 375°F. When the oil is ready, dip the fish, just a few pieces at a time, into the batter, shaking off any excess.

4 Deep-fry the fish in batches for 4–5 minutes, until golden brown. Drain on paper towels. Serve immediately, garnished with mint sprigs and lime halves for squeezing over the fritters.

Gray Mullet with Pork

This unusual combination makes a spectacular main dish with little effort.

Serves 4

INGREDIENTS

1 gray mullet, red snapper or
   pompano, about 2 lb, gutted
   and cleaned
2 oz lean pork
3 dried Chinese mushrooms,
   soaked in hot water until soft
½ tsp cornstarch
2 tbsp light soy sauce
1 tbsp vegetable oil
1 tbsp finely shredded fresh
   ginger root
1 tbsp shredded scallion
salt and ground black pepper
rice, to serve
sliced scallion, to garnish

*dried Chinese
mushrooms*

cornstarch   soy sauce

pork

gray mullet

*ginger
root*

scallion

*vegetable
oil*

COOK'S TIP
If the fish is too big to fit into
the steamer whole, simply cut
the fish in half for cooking, then
reassemble it to serve.

1 Make four diagonal cuts on either side of the fish and rub with a little salt; place the fish on a large shallow heatproof serving dish.

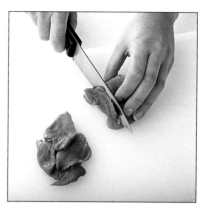

2 Cut the pork into thin strips. Place in a bowl. Drain the soaked mushrooms, remove and discard the stalks and slice the caps thinly.

3 Add the mushrooms to the pork, with the cornstarch and half the soy sauce. Stir in 1 teaspoon of the oil and a generous grinding of black pepper. Arrange the pork mixture along the length of the fish. Scatter the shredded ginger over the top.

4 Cover the fish loosely with foil. Have ready a large saucepan or roasting pan, with about 2 inches boiling water, that is big enough to fit the heatproof dish inside it on a metal trivet. Place the dish in the pan or roasting pan, cover and steam over high heat for 15 minutes.

5 Test the fish by pressing the flesh gently. If it comes away from the bone with slight resistance, the fish is cooked. Carefully pour away any excess liquid from the dish.

6 Heat the remaining oil in a small pan. When it is hot, fry the shredded scallion for a few seconds, then pour it over the fish, being very careful, because it will splatter. Drizzle with the remaining soy sauce, garnish with sliced scallion and serve immediately with rice.

Green Seafood Curry

This curry is based on a Thai classic. The lovely green color is imparted by the finely chopped chili and fresh herbs added during the last few moments of cooking.

COOK'S TIP
If you like more fiery curries, increase the amount of green curry paste used.

Serves 4

INGREDIENTS
8 oz small, cleaned squid
8 oz raw large shrimp
1¾ cups coconut milk
2 tbsp green curry paste
2 fresh kaffir lime leaves, finely shredded
2 tbsp Thai fish sauce (*nam pla*)
1 lb firm white fish fillets, skinned, boned and cut into chunks
2 fresh green chilies, seeded and finely chopped
2 tbsp torn basil or cilantro leaves
squeeze of lime juice
Thai jasmine rice, to serve

shrimp

green chilies

squid

white fish

basil

coconut milk

green curry paste

kaffir lime leaves

1 Rinse the squid and pat dry with paper towels. Cut the bodies into rings and halve the tentacles, if necessary.

2 Heat a wok until hot, add the shrimp and stir-fry without any oil for about 4 minutes, until they turn pink.

3 Remove the shrimp from the heat and when they are cool enough to handle, peel off the shells. Make a slit along the back of each one and remove the black vein.

4 Pour the coconut milk into the wok, then bring to a boil, stirring. Add the curry paste, shredded lime leaves and fish sauce. Reduce the heat to a simmer and cook for about 10 minutes, enough for the flavors to develop.

5 Add the squid, shrimp and white fish and cook for about 2 minutes until the seafood is tender. Take care not to overcook the squid, as it will become tough very quickly.

6 Just before serving, stir in the chilies and basil or cilantro. Taste and adjust the flavor with a squeeze of lime juice. Serve with Thai jasmine rice.

Gingered Seafood Stir-fry

A refreshing summer supper, served with plenty of crusty bread to mop up the juices and a glass of chilled dry white wine. It would also make a great appetizer for four people.

Serves 2

INGREDIENTS
1 tbsp sunflower oil
1 tsp sesame oil
1-in piece fresh ginger root, peeled
    and finely chopped
1 bunch scallions, sliced
1 red bell pepper, seeded and finely
    chopped
¼ lb small bay scallops
8 large uncooked shrimp, shelled
¼ lb squid rings
1 tbsp lime juice
1 tbsp light soy sauce
¼ cup coconut milk
salt and pepper
mixed lettuce leaves and crusty
    bread, to serve

lettuce leaves   *scallions*   *uncooked shrimp*   *bay scallops*

fresh ginger   *lime*   *squid rings*

light soy sauce   *red bell pepper*

sesame oil   *sunflower oil*   *coconut milk*

1 Heat the oils in a wok or large frying pan and cook the ginger and scallions for 2–3 minutes or until golden. Stir in the red bell pepper and cook for 3 more minutes.

2 Add the scallops, shrimp and squid rings and cook over medium heat for about 3 minutes, until the seafood is just cooked.

3 Stir in the lime juice, soy sauce and coconut milk. Simmer, uncovered, for 2 minutes, until the juices begin to thicken slightly.

4 Season well. Arrange the lettuce leaves on serving plates and spoon on the seafood mixture with the juices. Serve with plenty of crusty bread to mop up the juices.

Hot Spicy Crab Claws

Crab claws are used to delicious effect in this quick appetizer based on an Indonesian dish called *Kepiting Pedas*.

Serves 4

INGREDIENTS
12 fresh or frozen and thawed
  cooked crab claws
4 shallots, coarsely chopped
2–4 fresh red chilies, seeded and
  coarsely chopped
3 garlic cloves, coarsely chopped
1 tsp grated fresh ginger root
½ tsp ground coriander
3 tbsp peanut oil
4 tbsp water
2 tsp sweet soy sauce
  (*kecap manis*)
2–3 tsp lime juice
salt, to taste
fresh cilantro, to garnish

shallots

crab claws

sweet soy sauce

garlic

coriander

peanut oil

red chilies

lime

ginger

1 Crack the crab claws with the back of a heavy knife to make eating easier. Set aside. In a mortar, pound the chopped shallots with the pestle until pulpy. Add the chilies, garlic, ginger and ground coriander and pound until the mixture forms a coarse paste.

2 Heat the wok over medium heat. Add the oil and swirl it around. When it is hot, stir in the chili paste. Stir-fry for about 30 seconds. Increase the heat to high. Add the crab claws and stir-fry for another 3–4 minutes.

3 Stir in the water, sweet soy sauce, lime juice and salt to taste. Continue to stir-fry for 1–2 minutes. Serve at once, garnished with fresh cilantro. The crab claws are eaten with the fingers, so provide finger bowls.

COOK'S TIP
If whole crab claws are unavailable, look out for frozen prepared crab claws. These are shelled with just the tip of the claw attached to the white meat. Stir-fry for about two minutes until heated through.

Lemongrass-and-basil-scented Mussels

Thai flavorings of lemongrass and basil are used in this quick and easy dish.

Serves 4

INGREDIENTS
4–4½ lb fresh mussels
  in the shell
2 lemongrass stalks
handful of small fresh basil leaves
2-in piece fresh ginger root
2 shallots, finely chopped
¼ pint/⅔ cup fish stock

lemongrass

mussels

fish stock

shallots

ginger root

basil

COOK'S TIP

Mussels are best bought fresh and eaten on the day of purchase. Any that remain closed after cooking should be thrown away.

1 Scrub the mussels under cold running water, scraping off any barnacles with a small sharp knife. Pull or cut off the hairy "beards". Discard any with damaged shells and any that remain open when sharply tapped.

2 Cut each lemongrass stalk in half and bruise with a rolling pin.

3 Coarsely chop half the basil leaves; reserve the remainder for the garnish.

4 Put the mussels, lemongrass, chopped basil, ginger, shallots and stock in a wok. Bring to a boil, cover and simmer for 5 minutes. Discard any mussels that remain closed. Sprinkle over the reserved basil and serve at once.

Spiced Shrimp with Coconut

This spicy dish is based on *Sambal Goreng Udang*, which is Indonesian in origin. It is best served with plain boiled rice.

Serves 3-4

INGREDIENTS

2-3 fresh red chilies, seeded
   and chopped
3 shallots, chopped
1 lemongrass stalk, chopped
2 garlic cloves, chopped
thin sliver of dried shrimp paste
½ tsp ground galangal
1 tsp ground turmeric
1 tsp ground coriander
1 tbsp peanut oil
1 cup water
2 fresh kaffir lime leaves
1 tsp light brown sugar
2 tomatoes, peeled, seeded
   and chopped
1 cup coconut milk
1½ lb large raw shrimp,
   shelled and deveined
squeeze of lemon juice
salt, to taste
shredded scallions and
   flaked coconut, to garnish

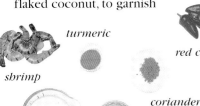

turmeric

shrimp

coconut milk *sugar*

red chilies

coriander

galangal

garlic

lemongrass

dried shrimp paste

peanut oil

tomatoes

kaffir lime leaves *shallots*

COOK'S TIP
Dried shrimp paste, much used in Southeast Asia, is available at Asian stores.

1 In a mortar pound the chilies, shallots, lemongrass, garlic, shrimp paste, galangal, turmeric and coriander with a pestle until it forms a paste.

2 Heat a wok until hot, add the oil and swirl it around. Add the spiced paste and stir-fry for about 2 minutes. Pour in the water and add the kaffir lime leaves, sugar and tomatoes. Simmer for 8–10 minutes, until most of the liquid has evaporated.

3 Add the coconut milk and shrimp and cook gently, stirring, for about 4 minutes until the shrimp are pink. Taste and adjust the seasoning with salt and a squeeze of lemon juice. Serve at once, garnished with shredded scallions and toasted flaked coconut.

Asian Scallops with Ginger Relish

If possible, buy scallops in their shells to be sure of their freshness; your fish dealer will open them for you if you find this difficult to do. Some specialty fish dealers will sell scallops with their roe.

Serves 4

INGREDIENTS
8 sea scallops
4 whole star anise
2 tbsp sweet butter
salt and freshly ground white pepper
fresh chervil sprigs and whole star
    anise, to garnish

FOR THE RELISH
½ cucumber, peeled
salt, for sprinkling
2 in piece ginger root, peeled
2 tsp superfine sugar
3 tbsp rice wine vinegar
2 tsp ginger juice, strained from a
    jar of stem ginger
sesame seeds, for sprinkling

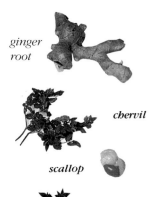

ginger root

chervil

scallop

star anise

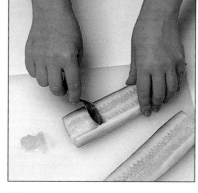

1 To make the relish, halve the cucumber lengthwise and scoop out the seeds with a teaspoon.

2 Cut the cucumber into 1 in pieces, place in a colander and sprinkle liberally with salt. Set aside for 30 minutes.

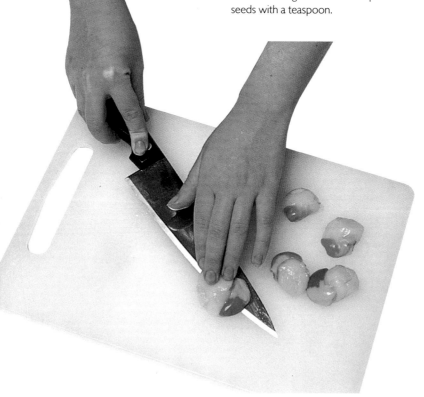

3 To prepare the scallops, cut each into 2–3 slices. Coarsely grind the star anise in a mortar and pestle.

4 Place the scallop slices with the roe in a bowl and marinate with the star anise and seasoning for about 1 hour.

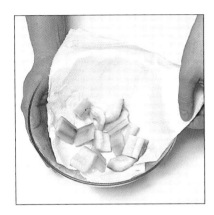

5 Rinse the cucumber under cold water and pat dry on paper towels. Cut the ginger into thin julienne strips and mix with the remaining relish ingredients. Cover and chill until needed.

6 Heat the wok and add the butter. When the butter is hot, add the scallop slices and stir-fry for 2–3 minutes. Garnish with sprigs of chervil and whole star anise, and serve with the cucumber relish, sprinkled with sesame seeds.

Fish Casserole with Lemongrass

Lemongrass gives this delicate fish casserole an aromatic flavor, perfect for a special treat.

Serves 4

INGREDIENTS

2 tbsp butter
6 oz onions, chopped
4 tsp flour
1²/₃ cups stock
²/₃ cup white wine
1-in piece fresh ginger root, peeled and finely chopped
2 lemongrass stalks, trimmed and finely chopped
1 lb new potatoes, scrubbed and halved if necessary
white fish fillets (1 lb), skinned
6 oz large shelled cooked shrimp
10 oz small broccoli florets
²/₃ cup heavy cream
¹/₄ cup chopped fresh chives
salt and pepper
crusty bread, to serve

butter

onions

white wine

white fish fillets

shrimp

broccoli

lemon grass

heavy cream

fresh ginger

flour

chives

potatoes

stock

1 Melt the butter in a large saucepan. Cook the onion for 3–4 minutes or until just tender. Stir in the flour and cook for 1 minute.

2 Stir in the stock, wine, ginger, lemongrass and potatoes. Season well and bring to a boil. Cover and cook for 15 minutes or until the potatoes are almost tender.

3 Cut the fish into large chunks. Add the fish to the pan, with the shrimp, broccoli and cream. Stir gently.

4 Simmer gently for 5 minutes, taking care not to break up the fish. Adjust the seasoning and stir in the chives. Serve with plenty of crusty bread.

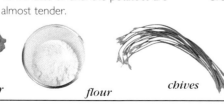

Stir-Fried Shrimp with Snow Peas

Shrimp and snow peas make a very pretty dish that needs no embellishment.

Serves 4

INGREDIENTS

1¼ cups fish stock
12 oz raw tiger shrimp, shelled
   and deveined
1 tbsp vegetable oil
1 garlic clove, finely chopped
8 oz (2 cups) snow peas
¼ tsp salt
1 tbsp dry sherry
1 tbsp oyster sauce
1 tsp cornstarch
1 tsp sugar
1 tbsp cold water
¼ tsp sesame oil

snow peas

shrimp

sherry   *cornstarch*

sugar

oyster sauce   *sesame oil*

garlic

fish stock

1 Bring the fish stock to a boil in a frying pan. Add the shrimp. Cook gently for 2 minutes, until the shrimp have turned pink, then drain and set aside.

2 Heat the vegetable oil in a nonstick frying pan or wok. Add the chopped garlic and cook for a few seconds, then add the snow peas. Sprinkle with the salt. Stir-fry for 1 minute.

3 Add the shrimp and sherry to the pan or wok. Stir-fry for a few seconds, then add the oyster sauce.

4 Mix the cornstarch and sugar to a paste with the water. Add the mixture to the pan and cook, stirring constantly, until the sauce thickens slightly. Drizzle with the sesame oil and serve.

Gong Boa Shrimp

A pleasantly spicy sweet-and-sour dish that takes only minutes to make.

Serves 4

INGREDIENTS

12 oz raw tiger shrimp
½ cucumber, about 3 oz
1¼ cups fish stock
1 tbsp vegetable oil
½ tsp crushed dried chilies
½ green bell pepper, seeded and cut into 1-in strips
1 small carrot, thinly sliced
2 tbsp ketchup
3 tbsp rice vinegar
1 tbsp sugar
⅔ cup vegetable stock
½ cup drained canned pineapple chunks
2 tsp cornstarch
1 tbsp cold water
salt

1 Shell and devein the shrimp. Rub them gently with ½ teaspoon salt; let sit for a few minutes and then wash and dry thoroughly.

2 Using a narrow peeler or zester, pare strips of skin off the cucumber to give a striped effect. Cut the cucumber in half lengthwise and scoop out the seeds with a teaspoon. Cut the flesh into ¼-inch crescents.

3 Bring the fish stock to a boil in a saucepan. Add the shrimp, lower the heat and poach the shrimp for about 2 minutes, until they turn pink, then drain and set aside.

green bell pepper *shrimp* *cucumber* *crushed dried chiles* *ketchup* *sugar* *vegetable stock* *pineapple chunks* *rice vinegar* *fish stock* *cornstarch* *carrot*

4 Heat the oil in a nonstick frying pan or wok over high heat. Fry the chilies for a few seconds, then add the pepper strips and carrot slices and stir-fry for 1 minute.

5 Mix together the ketchup, vinegar, sugar and vegetable stock with ¼ teaspoon salt. Pour into the pan and cook for 3 minutes more.

COOK'S TIP

Omit the chilies if you like,
or increase the quantity for
a spicier dish.

6 Add the shrimp, cucumber and
pineapple and cook for 2 minutes more.
Mix the cornstarch to a paste with the
water. Add the mixture to the pan and
cook, stirring constantly, until the sauce
thickens. Serve at once.

Spicy Seafood and Okra Stew

This spicy combination of seafood and vegetables is good served with herbed brown rice.

Serves 4–6

INGREDIENTS
2 tsp olive oil
1 onion, chopped
1 garlic clove, crushed
2 stalks celery, chopped
1 red bell pepper, seeded and diced
1 tsp each ground coriander,
ground cumin and ground ginger
½ tsp chili powder
½ tsp garam masala
2 tbsp whole-wheat flour
1¼ cups each fish stock and dry
white wine
1 can (8 oz) chopped tomatoes
1 can (8 oz) okra, trimmed
and sliced
3 cups mushrooms, sliced
1 lb frozen, cooked, shelled seafood,
defrosted
1 can (6 oz) corn kernels
8 oz long grain brown rice
2–3 tbsp chopped fresh mixed herbs
salt and ground black pepper
fresh parsley sprigs, to garnish

1 Heat the oil in a large saucepan. Add the onion, garlic, celery and pepper and cook for 5 minutes, stirring occasionally.

2 Add the spices and cook for 1 minute, stirring, then add the flour and cook for another 1 minute, stirring.

olive oil *onion* *garlic* *celery* *red bell pepper* *ground coriander*

ground cumin *ground ginger* *chili powder* *garam masala* *whole-wheat flour*

fish stock *dry white wine* *chopped tomatoes* *okra* *mushrooms*

seafood *corn* *long grain brown rice* *fresh mixed herbs*

3 Gradually stir in the stock and wine and add the tomatoes, okra and mushrooms. Bring to a boil, stirring constantly, then cover and simmer for 20 minutes, stirring occasionally.

4 Stir in the seafood and corn and cook for another 10–15 minutes, until piping hot.

COOK'S TIP
Use fresh cooked seafood in place of the frozen if it is available.

5 Meanwhile, cook the rice in a large saucepan of lightly salted boiling water for about 35 minutes, until tender.

6 Rinse the rice in fresh boiling water and drain thoroughly, then toss together with the mixed herbs. Season the stew and serve on a bed of herbed rice. Garnish with fresh parsley sprigs.

Broiled Jumbo Shrimp Bhoona

The unusual and delicious flavor of this dish is achieved by broiling the shrimp and then adding them to fried onions and peppers.

Serves 4

INGREDIENTS

3 tbsp plain low-fat yogurt
1 tsp paprika
1 tsp ginger pulp
salt
12–14 frozen cooked jumbo shrimp, thawed and shelled
1 tbsp corn oil
3 medium onions, sliced
½ tsp fennel seeds, crushed
1 cinnamon stick
1 tsp garlic pulp
1 tsp chili powder
1 medium yellow bell pepper, seeded and roughly chopped
1 medium red bell pepper, seeded and roughly chopped
1 tbsp cilantro leaves, to garnish

1 Blend together the yogurt, paprika, ginger, and salt to taste. Pour this mixture over the shrimp and let it marinate for 30–45 minutes.

fennel seeds *paprika*

chili powder *ginger pulp*

garlic pulp

jumbo shrimp

cinnamon stick

yogurt

cilantro

onions

red bell pepper

yellow bell pepper

2 Meanwhile, heat the oil in a nonstick wok or frying pan and stir-fry the onions with the fennel seeds and the cinnamon stick.

3 Lower the heat and add the garlic and chili powder.

4 Add the peppers and stir-fry gently for 3–5 minutes.

5 Remove from the heat and transfer to a serving dish, discarding the cinnamon bark.

6 Preheat the broiler and turn the heat to medium. Put the shrimp in a broiling pan or flameproof dish and place under the broiler to darken their tops and achieve a chargrilled effect. Add the shrimp to the onion mixture, garnish with the cilantro and serve.

Asparagus with Crabmeat Sauce

The subtle flavor of fresh asparagus is enhanced by the equally delicate taste of the crabmeat in this classic dish.

Serves 4

INGREDIENTS
1 lb asparagus, trimmed
1 tbsp vegetable oil
4 thin slices of fresh ginger root
2 garlic cloves, finely chopped
4 oz (⅔ cup) fresh or thawed frozen
   white crabmeat
1 tsp dry sherry
⅔ cup low-fat milk
1 tbsp cornstarch
3 tbsp cold water
salt and ground white pepper
1 scallion, thinly shredded,
   to garnish

garlic
ginger root
sherry
asparagus
vegetable oil
low-fat milk
crabmeat
cornstarch
scallion

1 Bring a large pan of lightly salted water to a boil. Poach the asparagus for about 5 minutes, until just crisp-tender. Drain well and keep hot in a shallow serving dish.

2 Heat the oil in a nonstick frying pan or wok. Cook the ginger and garlic for 1 minute to release their flavor, then lift them out with a slotted spoon and discard them.

3 Add the crabmeat, sherry and milk to the flavored oil and cook, stirring often, for 2 minutes.

4 In a small bowl, mix the cornstarch to a paste with the water and add to the pan. Cook, stirring constantly, until the sauce is thick and creamy. Season to taste with salt and pepper, spoon over the asparagus, garnish with shreds of scallion and serve.

Squid with Broccoli

The slightly chewy squid contrasts beautifully with the crisp crunch of the broccoli to give this dish the perfect combination of textures so beloved by the Chinese.

Serves 4

INGREDIENTS

1¼ cups fish stock
12 oz prepared squid, cut into
   large pieces
8 oz broccoli
1 tbsp vegetable oil
2 garlic cloves, finely chopped
1 tbsp dry sherry
2 tsp cornstarch
½ tsp sugar
3 tbsp cold water
1 tbsp oyster sauce
½ tsp sesame oil
noodles, to serve

fish stock

squid

broccoli

vegetable oil

garlic

sherry   cornstarch

sugar

oyster sauce   sesame oil

1 Bring the fish stock to a boil in a wok or saucepan. Cook the squid pieces for 2 minutes, until they are tender and have curled. Drain and set aside.

2 Trim the broccoli and cut into small florets. Cook in a saucepan of boiling water for 2 minutes, until crisp-tender. Drain thoroughly.

3 Heat the vegetable oil in a wok or nonstick frying pan. Stir-fry the garlic for a few seconds, then add the squid, broccoli and sherry. Stir-fry for about 2 minutes.

4 Mix the cornstarch and sugar to a paste with the water. Stir the mixture into the wok or pan, with the oyster sauce. Cook, stirring, until the sauce thickens slightly. Just before serving, stir in the sesame oil. Serve with noodles.

Sweet-and-sour Fish

The combination of sweet and sour is a popular one in many cuisines. The sauce can be made up to two days in advance.

Serves 3–4

INGREDIENTS
1 lb white fish fillets, skinned,
  boned and cubed
½ tsp Chinese five-spice
  powder
1 tsp light soy sauce
1 egg, lightly beaten
2–3 tbsp cornstarch
peanut oil, for deep-frying

FOR THE SAUCE
2 tsp cornstarch
4 tbsp water
4 tbsp pineapple juice
3 tbsp Chinese rice vinegar
3 tbsp sugar
2 tsp light soy sauce
2 tbsp tomato ketchup
2 tsp Chinese rice wine or
  medium-dry sherry
3 tbsp peanut oil
1 garlic clove, crushed
1 tbsp finely chopped
  fresh ginger root
6 scallions, sliced diagonally
  into 2-in lengths
1 green bell pepper, seeded and
  cut into ¾-in pieces
4 oz fresh pineapple,
  cut into ¾-in pieces
salt and ground black pepper

light soy sauce

white fish

scallion

garlic

cornstarch

egg

green bell pepper

Chinese rice wine

ginger root

Chinese five-spice powder

pineapple

tomato ketchup

COOK'S TIP
When buying the fish for this dish, select fillets which are ¾ in or more thick.

1 Put the fish in a bowl. Sprinkle over the five-spice powder and soy sauce, then toss gently. Cover and allow to marinate for about 30 minutes. Dip the fish in the egg, then in the cornstarch, shaking off any excess.

2 Half-fill a wok with oil and heat to 375°F. Deep-fry the fish in batches for about 2 minutes, until golden. Drain and keep warm. Carefully pour off all the oil from the wok and wipe clean.

4 Heat the wok until hot, add 2 tbsp of the oil and swirl it around. Add the garlic and ginger and stir-fry for a few seconds. Add the scallions and green pepper and stir-fry over medium heat for 2 minutes. Add the pineapple.

3 To make the sauce, blend together in a bowl the cornstarch, water, pineapple juice, rice vinegar, sugar, soy sauce, ketchup and rice wine or sherry. Mix well, then set aside.

5 Pour in the sauce and cook, stirring until thickened. Stir in the remaining 1 tbsp oil and add seasoning to taste. Pour the sauce over the fish and serve at once.

Clay Pot of Chili Squid and Noodles

This dish is delicious in its own right, or served as part of a larger Chinese meal, with other meat or fish dishes and rice.

Serves 2–4

INGREDIENTS
1½–1 lb fresh squid
2 tbsp oil
3 slices fresh ginger root,
    finely chopped
2 garlic cloves, finely chopped
1 red onion, finely sliced
1 carrot, finely sliced
1 celery rib, sliced
    diagonally
2 oz sugar snap peas, trimmed
pinch of salt
1 tsp sugar
1 tbsp chili bean paste
½ tsp chili powder
3 oz cellophane noodles,
    soaked in hot water until soft
½ cup chicken stock or water
1 tbsp light soy sauce
1 tbsp oyster sauce
1 tsp sesame oil
cilantro leaves, to garnish

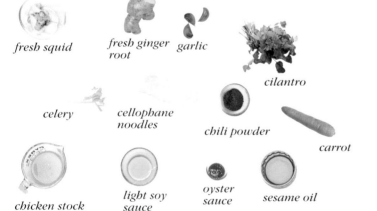

fresh squid *fresh ginger root* *garlic*

cilantro

celery *cellophane noodles* *chili powder* *carrot*

chicken stock *light soy sauce* *oyster sauce* *sesame oil*

1 Prepare the squid. Holding the body in one hand, gently pull away the head and tentacles. Discard the head; trim and reserve the tentacles. Remove the "quill" from inside the body of the squid. Peel off the brown skin on the outside. Rub salt into the squid and wash under water. Cut the body of the squid into rings or split it open lengthwise, score crisscross patterns on the inside of the body and cut it into 2 x 1½-inch pieces.

2 Heat the oil in a large, flameproof casserole or wok. Add the ginger, garlic and onion and cook for 1–2 minutes. Add the squid, carrot, celery and sugar snap peas. Cook until the squid curls up. Season with salt and sugar and then stir in the chili bean paste and chili powder. Transfer the mixture to a bowl and set aside until required. Drain the soaked noodles and add to the casserole or wok.

3 Stir in the chicken stock or water, light soy sauce and oyster sauce. Cover and cook over medium heat for 10 minutes, or until the noodles are tender. Return the squid and vegetable mixture to the pot.

4 Cover and cook for another 5–6 minutes, until all the flavors are combined. Season to taste.

5 Spoon the mixture into a warmed clay pot and drizzle with the sesame oil. Sprinkle with the cilantro leaves and serve immediately.

COOK'S TIP
These noodles have a smooth, light texture that readily absorbs the other flavors in the dish. To vary the flavor, the vegetables can be altered according to what is available.

MEAT AND POULTRY

In this section, the technique of stir-frying is often used. When using this method of cooking, the ingredients should be cut into small, thin slices or shreds of uniform size, so that they will all cook quickly, thus retaining their natural color, aroma and flavor.

Char-siu Pork

Marinated pork, roasted and glazed with honey, is irresistible on its own and can also be used as the basis for salads or stir-fries.

Serves 6

INGREDIENTS
1 tbsp vegetable oil
1 tbsp hoisin sauce
1 tbsp yellow bean sauce
¼ tsp five-spice powder
½ tsp cornstarch
1 tbsp sugar
¼ tsp salt
¼ tsp ground white pepper
1 lb pork tenderloin, trimmed
2 tsp honey
shredded scallion, to garnish
rice, to serve

pork
tenderloin

vegetable
oil

hoisin sauce

yellow
bean
sauce

five-spice
powder

sugar

cornstarch

honey

1 Mix the oil, sauces, five-spice powder, cornstarch, sugar and seasoning in a shallow dish. Add the pork and coat it with the mixture. Cover and chill for 4 hours or overnight.

2 Preheat the oven to 375°F. Drain the pork and place it on a wire rack over a deep roasting pan. Roast for 40 minutes, turning the pork over from time to time.

3 Check that the pork is cooked by inserting a skewer or fork into the meat; the juices should run clear. If they are still tinged with pink, roast the pork for 5–10 minutes more.

4 Remove the pork from the oven and brush it with the honey. Allow to cool for 10 minutes before cutting into thin slices. Garnish with scallions and serve hot or cold with rice.

Sticky Pork Ribs

A delicious dish that has to be eaten with the fingers to be enjoyed fully.

Serves 4

INGREDIENTS
2 tbsp sugar
½ tsp five-spice powder
3 tbsp hoisin sauce
2 tbsp yellow bean sauce
3 garlic cloves, finely chopped
1 tbsp cornstarch
½ tsp salt
16 pork ribs
chives and sliced scallions,
    to garnish
salad or rice, to serve

pork ribs

hoisin sauce

five-spice powder

yellow bean sauce

sugar

cornstarch

garlic

1 Combine the sugar, five-spice powder, hoisin sauce, yellow bean sauce, garlic, cornstarch and salt in a bowl, then mix together well.

2 Place the ribs in an ovenproof dish and pour the marinade over them. Mix thoroughly, cover and let sit in a cool place for 1 hour.

COOK'S TIP

The ribs cook on a barbecue well. Bake as described in Step 3, then transfer them to the grill to finish cooking. The sauce coating makes the ribs liable to burn, so watch them closely.

3 Preheat the oven to 350°F. Cover the dish tightly with foil and bake the ribs for 40 minutes. Baste the ribs from time to time with the cooking juices.

4 Remove the foil, baste the ribs and continue to cook for 20 minutes, until glossy and brown. Garnish with chives and scallions and serve with a salad or rice.

Sweet-and-Sour Pork

A wonderful low-fat version of this popular classic Chinese dish.

Serves 4

INGREDIENTS

1 tbsp dry sherry
12 oz lean center-cut pork chops
1 tbsp vegetable oil
1 garlic clove, finely chopped
½ onion, diced
1 small green bell pepper, seeded and cut into 1-inch squares
1 small carrot, sliced
½ cup drained canned pineapple chunks
2 tbsp malt vinegar
3 tbsp ketchup
⅔ cup pineapple juice
2 tsp sugar
2 tsp cornstarch
1 tbsp cold water
salt and ground black pepper
rice, to serve

garlic

sherry

pork chops

onion

sugar

carrot

pineapple juice

cornstarch

malt vinegar

green bell pepper

pineapple chunks

ketchup

COOK'S TIP

This is a great way of giving leftover pork from the Sunday roast a new lease on life. Proceed from Step 3.

1 Mix the sherry, ½ teaspoon salt and a large pinch of pepper in a shallow dish. Add the pork, turn to coat, then cover and let marinate in a cool place for 15 minutes.

2 Drain the pork chops and place them on a rack over a broiling pan. Broil under high heat for 5 minutes on each side or until cooked, then remove and let cool. Cut the cooked pork into bite-size pieces.

3 Heat the oil in a nonstick frying pan or wok until very hot. Stir-fry the garlic and onion for a few seconds, then add the green bell pepper and carrot and stir-fry for 1 minute.

4 Stir in the pineapple chunks, vinegar, ketchup, pineapple juice and sugar. Bring to a boil, lower the heat and simmer for 3 minutes.

5 Add the cooked pork to the vegetable mixture and cook for about 2 minutes.

6 Mix the cornstarch to a paste with the water. Add the mixture to the pan or wok and cook, stirring, until slightly thickened. Serve with rice.

Stir-fried Pork with Lychees

Lychees have a very pretty pink skin which, when peeled, reveals a soft fleshy berry with a hard shiny pit. If you cannot buy fresh lychees, this dish can be made with drained canned lychees.

Serves 4

INGREDIENTS

1 lb fatty pork, for example belly pork
2 tbsp hoisin sauce
4 scallions, sliced
6 oz lychees, peeled, pitted and cut
　　into slivers
salt and freshly ground pepper
fresh lychees and fresh parsley sprigs,
　　to garnish

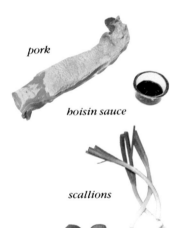

pork

hoisin sauce

scallions

lychees

1 Cut the pork into bite-size pieces.

2 Pour the hoisin sauce over the pork and marinate for 30 minutes.

3 Heat the wok, then add the pork and stir-fry for 5 minutes until crisp and golden. Add the scallions and stir-fry for a further 2 minutes.

4 Scatter the lychee slivers over the pork, and season well with salt and pepper. Garnish with fresh lychees and fresh parsley, and serve.

Glazed Lamb

Lemon and honey make a classically good combination in sweet dishes, and this lamb recipe shows how well they work together in savory dishes, too. Serve with a fresh mixed salad to complete this delicious dish.

Serves 4

INGREDIENTS
1 lb boneless lean lamb
1 tbsp grapeseed oil
6 oz snow peas, topped and
   tailed
3 scallions, sliced
2 tbsp honey
juice of half a lemon
2 tbsp fresh cilantro, chopped
1 tbsp sesame seeds
salt and freshly ground pepper

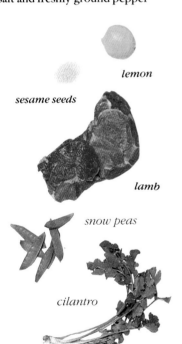

lemon

sesame seeds

lamb

snow peas

cilantro

1 Using a sharp knife, cut the lamb into thin strips.

2 Heat the wok, then add the oil. When the oil is hot, stir-fry the lamb until browned all over. Remove from the wok and keep warm.

3 Add the snow peas and scallions to the hot wok and stir-fry for 30 seconds.

4 Return the lamb to the wok and add the honey, lemon juice, cilantro and sesame seeds, and season well. Bring to a boil and bubble for 1 minute until the lamb is well coated in the honey mixture.

Stir-fried Pork with Mustard

Fry the apples for this dish very carefully, because they will disintegrate if they are overcooked.

Serves 4

INGREDIENTS

1¼ lb pork fillet
1 tart apple, such as Granny Smith
3 tbsp sweet butter
1 tbsp superfine sugar
1 small onion, finely chopped
2 tbsp Calvados, Applejack or
    other brandy
1 tbsp Meaux or coarse-grain
    mustard
⅔ cup heavy cream
2 tbsp fresh parsley, chopped
salt and freshly ground black pepper
flat-leaf parsley sprigs, to garnish

pork fillet

onion

mustard

apple

1 Cut the pork fillet into thin slices.

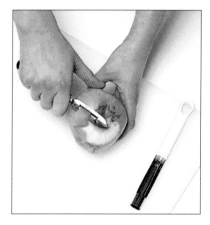

2 Peel and core the apple. Cut it into thick slices.

3 Heat the wok, then add half the butter. When the butter is hot, add the apple slices, sprinkle over the sugar, and stir-fry for 2–3 minutes. Remove the apple and set aside. Wipe out the wok with paper towels.

4 Heat the wok, then add the remaining butter and stir-fry the pork fillet and onion together for 2–3 minutes, until the pork is golden and the onion has begun to soften.

5 Stir in the Calvados, Applejack or other brandy and boil until it is reduced by half. Stir in the mustard.

6 Add the cream and simmer for 1 minute, then stir in the parsley. Serve garnished with sprigs of flat-leaf parsley.

Mu Shu Pork with Eggs and Wood Ears

Mu shu is the Chinese name for a bright yellow flower. Traditionally, this dish is served as a filling wrapped in thin pancakes, but it can also be served on its own with plain rice.

Serves 4

INGREDIENTS

½ oz dried wood ears
6–8 oz pork tenderloin
8 oz napa cabbage
4 oz bamboo shoots, drained
2 scallions
3 eggs
1 tsp salt
4 tbsp vegetable oil
1 tbsp light soy sauce
1 tbsp Chinese rice wine or
   dry sherry
few drops sesame oil

napa cabbage

bamboo shoots

scallions

pork

eggs

wood ears

1 Soak the wood ears in cold water for 25–30 minutes. Rinse and discard the hard stalks, if any. Squeeze dry, then thinly shred.

2 Cut the pork into matchsticks-size shreds. Thinly shred the napa cabbage, bamboo shoots and scallions.

3 Beat the eggs with a pinch of the salt and lightly scramble in a little of the warm oil until set but not too dry. Remove from the heat.

4 Heat the remaining oil in the wok and stir-fry the pork for about 1 minute, or until the color changes.

5 Add the vegetables to the wok, stir-fry for another minute, then add the remaining salt, the soy sauce and wine or sherry.

6 Stir for 1 more minute before adding the scrambled eggs. Break up the scrambled eggs and blend well. Sprinkle with sesame oil and serve.

Pork and Vegetable Stir-fry

A quick and easy stir-fry of pork and vegetables.

Serves 4

INGREDIENTS

1 can (8 oz) pineapple cubes
1 tbsp cornstarch
2 tbsp light soy sauce
1 tbsp each dry sherry, brown sugar
  and wine vinegar
1 tsp five-spice powder
2 tsp olive oil
1 red onion, sliced
1 garlic clove, crushed
1 fresh seeded red chili, chopped
1-in piece fresh ginger root
12 oz lean pork tenderloin, cut into
  thin strips
6 oz carrots
1 red bell pepper, seeded and sliced
6 oz snow peas, halved
½ cup bean sprouts
1 can (7 oz) corn kernels
2 tbsp chopped cilantro
salt
1 tbsp toasted sesame seeds,
  to garnish

pineapple cubes   *light soy sauce*   *dry sherry*

wine vinegar   *five-spice powder*   *olive oil*   *red onion*

garlic   *red chili*   *ginger*

carrots

red bell pepper

snow peas

pork tenderloin   *corn kernels*   *cilantro*

bean sprouts

1 Drain the pineapple, reserving the juice. In a small bowl, blend the cornstarch with the pineapple juice. Add the soy sauce, sherry, sugar, vinegar and spice, stir to mix and set aside.

2 Heat the oil in a large nonstick frying pan or wok. Add the onion, garlic, chili and ginger and stir-fry for 30 seconds. Add the pork and stir-fry for 2–3 minutes.

3 Cut the carrots into matchstick strips. Add to the wok with the pepper and stir-fry for 2–3 minutes. Add the snow peas, bean sprouts and corn and stir-fry for 1–2 minutes.

4 Pour in the sauce mixture and the reserved pineapple and stir-fry until the sauce thickens. Reduce the heat and stir-fry for another 1–2 minutes. Stir in the cilantro and season to taste. Sprinkle with sesame seeds and serve immediately.

Stir-fried Beef and Broccoli

This spicy beef may be served with noodles or on a bed of boiled rice for a speedy and low calorie Chinese meal.

Serves 4

INGREDIENTS

12 oz sirloin or lean London
    broil steak
1 tbsp cornstarch
1 tsp sesame oil
12 oz broccoli, cut into small
    florets
4 scallions, sliced on the diagonal
1 carrot, cut into matchstick strips
1 garlic clove, crushed
1 in piece ginger root, cut into very
    fine strips
½ cup low fat beef stock
2 tbsp soy sauce
2 tbsp dry sherry
2 tsp light brown sugar
scallion tassels, to garnish
noodles or rice, to serve

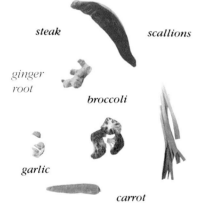

steak   *scallions*

*ginger
root*

broccoli

garlic

carrot

1 Trim the beef and cut into thin slices across the grain. Cut each slice into thin strips. Toss in the cornstarch to coat thoroughly.

2 Heat the sesame oil in a large non-stick frying pan or wok. Add the beef strips and stir-fry over a brisk heat for 3 minutes. Remove and set aside.

COOK'S TIP

To make scallion tassels, trim the bulb base then cut the green shoot so that the onion is 3 in long. Shred to within 1 in of the base and put into iced water for 1 hour.

3 Add the broccoli, scallions, carrot, garlic clove, ginger and stock to the frying pan or wok. Cover and simmer for 3 minutes. Uncover and cook, stirring until all the stock has reduced entirely.

4 Mix the soy sauce, sherry and brown sugar together. Add to the frying pan or wok with the beef. Cook for 2–3 minutes stirring continuously. Spoon into a warm serving dish and garnish with scallion tassels. Serve on a bed of noodles or rice.

Sizzling Beef with Celeriac Straw

The crisp celeriac matchsticks look like fine pieces of straw when cooked and have a mild celery-like flavor that is quite delicious.

Serves 4

INGREDIENTS
1 lb celeriac
⅔ cup vegetable oil
1 red bell pepper
6 scallions
1 lb round steak
4 tbsp beef stock
2 tbsp sherry vinegar
2 tsp Worcestershire sauce
2 tsp tomato paste
salt and freshly ground black pepper

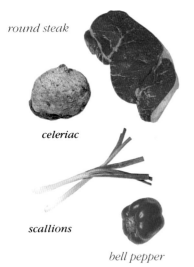

round steak

celeriac

scallions

bell pepper

1 Peel the celeriac and then cut it into fine matchsticks, using a cleaver.

2 Heat the wok, then add two-thirds of the oil. When the oil is hot, fry the celeriac matchsticks in batches until golden brown and crispy. Drain well on paper towels.

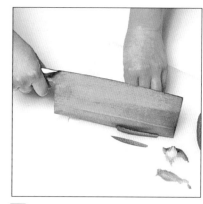

3 Chop the red bell pepper and the scallions into approximate 1 in lengths, using diagonal cuts.

4 Chop the beef into strips, across the grain of the meat.

5 Heat the wok, and then add the remaining oil. When the oil is hot, stir-fry the chopped scallions and red bell pepper for 2–3 minutes.

6 Add the beef strips and stir-fry for a further 3–4 minutes until well browned. Add the stock, vinegar, Worcestershire sauce and tomato paste. Season well and serve with the celeriac straw.

Hot-and-Sour Pork

Chinese five-spice powder is made from a mixture of ground star anise, Szechuan pepper, cassia, cloves and fennel seed and has a flavor similar to licorice. If you can't find any, use mixed spice instead.

Serves 4

INGREDIENTS
12 oz pork fillet
1 tsp sunflower oil
1 in piece ginger root, grated
1 red chili, seeded and finely chopped
1 tsp Chinese five-spice powder
1 tbsp sherry vinegar
1 tbsp soy sauce
8 oz can pineapple chunks in natural juice
¾ cup chicken stock
4 tsp cornstarch
1 small green bell pepper, seeded and sliced
4 oz baby corn, halved
salt and freshly ground black pepper
sprig of Italian parsley, to garnish
boiled rice, to serve

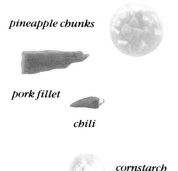

pineapple chunks

pork fillet

chili

cornstarch

soy sauce

bell pepper

baby corn

1 Preheat the oven to 325°F. Trim away any visible fat from the pork and cut into ½ in thick slices.

2 Brush the sunflower oil over the base of a flameproof casserole. Heat over a medium flame, then fry the meat for about 2 minutes on each side or until lightly browned.

3 Blend together the ginger, chili, five-spice powder, vinegar and soy sauce.

4 Drain the pineapple chunks, reserving the juice. Make the stock up to 1¼ cups with the reserved juice, mix together with the spices and pour over the pork.

5 Slowly bring to a boil. Blend the cornstarch with 1 tbsp of cold water and gradually stir into the pork. Add the vegetables and season to taste.

6 Cover and cook in the oven for 30 minutes. Stir in the pineapple and cook for a further 5 minutes. Garnish with Italian parsley and serve with boiled rice.

Beef with Peppers and Black Bean Sauce

A spicy, rich dish with the distinctive flavor of black bean sauce.

Serves 4

INGREDIENTS

12 oz round or sirloin steak,
  trimmed and thinly sliced
1 tbsp vegetable oil
1¼ cups beef stock
2 garlic cloves, finely chopped
1 tsp grated fresh ginger root
1 fresh red chili, seeded and
  finely chopped
1 tbsp black bean sauce
1 green bell pepper, seeded and cut
  into 1-in squares
1 tbsp dry sherry
1 tsp cornstarch
1 tsp sugar
3 tbsp cold water
salt
rice noodles, to serve

beef
stock

ginger
root

steak

garlic   black
         bean sauce

sherry

bell
pepper

cornstarch   chili   sugar

1 Place the steak in a bowl. Add 1 teaspoon of the oil and stir to coat.

2 Bring the stock to a boil in a saucepan. Add the beef and cook for 2 minutes, stirring constantly to prevent the slices from sticking together. Drain the beef and set aside.

COOK'S TIP

For extra color, use half each of a green and a red bell pepper or a mixture that includes yellow and orange bell peppers.

3 Heat the remaining oil in a nonstick frying pan or wok. Stir-fry the garlic, ginger and chili with the black bean sauce for a few seconds. Add the pepper squares and a little water. Cook for about 2 minutes more, then stir in the sherry. Add the beef slices to the pan and spoon the sauce over them.

4 Mix the cornstarch and sugar to a paste with the water. Pour the mixture into the pan. Cook, stirring, until the sauce has thickened. Season with salt. Serve at once, with rice noodles.

Beef with Tomatoes

Colorful and fresh-tasting, this is the perfect way of serving sun-ripened tomatoes from the garden.

Serves 4

INGREDIENTS

12 oz sirloin steak, trimmed
1 tbsp vegetable oil
1¼ cups beef stock
1 garlic clove, finely chopped
1 small onion, sliced into rings
5 tomatoes, quartered
1 tbsp tomato paste
1 tsp sugar
1 tbsp dry sherry
1 tbsp cold water
salt and ground white pepper
noodles, to serve

beef stock   *onion*

garlic

tomatoes

steak   *tomato paste*

sugar

sherry

1 Slice the steak thinly. Place the slices in a bowl, add 1 teaspoon of the vegetable oil and stir to coat.

2 Bring the stock to the boil in a saucepan. Add the beef and cook for 2 minutes, stirring constantly. Drain the beef and set it aside.

COOK'S TIP

Use plum tomatoes or vine tomatoes from the garden, if you can. The store-bought ones are a little more expensive than standard tomatoes but have a far better flavor.

3 Heat the remaining oil in a nonstick frying pan or wok until very hot. Stir-fry the garlic and onion for a few seconds.

4 Add the beef and tomatoes and cook for 1 minute more. Mix the tomato paste, sugar, sherry and water in a cup or small bowl. Stir the mixture into the pan, add salt and pepper to taste and mix thoroughly. Cook for 1 minute, then serve with noodles.

Chili Beef with Basil

This is a dish for chili lovers! It is very easy to prepare and cook.

Serves 2

INGREDIENTS
about 6 tbsp peanut oil
16–20 large fresh basil leaves
10 oz round steak
2 tbsp Thai fish sauce
  (*nam pla*)
1 tsp dark brown sugar
1–2 fresh red chilies, sliced
  into rings
3 garlic cloves, chopped
1 tsp finely chopped
  fresh ginger root
1 shallot, thinly sliced
2 tbsp finely chopped fresh
  basil leaves
squeeze of lemon juice
salt and ground black pepper
Thai jasmine rice, to serve

steak

shallot

Thai fish sauce

basil

garlic

sugar

ginger root

peanut oil

red chili

1 Heat the oil in a wok and, when hot, add the basil leaves and fry for about 1 minute, until crisp and golden. Drain on paper towels. Remove the wok from the heat and pour off all but 2 tbsp of the oil.

2 Cut the steak across the grain into thin strips. In a bowl mix together the fish sauce and sugar. Add the beef, mix well, then allow to marinate for about 30 minutes.

3 Reheat the oil until hot, add the chili(es), garlic, ginger and shallot and stir-fry for 30 seconds. Add the beef and chopped basil, then stir-fry for about 3 minutes. Flavor with lemon juice and add seasoning to taste.

4 Transfer to a serving plate, sprinkle over the basil leaves and serve immediately with Thai jasmine rice.

182

Lemongrass Pork

Chilies and lemongrass flavor this simple stir-fry, while peanuts add crunch.

Serves 4

INGREDIENTS

1½ lb boneless pork loin
2 lemongrass stalks,
    finely chopped
4 scallions, thinly sliced
1 tsp salt
12 black peppercorns,
    coarsely crushed
2 tbsp peanut oil
2 garlic cloves, chopped
2 fresh red chilies, seeded
    and chopped
1 tsp light brown sugar
2 tbsp Thai fish sauce (*nam pla*),
    or to taste
¼ cup roasted unsalted peanuts,
    chopped
salt and ground black pepper
rice noodles, to serve
coarsely torn cilantro leaves,
    to garnish

scallions

red chilies

peanuts

pork

sugar

cilantro

lemongrass

Thai fish sauce

garlic

peanut oil

1 Trim any excess fat from the pork. Cut the meat across into ¼-in thick slices, then cut each slice into ¼-in strips. Put the pork into a bowl with the lemongrass, scallions, salt and crushed peppercorns; mix well. Cover and allow to marinate for 30 minutes.

2 Heat a wok until hot, add the oil and swirl it around. Add the pork mixture and stir-fry for 3 minutes.

3 Add the garlic and chilies and stir-fry for another 5–8 minutes over medium heat until the pork no longer looks pink.

4 Add the sugar, fish sauce and peanuts, and toss to mix. Taste and adjust the seasoning if necessary. Serve immediately on a bed of rice noodles, garnished with coarsely torn cilantro leaves.

Beef with Noodles, Vegetables and Bean Curd

This Japanese dish is a meal in itself; the recipe incorporates all the traditional elements—meat, vegetables, noodles and tofu. If you want to do it all properly, eat the meal with chopsticks, and a spoon to collect the stock juices.

Serves 4

INGREDIENTS
1 lb thick round steak
7 oz Japanese rice noodles
1 tbsp peanut oil
7 oz firm tofu, cut
    into cubes
8 shiitake mushrooms, trimmed
2 medium leeks, sliced into 1 in
    lengths
3½ oz baby spinach, well washed,
    to serve

FOR THE STOCK
1 tbsp superfine sugar
6 tbsp rice wine
3 tbsp dark soy sauce
½ cup water

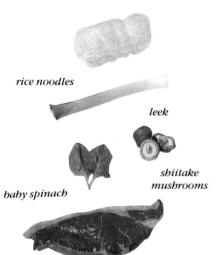

rice noodles

leek

baby spinach

shiitake mushrooms

round steak

1 Cut the beef into thin slices.

2 Blanch the noodles in boiling water for 2 minutes. Strain well.

3 Mix together all the stock ingredients in a bowl.

4 Heat the wok, then add the oil. When the oil is hot, stir-fry the beef for about 2–3 minutes, until it is cooked but still pink in color.

5 Pour the stock over the beef.

6 Add the remaining ingredients and cook for 4 minutes, until the leeks are tender. Serve a selection of the different ingredients, with a few baby spinach leaves, to each person.

Savory Chiffon Custards

The velvety smoothness of the egg combined with the coarse texture of the ground pork makes this a children's favorite.

Serves 4

INGREDIENTS
4 dried Chinese mushrooms
6 oz lean pork, roughly chopped
½ oz dried shrimp, soaked in
   warm water
3 large eggs
2 cups chicken stock
salt and ground white pepper
2 tbsp chopped chives
braided whole chives, to garnish

dried shrimp

eggs

pork

chicken stock

dried Chinese mushrooms

chives

VARIATION
For a delicious alternative, replace the pork mixture with fresh or frozen white crabmeat; this gives a more subtle taste. The crabmeat custards would make a great appetizer.

1 Soak the mushrooms in a bowl of hot water for 30 minutes, until soft. Drain, remove the hard stems, then cut the mushroom caps into small pieces.

2 Place the pork and mushrooms in a food processor. Drain the shrimp and add them to the processor with ¼ teaspoon salt and a pinch of pepper. Process until finely ground. Scrape into a bowl and set aside.

3 Break the eggs into a mixing bowl, then gradually whisk in the stock. Add ½ teaspoon salt and a large pinch of pepper. Beat well, then strain through a fine sieve into a pitcher.

4 Stir a little of the beaten egg mixture into the pork mixture to loosen it. Divide the pork among four 1¼-cup soufflé dishes and pour the remaining egg mixture on top, dividing it equally among the soufflé dishes.

5 Sprinkle the chopped chives over the tops. Cover the dishes tightly with plastic wrap and then foil and place in a steamer.

6 Have ready a pan with about 2 inches boiling water. Cover the steamer and steam over boiling water for about 10 minutes, then lower the heat and continue steaming for another 20 minutes, until the custards are just set. Serve immediately, garnished with braided whole chives.

Beef Stir-fry with a Cucumber Flower

A cucumber flower is a stunning Chinese garnish; the perfect decoration for a tasty stir-fry.

Serves 2–3

INGREDIENTS
1 tbsp sunflower oil
6-oz round steak, shredded
1 red onion, thinly sliced
1 red bell pepper, thinly sliced
4 oz broccoli florets
4 oz baby corn, cut in half
4 oz oyster mushrooms, sliced
½ cup bean sprouts
salt and freshly ground black
 pepper
6-in piece cucumber,
 to garnish

FOR THE SAUCE
3 tbsp honey
2 tbsp fresh lime juice
3 tbsp soy sauce
1 tsp crushed garlic
2 tbsp grated fresh ginger root

round steak
broccoli
red bell pepper
baby corn
bean sprouts
lime
oyster mushrooms
red onion
cucumber
fresh ginger root

1 First, cut the cucumber in half lengthwise and remove the seeds. Place each half cut-side down and cut at an angle into 3-inch lengths. Cut into very fine slices, stopping ¼ inch short of the cut side, so that all of the cucumber slices remain attached.

2 Fan the slices out. Turn in alternate slices to form a loop. Bend the length into a semicircle with the loops on the outside so that they resemble petals. Make more flowers in the same way.

3 Heat the sunflower oil in a wok. Mix the sauce ingredients in a bowl, add them to the wok and cook for 30 seconds. Add the onion and red pepper and stir-fry for 2 minutes.

4 Add the broccoli, baby corn and beef and stir-fry for 3–4 minutes. Finally add the oyster mushrooms and bean sprouts. Stir-fry for 2 minutes more. Adjust seasoning and add more soy sauce if necessary. Serve garnished with the cucumber flowers.

Pork, Peanut and Chili Saté

These delicious skewers of pork are popular street food in south-east Asia.

Serves 4

INGREDIENTS
2 cups long-grain rice
1 lb lean pork
pinch of salt
2 limes, quartered, to garnish
4 oz green salad, to serve

FOR THE BASTE AND DIP
1 tbsp vegetable oil
1 small onion, chopped
1 garlic clove, crushed
½ tsp hot chili sauce
1 tbsp sugar
2 tbsp soy sauce
2 tbsp lemon or lime juice
½ tsp anchovy paste (optional)
4 tbsp smooth peanut butter

lemon

lime

rice

peanut butter

pork

garlic

chili sauce

1 In a large saucepan, cover the rice with 3¾ cups of boiling salted water, stir and simmer uncovered for 15 minutes until the liquid has been absorbed. Switch off the heat, cover and stand for 5 minutes. Slice the pork into thin strips, then thread zig-zag fashion onto 16 bamboo skewers.

2 Heat the vegetable oil in a pan. Add the onion and cook over a gentle heat to soften without coloring for about 3–4 minutes. Add the next 5 ingredients and the anchovy paste, if using. Simmer briefly, then stir in the peanut butter.

3 Preheat a moderate broiler; spoon a third of the sauce over the pork and cook for 6–8 minutes, turning once. Spread the rice out onto a serving dish, place the pork saté on top and serve with the dipping sauce. Garnish with quartered limes and serve with a green salad.

VARIATION

This saté can be prepared with lean beef, chicken or shrimp.

Stir-fried Lamb with Pearl Onions and Peppers

The pearl onions are used whole in this recipe. Serve with rice or lentils.

Serves 4

INGREDIENTS

1 tbsp corn oil
8 pearl onions
8 oz boned lean lamb, cut
    into strips
1 tsp ground cumin
1 tsp ground coriander
1 tbsp tomato paste
1 tsp chili powder
1 tsp salt
1 tbsp lemon juice
½ tsp onion seeds
4 curry leaves
1¼ cups water
1 small red bell pepper, seeded and
    roughly sliced
1 small green bell pepper, seeded
    and roughly sliced
1 tbsp chopped cilantro
1 tbsp chopped fresh mint

onions

green/red bell peppers   *lamb*

onion seeds

lemon juice

cilantro

mint   *curry leaves*

ground cumin   *ground coriander*   *chili powder*

tomato paste   *salt*

1 Heat the oil in a nonstick wok or frying pan and stir-fry the onions for about 3 minutes. Using a slotted spoon, remove the onions from the wok and set aside to drain.

2 Mix together the lamb, cumin, ground coriander, tomato paste, chili powder, salt and lemon juice in a bowl and set aside.

3 Reheat the oil and stir-fry the onion seeds and curry leaves for 2–3 minutes.

4 Add the lamb and spice mixture and stir-fry for about 5 minutes, then pour in the water, lower the heat and cook gently for about 10 minutes, until the lamb is cooked through.

5 Add the peppers and half the cilantro and mint. Stir-fry for another 2 minutes.

6 Finally, add the onions and the remaining chopped cilantro and mint and serve.

COOK'S TIP
This dish benefits from being cooked a day in advance and kept in the refrigerator.

Pork Dumplings

When poached in large quantities, these dumplings (*jiao zi*) make a substantial main course. They can also be served on their own as a snack, if steamed, or as a good appetizer before a multicourse meal when fried.

Makes about 80–90 dumplings

INGREDIENTS
4 cups all-purpose flour, plus extra
    for dusting
2 cups water
flour, for dusting

FILLING
1 lb napa cabbage or white
    cabbage
1 lb ground pork
1 tbsp finely chopped scallions
1 tsp finely chopped fresh
    ginger root
2 tsp salt
1 tsp light brown sugar
2 tbsp light soy sauce
1 tbsp Chinese rice wine or
    dry sherry
2 tsp sesame oil

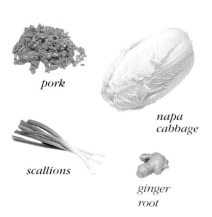

pork

napa cabbage

scallions

ginger root

1 Sift the flour into a bowl, then slowly pour in the water and mix to a firm dough. Knead until smooth and soft, then cover with a damp cloth and set aside for 25–30 minutes.

2 For the filling, blanch the cabbage leaves until soft. Drain and finely chop. Mix the cabbage with the remaining ingredients.

3 Lightly dust a work surface with the flour. Knead and roll the dough into a long sausage about 1 inch in diameter. Cut the sausage into 80–90 pieces and flatten each piece with the palm of your hand.

4 Using a rolling pin, roll out each piece into a thin pancake about 2½ inches in diameter.

5 Place about 1½ tbsp of the filling in the center of each pancake and fold into a half-moon-shaped pouch.

6 Pinch the edges firmly so that the dumpling is tightly sealed.

7 Cook the dumplings in about ²/₃ cup salted boiling water for 2 minutes. Remove from the heat and leave the dumplings in the water for about 15 minutes.

DIP SAUCE

2 tablespoons red chili oil
1 tablespoon light soy sauce
1 teaspoon finely chopped garlic
1 tablespoon finely chopped scallions

Combine all the ingredients in a small bowl, and serve with Pork Dumplings.

Pork Chow Mein

A perfect speedy meal, this is flavored with sesame oil for an authentic Asian taste.

Serves 4

INGREDIENTS

6 oz medium egg noodles
pork loin (12 oz)
2 tbsp sunflower oil
1 tbsp sesame oil
2 garlic cloves, crushed
8 scallions, sliced
1 red bell pepper, seeded and
 roughly chopped
1 green bell pepper, seeded and
 roughly chopped
2 tbsp dark soy sauce
3 tbsp dry sherry
3/4 cup bean sprouts
3 tbsp chopped fresh flat leaf
 parsley
1 tbsp toasted sesame seeds

red bell pepper

green bell pepper

scallions

garlic

medium egg noodles

flat leaf parsley

toasted sesame seeds

pork loin

dark soy sauce

dry sherry

sesame oil

sunflower oil

bean sprouts

1 Soak the noodles according to the package instructions. Drain well.

2 Thinly slice the pork. Heat the sunflower oil in a wok or large frying pan and cook the pork over high heat, until golden brown and cooked through.

3 Add the sesame oil to the pan, with the garlic, scallions and peppers. Cook over high heat for 3–4 minutes or until beginning to soften.

4 Reduce the heat slightly and stir in the noodles, with the soy sauce and sherry. Stir-fry for 2 minutes. Add the bean sprouts and cook for 1–2 more minutes. If the noodles begin to stick, add a splash of water. Stir in the parsley and serve sprinkled with the sesame seeds.

Paper-thin Lamb with Scallions

Scallions lend a delicious flavor to the lamb in this simple supper dish.

Serves 3-4

INGREDIENTS

1 lb lamb cutlet
2 tbsp Chinese rice wine
2 tsp light soy sauce
½ tsp roasted and ground
  Szechuan peppercorns
½ tsp salt
½ tsp dark brown sugar
4 tsp dark soy sauce
1 tbsp sesame oil
2 tbsp peanut oil
2 garlic cloves, thinly sliced
2 bunches scallions, cut
  into 3-in lengths,
  then shredded
2 tbsp chopped fresh cilantro

scallions

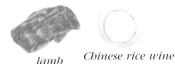

lamb   Chinese rice wine

sesame oil

light soy sauce

dark soy sauce

cilantro

garlic

brown sugar

1 Wrap the lamb and place in the freezer for about 1 hour, until just frozen. Cut the meat across the grain into paper-thin slices. Put the lamb slices in a bowl, add 2 tsp of the rice wine, the light soy sauce and ground Szechuan peppercorns. Mix well and allow to marinate for 15–30 minutes.

2 Make the sauce: in a bowl mix together the remaining rice wine, the salt, brown sugar, dark soy sauce and 2 tsp of the sesame oil. Set aside.

3 Heat a wok until hot, add the oil and swirl it around. Add the garlic and let it sizzle for a few seconds, then add the lamb. Stir-fry for about 1 minute, until the lamb is no longer pink. Pour in the sauce and stir briefly.

4 Add the scallions and cilantro and stir-fry for 15–20 seconds until the scallions just wilt. The finished dish should be slightly dry in appearance. Serve immediately, sprinkled with the remaining sesame oil.

Beef Stir-fry with Crisp Parsnips

Wonderful crisp shreds of parsnip add extra crunchiness to this stir-fry. This is a great supper dish to share with friends.

Serves 4

INGREDIENTS
¾ lb parsnips
1 lb round steak
1 lb trimmed leeks
2 red bell peppers, seeded
¾ lb zucchini
6 tbsp vegetable oil
2 garlic cloves, crushed
3 tbsp hoisin sauce
salt and pepper

vegetable oil

hoisin sauce

red bell peppers

leeks

round steak

garlic

zucchini

parsnips

1 Peel the parsnips. Cut in half lengthwise, place the flat surface on the board and cut into thin strips. Finely shred each piece. Rinse in cold water and drain thoroughly. Dry on paper towels if necessary.

2 Cut the steak into thin strips. Split the leeks in half lengthwise and thickly slice at an angle. Roughly chop the peppers and thinly slice the zucchini.

3 Heat the oil in a wok or large frying pan. Fry the parsnips until crisp and golden. You may need to do this in batches, adding a little more oil if necessary. Remove with a slotted spoon and drain on paper towels.

4 Stir-fry the steak in the wok until golden and cooked through. You may need to do this in batches, adding more oil if necessary. Remove and drain on paper towels.

5 Stir-fry the garlic, leeks, peppers and zucchini for about 10 minutes or until golden brown and beginning to soften but still retaining a little bite. Season the mixture well.

6 Return the meat to the pan with the hoisin sauce. Stir-fry for 2–3 minutes or until piping hot. Adjust the seasoning and serve with the crisp parsnips piled on top.

Beef in Oyster Sauce

The oyster sauce gives the beef extra richness and depth of flavor. To complete the dish, all you need is plain boiled rice or noodles.

Serves 4

INGREDIENTS

12 oz round or sirloin steak, trimmed
1 tbsp vegetable oil
1¼ cups beef stock
2 garlic cloves, finely chopped
1 small carrot, thinly sliced
3 celery ribs, sliced
1 tbsp dry sherry
1 tsp sugar
3 tbsp oyster sauce
1 tsp cornstarch
1 tbsp cold water
4 scallions, cut into 1-in lengths
ground white pepper
rice or noodles, to serve

steak

celery   *carrot*   *vegetable oil*

sugar   *garlic*

oyster sauce

scallions

cornstarch

beef stock   *sherry*

1 Slice the steak thinly. Place the slices in a bowl, add 1 teaspoon of the vegetable oil and stir to coat.

4 Stir in the sherry, sugar, oyster sauce and a large pinch of pepper. Add the steak to the pan with the reserved stock. Simmer for 2 minutes.

2 Bring the stock to a boil in a large saucepan. Add the beef and cook, stirring, for 2 minutes. Drain, reserving 3 tablespoons of the stock, and set aside.

5 Mix the cornstarch to a paste with the water. Add the mixture to the pan and cook, stirring, until thickened.

VARIATION

To increase the number of servings without upping the fat content of the dish, add more vegetables, such as bell peppers, snow peas, water chestnuts, baby corn and mushrooms.

3 Heat the remaining oil in a nonstick frying pan or wok. Stir-fry the garlic for a few seconds, then add the carrot and celery and stir-fry for 2 minutes.

6 Stir in the scallions, mixing well, then serve at once, with rice or noodles.

Sweet-and-Sour Pork Stir-fry

This is a great idea for a quick family supper. Remember to cut the carrots into thin strips so that they cook in time.

Serves 4

INGREDIENTS
pork tenderloin (1 lb)
2 tbsp flour
3 tbsp oil
1 onion, roughly chopped
1 garlic clove, crushed
1 green bell pepper, seeded and sliced
¾ lb carrots, cut into strips
1 can (8 oz) bamboo shoots, drained
1 tbsp white wine vinegar
1 tbsp brown sugar
2 tsp tomato paste
2 tbsp light soy sauce
salt and pepper

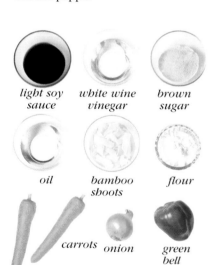

light soy sauce   *white wine vinegar*   *brown sugar*

oil   *bamboo shoots*   *flour*

carrots   *onion*   *green bell pepper*

tomato paste

garlic   *pork tenderloin*

1 Thinly slice the pork. Season the flour and toss the pork in it to coat.

2 Heat the oil in a wok or large frying pan and cook the pork over medium heat for about 5 minutes, until golden and cooked through. Remove with a slotted spoon and drain on paper towels. You may need to do this in batches.

3 Add the onion and garlic to the pan and cook for 3 minutes. Stir in the pepper and carrots and stir-fry over high heat for 6–8 minutes or until beginning to soften slightly.

4 Return the meat to the pan with the bamboo shoots. Add the remaining ingredients with ½ cup water and bring to a boil. Simmer gently for 2–3 minutes or until piping hot. Adjust the seasoning, if necessary, and serve immediately.

Minted Lamb Stir-fry

Lamb and mint have a long-established partnership that works particularly well in this full-flavored stir-fry. Serve with plenty of crusty bread.

Serves 2

INGREDIENTS

lamb shoulder (10 oz)
2 tbsp sunflower oil
2 tsp sesame oil
1 onion, roughly chopped
2 garlic cloves, crushed
1 red chili, seeded and
    finely chopped
3 oz green beans, halved
½ lb fresh spinach, shredded
2 tbsp oyster sauce
2 tbsp fish sauce
1 tbsp lemon juice
1 tsp superfine sugar
3 tbsp chopped fresh mint
salt and pepper
mint sprigs, to garnish
crusty bread, to serve

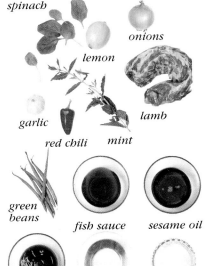

spinach

onions

lemon

garlic

lamb

red chili *mint*

green beans

fish sauce

sesame oil

oyster sauce

sunflower oil

superfine sugar

1 Trim the lamb of any excess fat and cut into thin slices. Heat the oils in a wok or large frying pan and cook the lamb over high heat, until browned. Remove with a slotted spoon and drain on paper towels.

2 Add the onion, garlic and chili to the wok and cook for 2–3 minutes. Add the beans to the wok and stir-fry for 3 minutes.

3 Stir in the spinach with the browned meat, oyster sauce, fish sauce, lemon juice and sugar. Stir-fry for 3–4 more minutes or until the lamb is cooked through.

4 Sprinkle in the mint, adjust the seasoning and garnish with mint sprigs. Serve piping hot, with plenty of crusty bread to mop up all the juices.

Asian Beef

This sumptuously rich beef melts in the mouth, and is perfectly complemented by the cool, crunchy relish.

Serves 4

INGREDIENTS
1 lb round steak

FOR THE MARINADE
1 tbsp sunflower oil
2 cloves garlic, crushed
4 tbsp dark soy sauce
2 tbsp dry sherry
2 tsp soft dark brown sugar

FOR THE RELISH
6 radishes
4 in piece cucumber
1 piece stem ginger
4 whole radishes, to garnish

round steak

brown sugar

soy sauce

garlic

radish

1 Cut the beef into thin strips. Place in a bowl.

2 To make the marinade, mix together the garlic, soy sauce, sherry and sugar in a bowl. Pour it over the beef and leave to marinate overnight.

3 To make the relish, chop the radishes and cucumber into matchsticks and the ginger into small matchsticks. Mix well together in a bowl.

4 Heat the wok, then add the oil. When the oil is hot, add the meat and marinade and stir-fry for 3–4 minutes. Serve with the relish, and garnish with a whole radish on each plate.

Stir-fried Duck with Blueberries

Serve this conveniently quick dinner party dish with sprigs of fresh mint, which will give a wonderful fresh aroma as you bring the meal to the table.

Serves 4

INGREDIENTS
2 duck breast portions, about 6 oz each
2 tbsp sunflower oil
1 tbsp red wine vinegar
1 tsp sugar
1 tsp red wine
1 tsp *crème de cassis* (black currant liqueur)
4 oz fresh blueberries
1 tbsp fresh mint, chopped
salt and freshly ground black pepper
fresh mint sprigs, to garnish
mixed green vegetables, steamed, to serve

duck

red wine vinegar

blueberries

red wine

mint

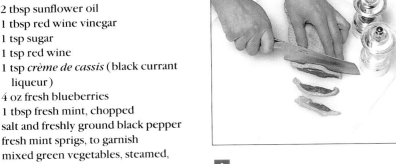

1 Cut the duck breast portions into neat slices. Season well with salt and pepper.

2 Heat the wok, then add the oil. When the oil is hot, stir-fry the duck for 3 minutes.

3 Add the red wine vinegar, sugar, red wine and *crème de cassis*. Bubble for 3 minutes, to reduce to a thick syrup.

4 Stir in the blueberries, sprinkle over the mint and serve garnished with sprigs of fresh mint.

Glazed Chicken with Cashew Nuts

Hoisin sauce lends a sweet yet slightly hot note to this chicken dish, while cashew nuts add a pleasing contrast of texture.

Serves 4

INGREDIENTS
¾ cup cashew nuts
1 red bell pepper
1 lb skinless and boneless
    chicken breast portions
3 tbsp peanut oil
4 garlic cloves, finely chopped
2 tbsp Chinese rice wine or
    medium-dry sherry
3 tbsp hoisin sauce
2 tsp sesame oil
5–6 scallions,
    green parts only,
    cut into 1-in lengths

scallions   *chicken*

Chinese rice wine   *red bell pepper*
                              cashew nuts

    garlic
hoisin sauce   *peanut oil*

sesame oil

1 Heat a wok until hot, add the cashew nuts and stir-fry over low to medium heat for 1–2 minutes, until golden brown. Remove and set aside.

2 Halve the pepper and remove the seeds. Slice the pepper and chicken into finger-length strips.

VARIATION
Use blanched almonds instead of cashew nuts if you prefer.

3 Heat the wok again until hot, add the oil and swirl it around. Add the garlic and let it sizzle in the oil for a few seconds. Add the pepper and chicken and stir-fry for 2 minutes.

4 Add the rice wine or sherry and hoisin sauce. Continue to stir-fry until the chicken is tender and all the ingredients are evenly glazed.

5 Stir in the sesame oil, toasted cashew nuts and scallion tips. Serve immediately with rice or noodles.

Chicken Liver Stir-fry

The final sprinkling of lemon, parsley and garlic granita gives this dish a delightful fresh flavor and wonderful aroma.

Serves 4

INGREDIENTS
1¼ lb chicken livers
6 tbsp butter
6 oz portabello mushrooms
2 oz chanterelle mushrooms
3 cloves garlic, finely chopped
2 shallots, finely chopped
⅔ cup medium sherry
3 fresh rosemary sprigs
2 tbsp fresh parsley, chopped
zest of 1 lemon, grated
salt and freshly ground pepper
fresh rosemary sprigs, to garnish
4 thick slices of white toast, to serve

1 Clean and trim the chicken livers to remove any gristle or muscle.

2 Season the livers generously with salt and freshly ground black pepper, tossing well to coat thoroughly.

chanterelle mushrooms

portabello mushroom

lemon

rosemary

3 Heat the wok and add 1 tbsp of the butter. When melted, add the livers in batches (melting more butter where necessary but reserving 2 tbsp for the vegetables) and flash-fry until golden brown. Drain with a slotted spoon and transfer to a plate, then place in a low oven to keep warm.

4 Cut the portabello mushrooms into thick slices and, depending on the size of the chanterelles, cut in half.

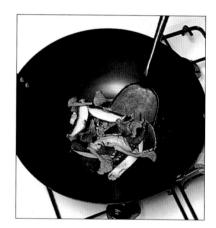

5 Heat the wok and add the remaining butter. When melted, stir in two-thirds of the chopped garlic and the shallots and stir-fry for 1 minute until golden brown. Stir in the mushrooms and continue to cook for a further 2 minutes.

6 Add the sherry, bring to a boil and simmer for 2–3 minutes until syrupy. Add the rosemary, salt and pepper and return livers to the pan. Stir-fry for 1 minute. Garnish with extra sprigs of rosemary, and serve sprinkled with a mixture of lemon, parsley and the remaining chopped garlic, with slices of toast.

Duck with Crêpes

Considerably lower in fat than traditional Peking duck, but just as delicious. Guests spread their crêpes with sauce, add duck and vegetables, then roll them up.

Serves 4

INGREDIENTS
1 tbsp honey
1¼ tsp five-spice powder
1 garlic clove, finely chopped
1 tbsp hoisin sauce
½ tsp salt
a large pinch of ground
   white pepper
2 small skinless duck breast portions
½ cucumber
10 scallions
3 Chinese cabbage leaves
12 Chinese crêpes (see Cook's Tip)

FOR THE SAUCE
1 tsp vegetable oil
2 garlic cloves, chopped
2 scallions, chopped
½-in piece of fresh ginger
   root, bruised
4 tbsp hoisin sauce
1 tbsp dry sherry
1 tbsp cold water
½ tsp sesame oil

1 Mix the honey, five-spice powder, garlic, hoisin sauce, salt and pepper in a shallow dish large enough to hold the duck breast portions side by side. Add the duck breast portions, turning them in the marinade. Cover and let sit in a cool place for 2 hours.

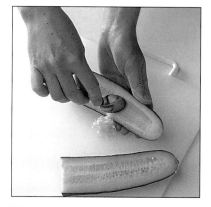

2 Cut the cucumber in half lengthwise. Using a teaspoon, scrape out and discard the seeds. Cut the flesh into thin sticks 2 inches long.

3 Cut off and discard the green tops from the scallions. Finely shred the white parts and place on a serving plate with the cucumber sticks.

sesame oil

duck breast portions

hoisin sauce

five-spice powder

ginger root

sherry

Chinese cabbage

scallions

honey

garlic

cucumber

Chinese crêpes

4 Make the sauce. Heat the oil in a small saucepan and gently cook the garlic for a few seconds without browning. Add the scallions, ginger, hoisin sauce, sherry and water. Cook gently for 5 minutes, stirring often, then strain and mix with the sesame oil.

5 Remove the duck breast portions from the marinade and drain them well. Place the duck breasts on a rack over a broiling pan. Broil under medium to high heat for 8–10 minutes on each side. Allow to cool for 5 minutes before cutting into thin slices. Arrange on a serving platter, cover and keep warm.

COOK'S TIP

Chinese crêpes can be bought frozen at Chinese markets. Allow to thaw before steaming.

6 Line a steamer with the Chinese cabbage and place the crêpes on top. Have ready a large pan with 2 inches boiling water. Cover the steamer and place on a trivet in the pan. Steam over high heat for 2 minutes, or until the pancakes are hot. Serve at once with the duck, cucumber, scallions and sauce.

Chicken with Cashew Nuts

An all-time favorite, this classic dish is no less tasty when given the low-fat treatment.

Serves 4

INGREDIENTS

12 oz skinless chicken
 breast fillets
¼ tsp salt
pinch of ground white pepper
1 tbsp dry sherry
1¼ cups chicken stock
1 tbsp vegetable oil
1 garlic clove, finely chopped
1 small carrot, cut into cubes
½ cucumber, about 3 oz, cut into
 ½-in cubes
½ cup drained canned bamboo
 shoots, cut into ½-in cubes
1 tsp cornstarch
1 tbsp light soy sauce
1 tsp sugar
¼ cup dry-roasted cashew nuts
½ tsp sesame oil
noodles, to serve

chicken breast fillets *garlic* *chicken stock*

cashew nuts *soy sauce* *vegetable oil*

sherry *cucumber*

sesame oil *cornstarch* *carrot* *bamboo shoots*

1 Cut the chicken into ¾-inch cubes. Place the cubes in a bowl and stir in the salt, pepper and sherry. Cover and marinate for 15 minutes.

2 Bring the stock to a boil in a large saucepan. Add the chicken and cook, stirring, for 3 minutes. Drain, reserving 6 tablespoons of the stock, and set aside.

3 Heat the vegetable oil in a nonstick frying pan until very hot, add the garlic and stir-fry for a few seconds. Add the carrot, cucumber and bamboo shoots and continue to stir-fry over medium heat for 2 minutes.

4 Stir in the chicken and reserved stock. Mix the cornstarch with the soy sauce and sugar and add the mixture to the pan. Cook, stirring, until the sauce thickens slightly. Finally, add the cashew nuts and sesame oil. Toss to mix thoroughly, then serve with noodles.

Chicken with Lemon Sauce

Succulent chicken with a refreshing lemony sauce and just a hint of lime is a sure winner.

Serves 4

INGREDIENTS

4 small skinless chicken breast fillets
1 tsp sesame oil
1 tbsp dry sherry
1 egg white, lightly beaten
2 tbsp cornstarch
1 tbsp vegetable oil
salt and ground white pepper
chopped cilantro leaves and
    scallions and lemon wedges,
    to garnish

FOR THE SAUCE

3 tbsp fresh lemon juice
2 tbsp lime cordial
3 tbsp sugar
2 tsp cornstarch
6 tbsp cold water

chicken breast fillets

sherry

lemon   *egg*

lime cordial

sesame oil

cornstarch   *sugar*

1 Arrange the chicken breast fillets in a single layer in a shallow bowl. Mix the sesame oil with the sherry and add ½ teaspoon salt and ¼ teaspoon pepper. Pour over the chicken, cover and marinate for 15 minutes.

2 Mix together the egg white and cornstarch. Add the mixture to the chicken and turn the chicken with tongs until thoroughly coated. Heat the vegetable oil in a nonstick frying pan or wok and fry the chicken fillets for about 15 minutes, until the fillets are golden brown on both sides.

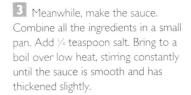

3 Meanwhile, make the sauce. Combine all the ingredients in a small pan. Add ¼ teaspoon salt. Bring to a boil over low heat, stirring constantly until the sauce is smooth and has thickened slightly.

4 Cut the chicken into pieces and arrange on a warm serving plate. Pour the sauce on top, garnish with the cilantro leaves, scallions and lemon wedges and serve.

Warm Chicken Salad with Shallots and Snow Peas

Succulent cooked chicken pieces are combined with vegetables in a light chili dressing.

Serves 6

INGREDIENTS

2 oz mixed lettuce leaves
2 oz baby spinach leaves
2 oz watercress
2 tbsp chili sauce
2 tbsp dry sherry
1 tbsp light soy sauce
1 tbsp ketchup
2 tsp olive oil
8 shallots, finely chopped
1 garlic clove, crushed
12 oz skinless, boneless chicken
   breast, cut into thin strips
1 red bell pepper, sliced
6 oz snow peas, trimmed
1 can (14 oz) baby corn, drained
   and halved
1 cup brown rice
salt and ground black pepper
parsley sprig to garnish

 mixed lettuce leaves
 spinach
 watercress
 chili sauce
 dry sherry
 light soy sauce
  ketchup
 olive oil
 shallots
 garlic
 brown rice
 chicken breast portions
 red bell pepper
 snow peas
baby corn

1 Arrange the mixed lettuce leaves, tearing up any large ones, and the spinach leaves on a serving dish. Add the watercress and toss to mix.

2 In a small bowl, mix together the chili sauce, sherry, soy sauce and ketchup and set aside.

3 Heat the oil in a large nonstick frying pan or wok. Add the shallots and garlic and stir-fry over medium heat for 1 minute.

4 Add the chicken and stir-fry for 3–4 minutes.

COOK'S TIP
Use other lean meat such as turkey breast, beef or pork in place of the chicken.

5 Add the pepper, snow peas, corn and rice and stir-fry for 2–3 minutes.

6 Pour in the chili sauce mixture and stir-fry for 2–3 minutes, until hot and bubbling. Season to taste. Spoon the chicken mixture over the salad leaves, toss together to mix and serve immediately, garnished with fresh parsley.

Turkey with Sage, Prunes and Brandy

This stir-fry has a very rich sauce based on a good brandy—use the best you can afford.

Serves 4

INGREDIENTS
4 oz prunes
3–3½ lb turkey breast portion
1¼ cups VSOP cognac or
  good brandy
1 tbsp fresh sage, chopped
5 oz smoked bacon, in one piece
4 tbsp butter
24 pearl onions, peeled and quartered
salt and freshly ground black pepper
fresh sage sprigs, to garnish

smoked bacon

prunes

pearl onion

sage

1 Pit the prunes and cut them into slivers. Remove the skin from the turkey and cut the breast into thin pieces.

2 Mix together the prunes, turkey, cognac and sage in a non-metallic dish. Cover and leave to marinate overnight.

3 Next day, strain the turkey and prunes, reserving the cognac mixture, and pat dry on paper towels.

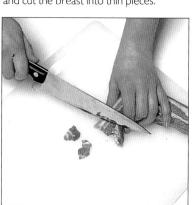

4 Cut the bacon into lardons (dice).

5 Heat the wok and add half the butter. When melted, add the onions and stir-fry for 4 minutes until crisp and golden. Set aside.

6 Heat the wok, add the lardons and stir-fry for 1 minute until the bacon begins to release some fat. Add the remaining butter and stir-fry the turkey and prunes for 3–4 minutes until crisp and golden. Push the turkey mixture to one side in the wok, add the cognac and simmer until thickened. Stir the turkey into the sauce, season well with salt and ground black pepper, and serve garnished with sage.

Lemon Chicken Stir-fry

It is essential to prepare all the ingredients before you begin so they are ready to cook. This dish is cooked in minutes.

Serves 4

INGREDIENTS

4 boned and skinned chicken
   breast portions
1 tbsp light soy sauce
5 tbsp cornstarch
1 bunch scallions
1 lemon
1 garlic clove, crushed
1 tbsp superfine sugar
2 tbsp sherry
⅔ cup fresh or canned chicken stock
4 tbsp olive oil
salt and freshly ground black pepper

superfine sugar

garlic

olive oil

scallions

lemon

soy sauce

cornstarch

*chicken breast
portions*

1 Divide the chicken breast portions into two natural fillets. Place each between two sheets of plastic wrap and flatten to a thickness of ¼ in with a rolling pin.

2 Cut into 1 in strips across the grain of the fillets. Put the chicken into a bowl with the soy sauce and toss to coat thoroughly, then sprinkle over 4 tbsp cornstarch to coat each piece.

3 Trim the roots off the scallions and cut diagonally into ½ in pieces. With a vegetable peeler, remove the lemon zest in thin strips and cut into fine shreds. Reserve the lemon juice. Have ready the garlic clove, sugar, sherry, stock, lemon juice and the remaining cornstarch blended to a paste with cold water.

4 Heat the oil in a wok or large frying pan and cook the chicken very quickly in small batches for 3–4 minutes until lightly colored. Remove and keep warm while frying the rest of the chicken.

5 Add the scallions and garlic to the pan and cook for 2 minutes.

6 Add the remaining ingredients and bring to a boil, stirring until thickened. Add more sherry or stock if necessary and stir until the chicken is evenly covered with sauce. Reheat for 2 more minutes. Serve immediately.

Stir-fried Turkey with Broccoli and Mushrooms

This is a really easy, tasty supper dish which works well with chicken too.

Serves 4

INGREDIENTS
4 oz broccoli florets
4 scallions
1 tsp cornstarch
3 tbsp oyster sauce
1 tbsp dark soy sauce
½ cup chicken stock,
    or bouillon cube
    and water
2 tsp lemon juice
3 tbsp peanut oil
1 lb turkey fillets, cut into
    strips, about ¼ x 2 in
1 small onion, chopped
2 garlic cloves, crushed
2 tsp fresh ginger root,
    finely grated
4 oz fresh shiitake
    mushrooms, sliced
3 oz canned baby corn,
    halved lengthwise
1 tbsp sesame oil
salt and ground black pepper
egg noodles, to serve

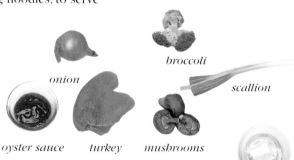

broccoli

onion

scallion

oyster sauce   turkey   mushrooms

lemon

dark soy sauce

baby corn

peanut oil

garlic

chicken stock

1 Divide the broccoli florets into smaller sprigs and cut the stalks into thin diagonal slices.

2 Finely chop the white parts of the scallions and slice the green parts into thin shreds.

3 In a bowl, blend together the cornstarch, oyster sauce, soy sauce, stock and lemon juice. Set aside.

4 Heat a wok until hot, add 2 tbsp of the peanut oil and swirl it around. Add the turkey and stir-fry for about 2 minutes, until golden and crispy at the edges. Remove the turkey from the wok and keep warm.

5 Add the remaining peanut oil to the wok and stir-fry the chopped onion, garlic and ginger over medium heat for about 1 minute. Increase the heat to high, add the broccoli, mushrooms and corn and stir-fry for 2 minutes.

6 Return the turkey to the wok, then add the sauce with the chopped scallion and seasoning. Cook, stirring, for about 1 minute, until the sauce has thickened. Then stir in the sesame oil. Serve immediately on a bed of egg noodles with the finely shredded scallion sprinkled on top.

Spiced Honey Chicken Wings

Be prepared to get very sticky when you eat these wings, as the best way to enjoy them is by eating them with your fingers. Provide individual finger bowls for your guests.

Serves 4

INGREDIENTS
1 red chili, finely chopped
1 tsp chili powder
1 tsp ground ginger
zest of 1 lime, finely grated
12 chicken wings
4 tbsp sunflower oil
1 tbsp fresh cilantro, chopped
2 tbsp soy sauce
3½ tbsp honey
lime zest and fresh cilantro sprigs, to garnish

lime

cilantro

honey

chicken wing

1 Mix the fresh chili, chili powder, ground ginger and lime zest together. Rub the mixture into the chicken skins and leave for at least 2 hours to allow the flavors to penetrate.

2 Heat the wok and add half of the oil. When the oil is hot, add half the wings and stir-fry for 10 minutes, turning regularly until crisp and golden. Drain on paper towels. Repeat with the remaining wings.

3 Add the cilantro to the hot wok and stir-fry for 30 seconds, then return the wings to the wok and stir-fry for about 1 minute.

4 Stir in the soy sauce and honey, and stir-fry for 1 minute. Serve the chicken wings hot with the sauce drizzled over them, garnished with lime rind and cilantro sprigs.

Stir-fried Crisp Duck

This stir-fry would be delicious wrapped in flour tortillas or steamed Chinese crêpes, with a little extra warm plum sauce.

Serves 2

INGREDIENTS
boneless duck breast portion
    (¾ lb)
2 tbsp flour
¼ cup oil
1 bunch scallions, halved
    lengthwise and cut into
    2-in strips
2½ cups green cabbage, finely
    shredded
1 can (8 oz) water chestnuts,
    drained and sliced
⅓ cup unsalted cashews
¼ lb cucumber, cut into strips
3 tbsp plum sauce
1 tbsp light soy sauce
salt and pepper
sliced scallions, to garnish

plum sauce   cashews   oil

water
chestnuts   flour   light soy
sauce

green
cabbage   scallions

duck
breast
portion   cucumber

1 Trim a little of the fat from the duck and thinly slice the meat. Season the flour well and use it to coat each piece of duck.

2 Heat the oil in a wok or large frying pan and cook the duck over high heat until golden and crisp. Keep stirring to prevent the duck from sticking. Remove with a slotted spoon and drain on paper towels. You may need to do this in batches.

3 Add the scallions to the pan and cook for 2 minutes. Stir in the cabbage and cook for 5 minutes or until softened and golden.

4 Return the duck to the pan with the water chestnuts, cashews and cucumber. Stir-fry for 2 minutes. Add the plum sauce and soy sauce with plenty of seasoning, and heat for 2 minutes. Serve piping hot, garnished with sliced scallions.

Indonesian-style Saté Chicken

Use boneless chicken thighs to give a good flavor to these satés.

Serves 4

INGREDIENTS
½ cup raw peanuts
3 tbsp vegetable oil
1 small onion, finely chopped
1 in piece ginger root, peeled and
  finely chopped
1 clove garlic, crushed
1½ lb chicken thighs, skinned and cut
  into cubes
3½ oz creamed coconut, chopped
1 tbsp chili sauce
4 tbsp chunky peanut butter
1 tsp soft dark brown sugar
⅔ cup milk
¼ tsp salt

creamed coconut

peanuts

chili sauce

peanut butter

1 Shell and rub the skins from the peanuts, then soak them in enough water to cover, for 1 minute. Drain the nuts and cut them into slivers.

2 Heat the wok and add 1 tsp oil. When the oil is hot, stir-fry the peanuts for 1 minute until crisp and golden. Remove with a slotted spoon and drain on paper towels.

3 Add the remaining oil to the hot wok. When the oil is hot, add the onion, ginger and garlic and stir-fry for 2–3 minutes until softened but not browned. Remove with a slotted spoon and drain on paper towels.

4 Add the chicken pieces and stir-fry for 3–4 minutes until crisp and golden on all sides. Thread on to pre-soaked bamboo skewers and keep warm.

5 Add the creamed coconut to the hot wok in small pieces and stir-fry until melted. Add the chili sauce, peanut butter and cooked ginger and garlic, and simmer for 2 minutes. Stir in the sugar, milk and salt, and simmer for a further 3 minutes. Serve the skewered chicken hot, with a dish of the hot dipping sauce sprinkled with the roasted peanuts.

Sweet-sour Duck with Mango

Mango adds natural sweetness to this colorful stir-fry. Crispy deep-fried noodles make the perfect accompaniment.

Serves 4

INGREDIENTS
8–12 oz duck breast portions
3 tbsp dark soy sauce
1 tbsp Chinese rice wine
1 tsp sesame oil
1 tsp Chinese five-
   spice powder
1 tbsp brown sugar
2 tsp cornstarch
3 tbsp Chinese rice vinegar
1 tbsp tomato ketchup
1 mango, not too ripe
3 baby eggplant
1 red onion
1 carrot
4 tbsp peanut oil
1 garlic clove, sliced
1-in piece fresh ginger root,
   cut into shreds
3 oz sugar snap peas

duck breast portions

peanut oil

carrot

dark soy sauce

eggplant

Chinese rice wine

mango

sesame oil

sugar snap peas

ginger

sugar

red onion

garlic

tomato ketchup

Chinese five-spice powder

1 Thinly slice the duck breast portions and place in a bowl. Mix together 1 tbsp of the soy sauce with the rice wine or sherry, sesame oil and five-spice powder. Pour over the duck, cover and allow to marinate for 1–2 hours. In a separate bowl, blend together the sugar, cornstarch, rice vinegar, ketchup and remaining soy sauce. Set aside.

2 Peel the mango, slice the flesh from the pit, then cut into thick strips. Slice the eggplant, onion and carrot into similar-sized pieces.

4 Add the remaining oil and fry the onion, garlic, ginger and carrot for 2–3 minutes, then add the sugar snap peas and stir-fry for another 2 minutes.

VARIATION
If baby eggplants are not available, use one small to medium eggplant instead.

3 Heat a wok until hot, add 2 tbsp of the oil and swirl it around. Drain the duck, reserving the marinade. Stir-fry the duck slices over high heat until the fat is crisp and golden. Remove and keep warm. Add 1 tbsp of the oil to the wok and stir-fry the eggplant for 3 minutes until golden.

5 Add the mango and return the duck with the sauce and reserved marinade to the wok. Cook, stirring, until the sauce thickens slightly. Serve immediately.

Thai Red Chicken Curry

Here chicken and potatoes are simmered in spiced coconut milk, then garnished with shredded kaffir lime leaves and red chilies.

Serves 4

INGREDIENTS
1 onion
1 tbsp peanut oil
1⅓ cups coconut milk
2 tbsp red curry paste
2 tbsp Thai fish sauce
  (*nam pla*)
1 tbsp light brown sugar
8 oz tiny new potatoes
1 lb skinless chicken breast
  portions, cut into chunks
1 tbsp lime juice
2 tbsp fresh mint,
  finely chopped
1 tbsp fresh basil,
  finely chopped
2 kaffir lime leaves, shredded
1–2 fresh red chilies, seeded and
  finely shredded
salt and ground black pepper

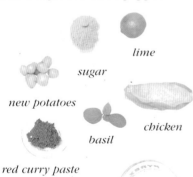

lime

sugar

new potatoes

basil

chicken

red curry paste

onion

coconut milk

mint

Thai fish sauce

VARIATION
You can use boneless chicken thighs instead of breast portions. Simply skin them, cut the flesh into chunks and cook in the coconut milk with the potatoes.

1 Cut the onion into wedges.

2 Heat a wok until hot, add the oil and swirl it around. Add the onion and stir-fry for 3–4 minutes.

3 Pour in the coconut milk, then bring to a boil, stirring. Stir in the curry paste, fish sauce and sugar.

4 Add the potatoes and seasoning and simmer gently, covered, for about 20 minutes.

5 Add the chicken chunks and cook, covered, over low heat for another 5–10 minutes, until the chicken and potatoes are tender.

6 Stir in the lime juice, chopped mint and basil. Serve at once, sprinkled with the shredded kaffir lime leaves and red chilies.

Chicken with Mixed Vegetables

A riot of color, this delectable dish has plenty of contrasts in terms of texture and taste.

Serves 4

INGREDIENTS
12 oz skinless chicken breast fillets
4 tsp vegetable oil
1¼ cups chicken stock
¾ cup drained canned straw mushrooms
½ cup sliced, drained, canned bamboo shoots
⅓ cup drained, canned water chestnuts, sliced
1 small carrot, sliced
½ cup snow peas
1 tbsp dry sherry
1 tbsp oyster sauce
1 tsp sugar
1 tsp cornstarch
1 tbsp cold water
salt and ground white pepper

chicken stock

chicken breast fillets

straw mushrooms

bamboo shoots

water chestnuts

snow peas

cornstarch

sherry

sugar

oyster sauce

carrot

1 Put the chicken in a shallow bowl. Add 1 teaspoon of the oil, ¼ teaspoon salt and a pinch of pepper. Cover and set aside for 10 minutes in a cool place.

2 Bring the stock to a boil in a saucepan. Add the chicken and cook for 12 minutes, or until tender. Drain and slice, reserving 5 tablespoons of the stock.

3 Heat the remaining oil in a nonstick frying pan or wok, add all the vegetables and stir-fry for 2 minutes. Stir in the sherry, oyster sauce, sugar and reserved stock. Add the chicken to the pan and cook for 2 minutes more.

4 Mix the cornstarch to a paste with the water. Add the mixture to the pan and cook, stirring, until the sauce thickens slightly. Season to taste with salt and pepper and serve immediately.

Duck with Pineapple

Duck and pineapple is a favorite combination, but the fruit must not be allowed to dominate. Here the proportions are perfect, and the dish has a wonderfully subtle sweet-sour flavor.

Serves 4

INGREDIENTS

1 tbsp dry sherry
1 tbsp dark soy sauce
2 small skinless duck breast portions
1 tbsp vegetable oil
2 garlic cloves, finely chopped
1 small onion, sliced
1 red bell pepper, seeded and cut into 1-in squares
½ cup drained, canned pineapple chunks
6 tbsp pineapple juice
1 tbsp rice vinegar
1 tsp cornstarch
1 tbsp cold water
1 tsp sesame oil
salt and ground white pepper
1 scallion, shredded, to garnish

red bell pepper
duck breasts
onion
garlic
sherry
rice vinegar
soy sauce
pineapple juice
cornstarch
pineapple chunks
sesame oil

1 Mix together the sherry and soy sauce. Stir in ½ teaspoon salt and ¼ teaspoon pepper. Put the duck breast portions in a bowl and add the marinade. Cover and let sit in a cool place for 1 hour.

2 Drain the duck breast portions and place them on a rack in a broiling pan. Broil under medium to high heat for 10 minutes on each side. Allow to cool for 10 minutes, then cut into bite-size pieces.

3 Heat the vegetable oil in a nonstick frying pan or wok and stir-fry the garlic and onion for 1 minute. Add the red bell pepper, pineapple chunks, duck, pineapple juice and vinegar and stir-fry for 2 minutes.

4 Mix the cornstarch to a paste with the water. Add the mixture to the pan with ¼ teaspoon salt. Cook, stirring, until the sauce thickens. Stir in the sesame oil and serve at once, garnished with shredded scallion.

Spicy Chicken Stir-fry

The chicken is marinated in an aromatic blend of spices and stir-fried with crisp vegetables. If you find it too spicy, serve with a spoonful of sour cream or yogurt. It's just as delicious hot or cold.

Serves 4

INGREDIENTS

½ tsp each ground turmeric and
   ground ginger
1 tsp each salt and ground
   black pepper
2 tsp ground cumin
1 tbsp ground coriander
1 tbsp superfine sugar
boneless, skinless chicken breast
   portions (1 lb)
1 bunch scallions
4 celery sticks
2 red bell peppers, seeded
1 yellow bell pepper, seeded
6 oz zucchini
6 oz snow peas or sugar
   snap peas
2 tbsp sunflower oil
1 tbsp lime juice
1 tbsp clear honey

1 Combine the turmeric, ginger, salt, pepper, cumin, coriander and sugar in a bowl.

2 Cut the chicken into bite-sized strips. Add to the spice mixture and stir to coat the chicken pieces thoroughly. Set aside.

yellow bell pepper

sunflower oil

lime

celery

zucchini

scallions

clear honey

red bell peppers

ground coriander

salt

sugar

chicken breast portions

snow peas

ground turmeric

ground ginger

ground black pepper

ground cumin

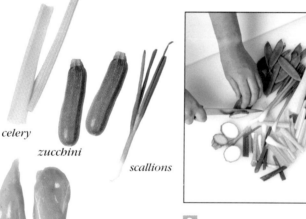

3 Prepare the vegetables. Cut the scallions, celery and peppers into 2-inch long, thin strips. Cut the zucchini at a slight angle into thin rounds and trim the snow peas or sugar snap peas.

4 Heat 2 tablespoons oil in a large frying pan or wok. Stir-fry the chicken in batches until cooked through and golden brown, adding a little more oil if necessary. Remove from the pan and keep warm.

5 Add a little more oil to the pan and cook the onions, celery, peppers and zucchini over medium heat for 8–10 minutes, until beginning to soften and turn golden. Add the snow peas or sugar snap peas and cook for 2 more minutes.

6 Return the chicken to the pan, with the lime juice and honey. Cook for 2 minutes. Adjust the seasoning and serve immediately.

Duck and Ginger Chop Suey

Chicken can also be used in this recipe, but duck gives a richer contrast of flavors.

Serves 4

INGREDIENTS
2 duck breast portions, 6 oz each
3 tbsp sunflower oil
1 medium egg, lightly beaten
1 clove garlic
6 oz/2 cups bean sprouts
2 slices ginger root, cut into
    matchsticks
2 tsp oyster sauce
2 scallions, cut into matchsticks
salt and freshly ground pepper

FOR THE MARINADE
1 tbsp honey
2 tsp rice wine
2 tsp light soy sauce
2 tsp dark soy sauce

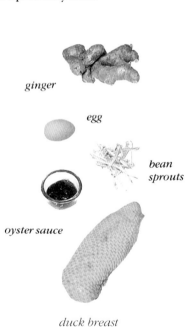

ginger

egg

*bean
sprouts*

oyster sauce

*duck breast
portion*

1 Remove the fat from the duck, cut the breasts into thin strips and place in a bowl. Mix the marinade ingredients together, pour over the duck, cover, chill and marinate overnight.

2 Next day, make the egg omelette. Heat a small frying pan and add 1 tbsp of the oil. When the oil is hot, pour in the egg and swirl around to make an omelet. Once cooked, leave it to cool and cut into strips. Drain the duck and discard the marinade.

3 Bruise the garlic with the flat blade of a knife. Heat the wok, then add 2 tsp oil. When the oil is hot, add the garlic and fry for 30 seconds, pressing it to release the flavor. Discard. Add the bean sprouts with seasoning and then stir-fry for about 30 seconds. Transfer to a heated dish, draining off any liquid.

4 Heat the wok and add the remaining oil. When the oil is hot, stir-fry the duck for 3 minutes until cooked. Add the ginger and oyster sauce and stir-fry for a further 2 minutes. Add the bean sprouts, egg strips and scallions, stir-fry briefly and serve immediately.

Chicken with Orange

A bowl of boiled rice is the ideal accompaniment to this chicken dish.

Serves 4

INGREDIENTS
1 lb boneless, skinless chicken
   breast portions

FOR THE MARINADE
1 tsp sugar
1 tbsp sake or rice wine
1 tbsp rice wine or dry sherry
2 tbsp dark soy sauce
zest of 1 orange, grated
orange segments and cress,
   to garnish

orange

rice wine

soy sauce

*chicken breast
portion*

1 Finely slice the chicken.

2 Mix all the marinade ingredients together in a bowl.

COOK'S TIP
Make sure the marinade is brought to a boil and cooked for 4–5 minutes, because it has been in contact with raw chicken.

3 Place the chicken in a bowl, pour over the marinade and leave to marinate for 15 minutes.

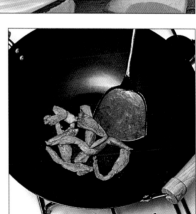

4 Heat the wok, add the chicken and marinade and stir-fry for 4–5 minutes. Serve garnished with orange segments and cress.

Crisp and Aromatic Duck

Because this dish is served with crêpes, scallions, cucumber and duck sauce (a sweet bean paste), many people mistakenly think this is Peking Duck. This recipe, however, uses quite a different cooking method. The result is just as crisp, with a delightful aroma.

DUCK SAUCE

2 tbsp sesame oil
6–7 tbsp crushed yellow bean sauce
2–3 tbsp light brown sugar

Heat the sesame oil in a saucepan. Add the bean sauce and light brown sugar. Stir until smooth and allow to cool. Serve at room temperature.

Serves 6-8

INGREDIENTS
1 oven-ready duckling, weighing
   about 4½–5 lb
2 tsp salt
5 or 6 whole star anise
1 tbsp Szechuan peppercorns
1 tsp cloves
2–3 cinnamon sticks
3–4 scallions
3–4 slices fresh ginger root, unpeeled
5–6 tbsp Chinese rice wine or
   dry sherry
vegetable oil, for deep-frying
lettuce leaves, to serve

duckling

rice wine

scallions

ginger root

cloves

star anise

cinnamon sticks

1 Remove the wings from the duck. Split the body in half down the backbone.

2 Rub salt all over the two duck halves, taking care to rub it in well.

3 Marinate in a dish with the spices, scallions, ginger and wine or sherry for at least 4–6 hours.

4 Vigorously steam the duck with the marinade for 3–4 hours (longer if possible), then remove from the cooking liquid and set aside to cool for at least 5–6 hours. The duck must be completely cool and dry or the skin will not be crispy.

5 Heat the oil in a wok until smoking. Place the duck pieces in the oil, skin side down, and deep-fry for 5–6 minutes, or until crisp and brown, turning just once at the very last minute.

6 Remove, drain and place on a bed of lettuce leaves. To serve, scrape the meat off the bone and wrap a portion in each crêpe with a little sauce, shredded scallions and cucumber. Eat with your fingers.

Warm Stir-fried Salad

Warm salads are becoming increasingly popular because they are delicious and nutritious. Arrange the salad leaves on four individual plates, so the hot stir-fry can be served quickly on to them, ensuring the lettuce remains crisp and the chicken warm.

Serves 4

INGREDIENTS

1 tbsp fresh tarragon
2 boneless, skinless chicken breast
    portions, about 8 oz each
2 in piece ginger root, peeled and
    finely chopped
3 tbsp light soy sauce
1 tbsp sugar
1 tbsp sunflower oil
1 Napa cabbage
½ chicory lettuce, torn into
    bite-size pieces
1 cup unsalted cashews
2 large carrots, peeled and cut into
    fine strips
salt and freshly ground black pepper

chicken breast portion

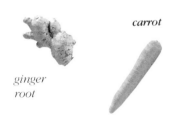

carrot

ginger root

cashews

1 Chop the tarragon.

2 Cut the chicken into fine strips and place in a bowl.

3 To make the marinade, mix together in a bowl the tarragon, ginger, soy sauce, sugar and seasoning.

4 Pour the marinade over the chicken strips and leave for 2–4 hours.

5 Strain the chicken from the marinade. Heat the wok, then add the oil. When the oil is hot, stir-fry the chicken for 3 minutes, add the marinade and bubble for 2–3 minutes.

6 Slice the Napa cabbage and arrange on a plate with the chicory. Toss the cashews and carrots together with the chicken, pile on top of the bed of lettuce and serve immediately.

Salt "Baked" Chicken

This is a wonderful way of cooking chicken. All the delicious, succulent juices are sealed inside the salt crust—yet the flavor isn't salty.

Serves 8

INGREDIENTS

3–3½ lb free-range chicken
¼ tsp fine sea salt
5 lb coarse rock salt
1 tbsp vegetable oil
1-in piece fresh ginger root,
   finely chopped
4 scallions, cut into fine rings
boiled rice, garnished with
   shredded scallions, to serve

chicken

scallions

ginger root   rock salt

COOK'S TIP
To reduce the fat content, remove and discard the skin from the chicken before eating.

1 Rinse the chicken. Pat it dry, both inside and out, with paper towels, then rub the inside with the sea salt.

4 Pour the remaining salt over the chicken until it is completely covered. Dampen six more pieces of paper towel and place them around the rim of the pan or wok. Cover with a tight-fitting lid. Set the pan or wok over high heat for 10 minutes, or until it gives off a slightly smoky smell.

2 Place four pieces of damp paper towels on the bottom of a heavy frying pan or wok just large enough to hold the chicken.

5 Immediately reduce the heat to medium and continue to cook the chicken for 30 minutes without lifting the lid. After 30 minutes, turn off the heat and let sit for 10 minutes more before carefully lifting the chicken out of the salt. Brush off any salt still clinging to the chicken and allow the bird to cool for 20 minutes before cutting it into serving-size pieces.

COOK'S TIP
The dry salt around the top of the chicken can be used again, but the salt from under the bird should be thrown away, as it will have absorbed fat and cooking juices.

3 Sprinkle a layer of rock salt over the paper towels, about ½ inch thick. Place the chicken on top of the salt.

6 Heat the oil in a small saucepan until very hot. Add the ginger and scallions and fry for a few seconds, then pour into a heatproof bowl and use as a dipping sauce for the chicken. Serve the chicken with boiled rice, garnished with shredded scallions.

VEGETABLE AND VEGETARIAN DISHES

Fresh vegetables, whether stir-fried or steamed, are fundamental to Asian cuisine. Color plays an essential role in the overall experience of eating Asian food. Be sure to choose the vegetables carefully, checking their freshness, texture and aroma to ensure that every aspect of the dish is pleasing.

Szechuan Eggplant

This dish is also known as fish-fragrant eggplant, as the eggplant is cooked with flavorings that are often used with fish.

Serves 4

INGREDIENTS

2 small eggplant
1 tsp salt
3 dried red chilies
peanut oil, for deep frying
3–4 garlic cloves, finely chopped
½-in piece fresh ginger root, finely chopped
4 scallions, cut into 1-in lengths (white and green parts separated)
1 tbsp Chinese rice wine or medium-dry sherry
1 tbsp light soy sauce
1 tsp sugar
¼ tsp ground roasted Szechuan peppercorns
1 tbsp Chinese rice vinegar
1 tsp sesame oil

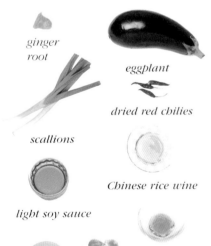

ginger root

eggplant

dried red chilies

scallions

Chinese rice wine

light soy sauce

sesame oil

garlic

peanut oil

1 Trim the eggplant and cut into strips, about 1½ in wide and 3 in long. Place the eggplant in a colander and sprinkle over the salt. Set aside for 30 minutes, then rinse them thoroughly under cold running water. Pat dry with paper towels.

2 Meanwhile, soak the chilies in warm water for 15 minutes. Drain, then cut each chili into three or four pieces, discarding the seeds.

3 Half-fill a wok with oil and heat to 350°F. Deep-fry the eggplant, until golden brown. Drain on paper towels. Pour off most of the oil from the wok. Reheat the oil and add the garlic, ginger and white scallion.

4 Stir-fry for 30 seconds. Add the eggplant and toss, then add the rice wine or sherry, soy sauce, sugar, ground Szechuan peppercorns and rice vinegar. Stir-fry for 1–2 minutes. Sprinkle over the sesame oil and green scallion.

Chinese Greens with Soy Sauce

Here Chinese greens are prepared in a very simple way—stir-fried and served with soy sauce. The combination makes a simple, quickly prepared, tasty accompaniment.

Serves 3-4

INGREDIENTS
1 lb Chinese greens
  (*bok choy*)
2 tbsp peanut oil
1–2 tablespoons soy sauce

Chinese greens

peanut oil

soy sauce

VARIATION

You can replace the Chinese greens with Chinese flowering cabbage, or Chinese broccoli, which is also known by its Cantonese name *choi sam*. It has green leaves and tiny yellow flowers, which are also eaten along with the leaves and stalks. It is available at Asian markets.

1 Trim the Chinese greens, removing any discolored leaves and damaged stems. Tear into manageable pieces.

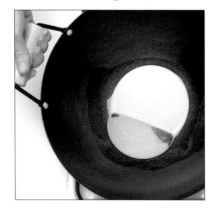

2 Heat a wok until hot, add the oil and swirl it around.

3 Add the Chinese greens and stir-fry for 2–3 minutes, until the greens have wilted a little.

4 Add the soy sauce and continue to stir-fry a few seconds more until the greens are cooked but still slightly crisp. Serve immediately.

Crisp Spring Rolls with Sweet Chili Dipping Sauce

Miniature spring rolls make delicious appetizers or party finger food.

Makes 20–24

INGREDIENTS

1 oz rice vermicelli noodles
peanut oil
1 tsp fresh ginger root, finely grated
2 scallions, finely shredded
2 oz carrot, finely shredded
2 oz snow peas, shredded
1 oz young spinach leaves
2 oz fresh bean sprouts
1 tbsp fresh mint, finely chopped
1 tbsp fresh cilantro, finely chopped
2 tbsp Thai fish sauce (*nam pla*)
20–24 spring roll wrappers, each 5 in square
1 egg white, lightly beaten

FOR THE DIPPING SAUCE

4 tbsp sugar
¼ cup rice vinegar
2 fresh red chilies, seeded and finely chopped

COOK'S TIP

You can cook the spring rolls for 2–3 hours in advance, then all you have to do is reheat them on a foil-lined baking sheet at 400°F for about 10 minutes.

1 First make the dipping sauce: place the sugar and vinegar in a small pan with 2 tbsp water. Heat gently, stirring until the sugar dissolves, then boil rapidly until it forms a light syrup. Stir in the chilies and leave to cool.

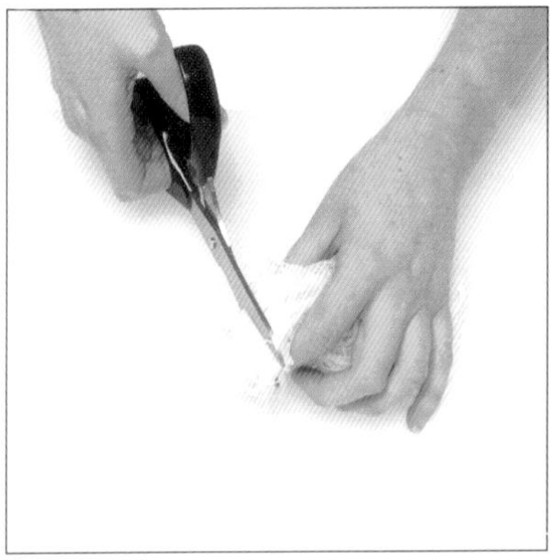

2 Soak the noodles according to the package instructions; rinse and drain well. Using scissors, snip the noodles into short lengths.

3 Heat a wok until hot. Add 1 tbsp oil and swirl it around. Add the ginger and scallions and stir-fry for 15 seconds. Add the carrot and snow peas and stir-fry for 2–3 minutes. Add the spinach, bean sprouts, mint, cilantro, fish sauce and noodles and stir-fry for another minute. Set aside to cool.

4 Take one spring roll wrapper and arrange it so that it faces you in a diamond shape. Place a spoonful of filling just below the center, then fold up the bottom point over the filling.

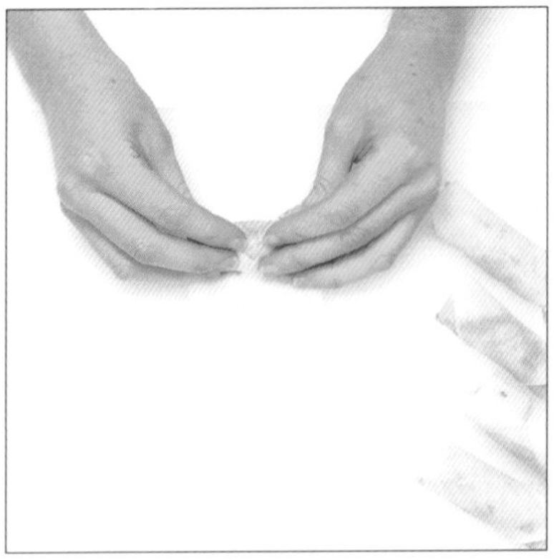

5 Fold in each side, then roll up tightly. Brush the end with beaten egg white to seal. Repeat until all the filling has been used.

6 Half-fill a wok with oil and heat to 350°F. Deep-fry the spring rolls in batches for 3–4 minutes, until golden and crisp. Drain on paper towels. Serve hot with the sweet chili dipping sauce.

Tofu Stir-fry

The tofu has a pleasant creamy texture, which contrasts well with crunchy stir-fried vegetables. Make sure that you buy firm tofu, as this is easy to cut neatly.

Serves 2–4

INGREDIENTS
4 oz cabbage
2 green chilies
8 oz firm tofu
3 tbsp vegetable oil
2 cloves garlic, crushed
3 scallions, chopped
6 oz green beans, topped and tailed
6 oz baby corn, halved
4 oz bean sprouts
3 tbsp smooth peanut butter
1½ tbsp dark soy sauce
1¼ cups coconut milk

baby corn

bean sprouts

chili

tofu

green beans

1 Shred the cabbage. Carefully remove the seeds from the chilies and chop finely. Wear rubber gloves to protect your hands, if necessary.

2 Cut the tofu into strips.

3 Heat the wok, then add 2 tbsp of the oil. When the oil is hot, add the bean curd, stir-fry for 3 minutes and remove. Set aside. Wipe out the wok with paper towels.

4 Add the remaining oil. When it is hot, add the garlic, scallions and chilies and stir-fry for 1 minute. Add the green beans, corn and bean sprouts and stir-fry for a further 2 minutes.

5 Add the peanut butter and soy sauce. Stir well to coat the vegetables. Add the bean curd to the vegetables.

6 Pour the coconut milk over the vegetables, simmer for 3 minutes and serve immediately.

Crisp Cabbage

This makes a wonderful accompaniment to meat or vegetable dishes—just a couple of spoonfuls will add a crisp texture to a meal. It goes especially well with shrimp dishes.

Serves 2–4 as an accompaniment

INGREDIENTS
4 juniper berries
1 large Savoy cabbage
4 tbsp vegetable oil
1 clove garlic, crushed
1 tsp superfine sugar
1 tsp salt

cabbage

vegetable oil

garlic

juniper berries

1 Finely crush the juniper berries, using a pestle and mortar.

2 Finely shred the cabbage.

3 Heat the wok., then add the oil. When the oil is hot, stir-fry the garlic for 1 minute. Add the cabbage and stir-fry for 3–4 minutes until crisp. Remove and pat dry with paper towels.

4 Return the cabbage to the wok. Toss the cabbage in sugar, salt and crushed juniper berries and serve hot or cold.

Sautéed Green Beans

The smoky flavor of the dried shrimp adds an extra dimension to green beans cooked this way.

Serves 4

INGREDIENTS

1 lb green beans
1 tbsp vegetable oil
3 garlic cloves, finely chopped
5 scallions, cut into 1-in lengths
1 oz dried shrimp, soaked in warm water and drained
1 tbsp light soy sauce
salt

green beans

soy sauce   *garlic*

scallions   *dried shrimp*

1 Trim the green beans and cut them in half crosswise.

2 Bring a saucepan of lightly salted water to a boil and cook the beans for 3–4 minutes, until crisp-tender. Drain, refresh under cold water and drain again.

COOK'S TIP

Don't be tempted to use too many dried shrimp. Their flavor is very strong and could overwhelm the more delicate taste of the beans.

3 Heat the oil in a nonstick frying pan or wok until very hot. Stir-fry the garlic and scallions for 30 seconds, then add the shrimp. Mix lightly.

4 Add the green beans and soy sauce. Toss the mixture over the heat until the beans are hot. Serve at once.

Stir-fried Vegetables with Cilantro Omelet

This is a great supper dish for vegetarians. The glaze is added here only to make the mixture shine, it is not intended as a sauce.

Serves 3-4

INGREDIENTS

FOR THE OMELET
2 eggs
2 tbsp water
3 tbsp chopped cilantro
salt and ground black pepper
1 tbsp peanut oil

FOR THE GLAZED VEGETABLES
1 tbsp cornstarch
2 tbsp dry sherry
1 tbsp sweet chili sauce
½ cup vegetable stock, or
  vegetable bouillon cube
  and water
2 tbsp peanut oil
1 tsp fresh ginger root,
  finely grated
6-8 scallions, sliced
4 oz bean sprouts
1 yellow bell pepper,
  seeded and sliced
4 oz fresh shiitake or
  button mushrooms
3 oz (drained weight)
  canned water chestnuts, rinsed
4 oz bean sprouts
½ small Chinese cabbage,
  coarsely shredded

cilantro

egg

snow peas

peanut oil

scallion   *mushrooms*

yellow bell pepper

stock   *sweet chili sauce*   *Chinese cabbage*   *bean sprouts*

1 Make the omelet: whisk the eggs, water, cilantro and seasoning in a small bowl. Heat the oil in a wok. Pour in the eggs, then tilt the wok so that the mixture spreads to an even layer. Cook over high heat until the edges are slightly crisp.

2 With a wok or spatula, flip the omelet over and cook the other side for about 30 seconds, until lightly browned. Turn the omelet onto a board and allow to cool. When cold, roll up loosely and cut into thin slices. Wipe the wok clean.

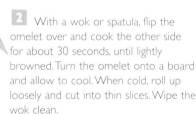

3 In a bowl, blend together the cornstarch, soy sauce, chili sauce and stock. Set aside.

4 Heat the wok until hot, add the oil and swirl it around, add the ginger and scallions and stir-fry for a few seconds to flavor the oil. Add the snow peas, pepper, mushrooms and water chestnuts and stir-fry for 3 minutes.

VARIATION

Vary the combination of vegetables used according to availability and taste.

5 Add the bean sprouts and Chinese cabbage and stir-fry for 2 minutes.

6 Pour in the glaze ingredients and cook, stirring, for about 1 minute until the glaze thickens and coats the vegetables. Turn the vegetables onto a warmed serving plate and top with the omelet shreds. Serve at once.

Red-cooked Tofu with Chinese Mushrooms

Red-cooked is a term applied to Chinese dishes cooked with dark soy sauce. This tasty dish can be served as either a side dish or main meal.

Serves 2–4

INGREDIENTS

8 oz firm tofu
3 tbsp dark soy sauce
2 tbsp Chinese rice wine or
   medium-dry sherry
2 tsp dark brown sugar
1 garlic clove, crushed
1 tbsp fresh ginger root,
   finely grated
½ tsp Chinese five-spice powder
pinch of ground roasted
   Szechuan peppercorns
6 dried Chinese black mushrooms
1 tsp cornstarch
2 tbsp peanut oil
5–6 scallions, sliced into
   1-in lengths
rice noodles, to serve
small basil leaves, to garnish

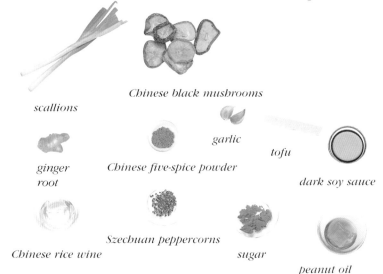

Chinese black mushrooms

scallions

ginger
root

garlic

tofu

Chinese five-spice powder

dark soy sauce

Chinese rice wine

Szechuan peppercorns

sugar

peanut oil

1 Drain the tofu, pat dry with paper towels and cut into 1-in cubes. Place in a shallow dish. In a small bowl, mix together the soy sauce, rice wine or sherry, sugar, garlic, ginger, five-spice powder and Szechuan peppercorns. Pour the marinade over the tofu, toss well and let marinate for about 30 minutes. Drain, reserving the marinade.

2 Meanwhile, soak the dried black mushrooms in warm water for 20–30 minutes until soft. Drain, reserving 6 tbsp of the soaking liquid. Squeeze out any excess liquid from the mushrooms, remove the tough stalks and slice the caps. In a small bowl, blend the cornstarch with the reserved marinade and mushroom soaking liquid.

3 Heat a wok until hot, add the oil and swirl it around. Add the tofu and fry for 2–3 minutes, until evenly golden. Remove from the wok and set aside.

4 Add the mushrooms and white scallions to the wok and stir-fry for 2 minutes. Pour in the marinade mixture and stir for 1 minute, until thickened.

5 Return the tofu to the wok with the green scallions. Simmer gently for 1–2 minutes. Serve at once with rice noodles and sprinkled with basil leaves.

Spiced Vegetables with Coconut

This spicy and substantial dish could be served as an appetizer, or as a vegetarian main course for two. Eat it with spoons and forks, and hunks of whole-wheat bread for mopping up the delicious coconut milk.

Serves 2–4 as a starter

INGREDIENTS
1 red chili
2 large carrots
6 stalks celery
1 bulb fennel
2 tbsp grapeseed oil
1 in piece ginger root, peeled and grated
1 clove garlic, crushed
3 scallions, sliced
1 × 14 fl oz can thin coconut milk
1 tbsp fresh cilantro, chopped
salt and freshly ground black pepper
cilantro sprigs, to garnish

celery

scallions

fennel

carrot

1 Halve, deseed and finely chop the chili. If necessary, wear rubber gloves to protect your hands.

2 Slice the carrots on the diagonal. Slice the celery stalks on the diagonal.

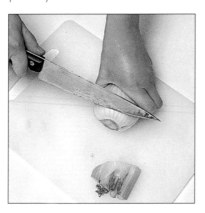

3 Trim the fennel head and slice roughly, using a sharp knife.

4 Heat the wok, then add the oil. When the oil is hot, add the ginger and garlic, chili, carrots, celery, fennel and scallions and stir-fry for 2 minutes.

5 Stir in the coconut milk with a large spoon and bring to a boil.

6 Stir in the cilantro and salt and pepper, and serve garnished with cilantro sprigs.

Spiced Tofu Stir-fry

You could add any quickly cooked vegetable to this stir-fry—try snow peas, sugar snap peas, leeks or thin slices of carrot.

Serves 4

INGREDIENTS

2 tsp ground cumin
1 tbsp paprika
1 tsp ground ginger
good pinch of cayenne pepper
1 tbsp superfine sugar
10 oz tofu
¼ cup oil
2 garlic cloves, crushed
1 bunch scallions, sliced
1 red bell pepper, seeded and sliced
1 yellow bell pepper, seeded and sliced
generous 3 cups cremini
    mushrooms, halved or
    quartered, if necessary
1 large zucchini, sliced
¼ lb green beans, halved
scant ½ cup pine nuts
1 tbsp lime juice
1 tbsp clear honey
salt and pepper

red bell pepper
tofu
paprika
pine nuts
cayenne pepper
scallions *ground cumin* *clear honey* *oil*
ground ginger
lime
garlic
yellow bell pepper
fine green beans
zucchini
superfine sugar
cremini mushrooms

1 Combine the cumin, paprika, ginger, cayenne and sugar with plenty of seasoning. Cut the tofu into cubes and coat them in the spice mixture.

2 Heat some oil in a wok or large frying pan. Cook the tofu over high heat for 3–4 minutes, turning occasionally (be careful not to break up the tofu too much). Remove with a slotted spoon. Wipe out the pan with paper towels.

3 Add a little more oil to the pan and cook the garlic and scallions for 3 minutes. Add the remaining vegetables and cook over medium heat for 6 minutes or until beginning to soften and turn golden. Season well.

4 Return the tofu to the pan with the pine nuts, lime juice and honey. Heat through and serve immediately.

Zucchini in Ginger Orange Sauce

If baby zucchini are unavailable, use larger ones, but cook whole so that they don't absorb too much water. Once cooked, halve them lengthwise and cut into 4-inch lengths.

Serves 4

INGREDIENTS

12 oz baby zucchini
4 scallions, finely sliced
1 in fresh ginger root, grated
2 tbsp cider vinegar
1 tbsp light soy sauce
1 tsp light brown sugar
3 tbsp vegetable stock
finely grated zest and juice of
    ½ lemon and ½ orange
1 tsp cornstarch
salt

orange

zucchini

lemon

fresh ginger root

scallions

1 Cook the zucchini in lightly salted boiling water for 3–4 minutes, or until just tender. Drain well and return to pan.

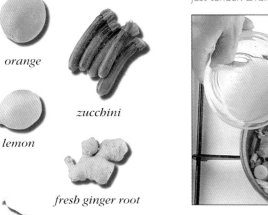

2 Meanwhile, put all the remaining ingredients, except the cornstarch, into a small saucepan and bring to a boil. Simmer for 3 minutes.

3 Blend the cornstarch with 2 teaspoons of cold water and add to the sauce. Bring to a boil, stirring constantly, until the sauce has thickened.

4 Pour the sauce over the zucchini and heat gently, shaking the pan to coat evenly. Transfer to a warmed serving dish and serve.

Yellow Flower Vegetables

To serve, each person spreads hoisin sauce on a crêpe, adds filling and rolls it up.

Serves 4

INGREDIENTS

3 eggs
2 tbsp water
4 tbsp peanut oil
1 oz dried Chinese black
　mushrooms
1 oz dried wood ears
2 tsp cornstarch
2 tbsp light soy sauce
2 tbsp Chinese rice wine or
　medium-dry sherry
2 tsp sesame oil
2 garlic cloves, finely chopped
½-in piece fresh ginger root,
　cut into thin shreds
3 oz canned sliced bamboo
　shoots (drained weight), rinsed
6 oz bean sprouts
4 scallions, finely shredded
salt and ground black pepper
Chinese crêpes and hoisin
　sauce, to serve

COOK'S TIP
Chinese crêpes are available at
Asian markets. Reheat them in a
bamboo steamer for 2–3 minutes
before serving.

1 Whisk the eggs, water and seasoning in a small bowl. Heat 1 tbsp of the peanut oil in a wok and swirl it around. Pour in the eggs, then tilt the wok so that they spread to an even layer. Continue to cook over high heat for about 2 minutes, until set. Turn onto a board and, when cool, roll up and cut into thin strips. Wipe the wok clean.

2 Meanwhile, put the black mushrooms and wood ears into separate bowls. Pour over enough warm water to cover, then allow to soak for 20–30 minutes, until soft. Drain the dried mushrooms, reserving their soaking liquid. Squeeze the excess liquid from each of them.

3 Remove the tough stalks and thinly slice the black mushrooms. Finely shred the wood ears. Set aside. Strain the reserved soaking liquid through muslin into a measuring cup; reserve ½ cup of the liquid. Then, in a bowl, blend the cornstarch with the reserved liquid, soy sauce, rice wine or sherry and sesame oil.

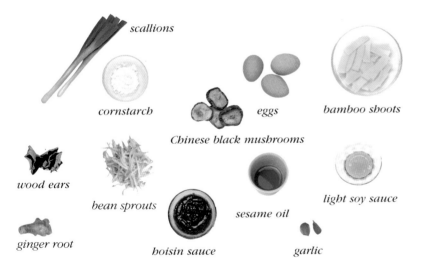

scallions

cornstarch

eggs

bamboo shoots

Chinese black mushrooms

wood ears

bean sprouts

sesame oil

light soy sauce

ginger root

hoisin sauce

garlic

4 Heat the wok over medium heat, add the remaining peanut oil and swirl it around. Add the wood ears and black mushrooms and stir-fry for about 2 minutes. Add the garlic, ginger, bamboo shoots and bean sprouts and stir-fry for 1–2 minutes.

5 Pour in the cornstarch mixture and cook, stirring, for 1 minute until thickened. Add the scallions and omelet strips and toss gently. Adjust the seasoning, adding more soy sauce, if needed. Serve at once with the Chinese crêpes and hoisin sauce.

Stir-fried Chickpeas

Buy canned chickpeas and you will save all the time needed for soaking and then thoroughly cooking dried chickpeas. Served with a crisp green salad, this dish makes a filling vegetarian main course for two, or could be served in smaller quantities as an appetizer or side dish.

Serves 2–4 as an accompaniment

INGREDIENTS
2 tbsp sunflower seeds
1 × 14 oz can chickpeas, drained
    and rinsed
1 tsp chili powder
1 tsp paprika
2 tbsp vegetable oil
1 clove garlic, crushed
7 oz canned chopped tomatoes
8 oz fresh spinach, well washed and
    coarse stalks removed
salt and freshly ground black pepper
2 tsp chili oil

spinach

garlic

sunflower seeds

chickpeas

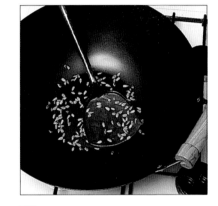

1 Heat the wok, and then add the sunflower seeds. Dry-fry until the seeds are golden and toasted.

2 Remove the sunflower seeds and set aside. Toss the chickpeas in chili powder and paprika. Remove and reserve.

3 Heat the wok, then add the oil. When the oil is hot, stir-fry the garlic for 30 seconds, add the chickpeas and stir-fry for 1 minute.

4 Stir in the tomatoes and stir-fry for 4 minutes. Toss in the spinach, season well and stir-fry for 1 minute. Drizzle chili oil and scatter sunflower seeds over the vegetables, then serve.

Balti Stir-fried Vegetables with Cashew Nuts

This versatile stir-fry will accommodate most other combinations of vegetables—you do not have to use the selection suggested here.

Serves 4

INGREDIENTS
2 medium carrots
1 medium red bell pepper, seeded
1 medium green bell pepper, seeded
2 zucchini
4 oz green beans, halved
1 medium bunch scallions
1 tbsp virgin olive oil
4–6 curry leaves
½ tsp white cumin seeds
4 dried red chilies
10–12 cashew nuts
1 tsp salt
2 tbsp lemon juice
fresh mint leaves, to garnish

scallions beans cashew nuts

carrots red chilies

zucchini peppers curry leaves

1 Prepare the vegetables: Cut the carrots, peppers and zucchini into short, thin sticks, halve the beans and chop the scallions. Set aside.

2 Heat the oil in a nonstick wok or frying pan and stir-fry the curry leaves, cumin seeds and dried chilies for about 1 minute.

3 Add the vegetables and nuts and stir-fry them gently. Add the salt and lemon juice. Continue to stir-fry and cook for 3–5 minutes.

4 Transfer to a serving dish and serve immediately. Garnish with mint leaves.

COOK'S TIP
If you are very short of time, use frozen mixed vegetables, which also work well in this dish.

Daikon, Beet and Carrot Stir-fry

This is a dazzling colorful dish with a crunchy texture and fragrant taste.

Serves 4 as an accompaniment

INGREDIENTS
¼ cup pine nuts
4 oz daikon, peeled
4 oz beets, peeled
4 oz carrots, peeled
1½ tbsp vegetable oil
juice of 1 orange
2 tbsp cilantro, chopped
salt and freshly ground black pepper

carrot

pine nuts   daikon

beet

1 Heat the wok, then add the pine nuts and toss until golden brown. Remove and set on one side.

2 Cut the daikon, beets and carrots into long thin strips.

3 Heat the wok and add one-third of the oil. When the oil is hot, stir-fry the daikon, beets and carrots for 2–3 minutes. Remove and set aside.

4 Pour the orange juice into the wok and simmer for 2 minutes. Remove and keep warm.

5 Arrange the vegetables in bundles, and sprinkle over the cilantro and salt and pepper.

6 Drizzle over the orange juice, sprinkle in the pine nuts, and serve.

Spicy Vegetable Fritters with Salsa

The salsa goes just as well with plain stir-fried salmon strips or stir-fried beef as it does with these zucchini fritters.

Serves 2–4 as an appetizer

INGREDIENTS
2 tsp cumin seeds
2 tsp coriander seeds
1 lb zucchini
1 cup chickpea (gram) flour
½ tsp baking soda
½ cup peanut oil
fresh mint sprigs, to garnish

FOR THE SALSA

½ cucumber, diced
3 scallions, chopped
6 radishes, cubed
2 tbsp fresh mint, chopped
1 in piece ginger root, peeled and grated
3 tbsp lime juice
2 tbsp superfine sugar
3 cloves garlic, crushed

cucumber

mint   *ginger root*

radishes

zucchini

1 Heat the wok, then toast the cumin and coriander seeds. Cool them, then grind well, using a mortar and pestle.

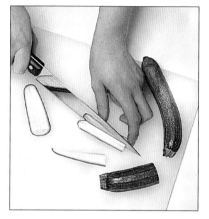

2 Cut the zucchini into 3 in sticks. Place in a bowl.

3 Blend the flour, baking soda, spices and salt and pepper in a food processor. Add ¼ cup warm water with 1 tbsp peanut oil, and blend again.

4 Coat the zucchini in the batter, then leave to stand for 10 minutes.

5 To make the salsa, mix all the ingredients together in a bowl.

6 Heat the wok, then add the remaining oil. When the oil is hot, stir-fry the zucchini in batches. Drain well on paper towels, then serve hot with the salsa, garnished with fresh mint sprigs.

Spring Vegetable Stir-fry

A colorful, dazzling medley of fresh and sweet young vegetables.

Serves 4

INGREDIENTS
1 tbsp peanut oil
1 garlic clove, sliced
1 in piece of fresh ginger root, finely
   chopped
4 oz baby carrots
4 oz patty pan squash
4 oz baby corn
4 oz green beans, ends removed
4 oz sugar-snap peas, ends removed
4 oz young asparagus, cut into 3 in
8 scallions, trimmed and cut into 2 in
   pieces
4 oz cherry tomatoes

FOR THE DRESSING
juice of 2 limes
1 tbsp honey
1 tbsp soy sauce
1 tsp sesame oil

1 Heat the peanut oil in a wok or large frying pan.

2 Add the garlic and ginger and stir-fry over a high heat for 1 minute.

3 Add the carrots, patty pan squash, baby corn and beans and stir-fry for another 3–4 minutes.

4 Add the sugar-snap peas, asparagus, scallions and cherry tomatoes and stir-fry for a further 1–2 minutes.

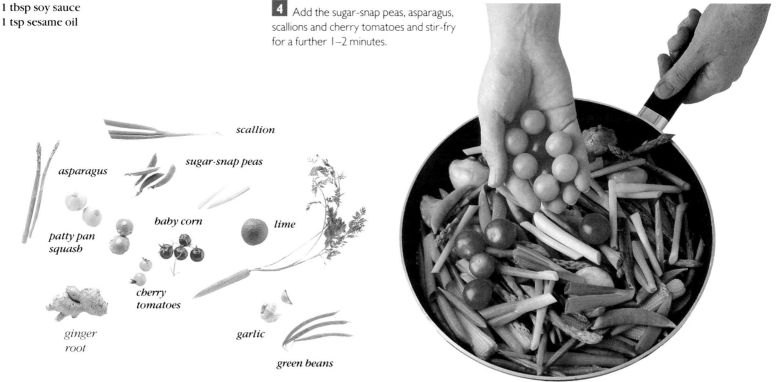

scallion

sugar-snap peas

asparagus

baby corn

lime

patty pan
squash

cherry
tomatoes

ginger
root

garlic

green beans

5 Mix the dressing ingredients together and add to the pan.

6 Stir well then cover the pan. Cook for 2–3 minutes more until the vegetables are just tender but still crisp.

COOK'S TIP

Stir-fries take only moments to cook so prepare this dish at the last minute.

Braised Eggplant and Zucchini

Eggplant, zucchini and some fresh red chilies form the basis of a dish that is simple, spicy and quite sensational.

Serves 4

INGREDIENTS

1 eggplant, about 12 oz
2 small zucchini
1 tbsp vegetable oil
2 garlic cloves, finely chopped
2 fresh red chilies, seeded
   and finely chopped
1 small onion, diced
1 tbsp black bean sauce
1 tbsp dark soy sauce
3 tbsp cold water
salt
chili flowers (optional), to garnish
   (see Cook's Tip)

1 Trim the eggplant and slice it in half lengthwise, then across into ½-inch-thick slices. Layer the slices in a colander, sprinkling each layer with salt. Set the colander in the sink and let stand for about 20 minutes.

2 Roll-cut the zucchini by slicing off one end diagonally, then rolling the zucchini through 180° and taking off another diagonal slice, which will form a triangular wedge. Make more wedges of zucchini in the same way.

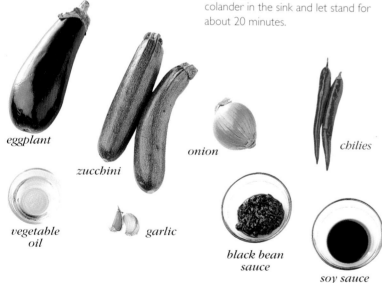

eggplant

zucchini

onion

chilies

vegetable oil

garlic

black bean sauce

soy sauce

3 Rinse the eggplant slices well, drain and dry thoroughly on paper towels.

4 Heat the oil in a wok or nonstick frying pan. Stir-fry the garlic, chilies and onion with the black bean sauce for a few seconds.

COOK'S TIP

Chili flowers make a pretty garnish. Using a small pair of scissors, slit a fresh red chili from the tip to within ½-in of the stem end. Repeat this at regular intervals around the chili so that you have slender "petals" attached at the stem. Rinse the chili to remove the seeds, then place it in a bowl of ice water for at least 4 hours, until the "petals" curl.

5 Add the eggplant slices and stir-fry for 2 minutes, sprinkling with a little water to prevent them from burning.

6 Stir in the zucchini, soy sauce and measured water. Cook, stirring occasionally, for 5 minutes. Serve hot, garnished with chili flowers.

Carrot and Cauliflower Stir-fry

The carrots are thinly sliced, which means that they cook quickly. This dish has a crunchy texture with only a few whole spices.

Serves 4

INGREDIENTS
2 large carrots
1 small cauliflower
1 tbsp olive oil
1 bay leaf
2 cloves
1 small cinnamon stick
2 cardamom pods
3 black peppercorns
1 tsp salt
2 oz frozen peas
2 tsp lemon juice
1 tbsp chopped cilantro
cilantro leaves, to garnish

frozen peas *lemon juice* *salt* *cinnamon* *cardamom* *cloves* *peppercorns* *bay leaf* *cauliflower* *cilantro* *carrots*

1 Cut the carrots into thin sticks about 1 inch long. Separate the cauliflower into small florets.

2 Heat the oil in a nonstick wok or frying pan and add the bay leaf, cloves, cinnamon, cardamom and peppercorns. Stir-fry over medium heat for 30–35 seconds, then add the salt.

3 Next add the carrot and cauliflower and continue to stir-fry for 3–5 minutes.

4 Add the peas, lemon juice and chopped cilantro and cook for another 2–3 minutes. Serve garnished with the whole cilantro leaves.

Nut Pilaf with Omelet Rolls

A wonderful mixture of textures—soft, fluffy rice with crunchy nuts and omelet rolls.

Serves 2

INGREDIENTS
1 cup basmati rice
1 tbsp sunflower oil
1 small onion, chopped
1 red bell pepper, finely diced
1½ cups hot vegetable bouillon,
  made from a cube
2 eggs
¼ cup salted peanuts
1 tbsp soy sauce
salt and freshly ground black pepper
parsley sprigs, to garnish

salted peanuts   *parsley*   *onion*

eggs

bouillon cube

red bell pepper

basmati rice

soy sauce

1 Wash the rice several times under cold running water. Drain thoroughly. Heat half the oil in a large frying pan. Fry the onion and bell pepper for 2–3 minutes. Then stir in the rice and bouillon. Bring to a boil, and cook for 10 minutes until the rice is tender.

2 Meanwhile, beat the eggs lightly with salt and pepper to taste. Heat the remaining oil in a second large frying pan. Pour in the eggs, and tilt the pan to cover the base thinly. Cook the omelet for 1 minute. Then flip it over, and cook the other side for 1 minute.

3 Carefully slide the omelet on to a clean board, and roll it up tightly. Cut the omelet roll into eight slices.

4 Stir the peanuts and soy sauce into the pilaf, and add black pepper to taste. Turn the pilaf into a serving dish. Arrange the omelet rolls on top, and garnish with the parsley. Serve at once.

Bok Choy and Mushroom Stir-fry

Try to buy all the varieties of mushroom for this dish; the wild oyster and shiitake mushrooms have particularly distinctive, delicate flavors.

Serves 4 as an accompaniment

INGREDIENTS
4 dried black Chinese mushrooms
1 lb bok choy
2 oz oyster mushrooms
2 oz shiitake mushrooms
1 tbsp vegetable oil
1 clove garlic, crushed
2 tbsp oyster sauce

Chinese mushrooms

shiitake mushrooms

bok choy

oyster mushrooms

1 Soak the black Chinese mushrooms in ⅔ cup boiling water for 15 minutes to soften them.

2 Tear the bok choy into bite-size pieces with your fingers.

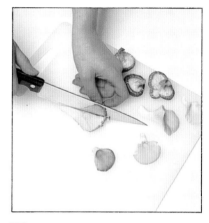

3 Halve any large oyster or shiitake mushrooms, using a sharp knife.

4 Strain the Chinese mushrooms. Heat the wok, then add the oil. When the oil is hot, stir-fry the garlic until softened but not colored.

5 Add the bok choy and stir-fry for 1 minute. Mix in all the mushrooms and stir-fry for 1 minute.

6 Add the oyster sauce, toss well and serve immediately.

Mixed Vegetables Monk-style

Chinese monks eat neither meat nor fish, so "monk-style" dishes are fine for vegetarians.

Serves 4

INGREDIENTS
2 oz dried bean curd sticks
4 oz fresh lotus root, or
    2 oz dried
¼ oz dried wood ears
8 dried Chinese mushrooms
1 tbsp vegetable oil
¾ cup drained canned straw
    mushrooms
4 oz (1 cup) baby corn,
    cut in half
2 tbsp light soy sauce
1 tbsp dry sherry
2 tsp sugar
⅔ cup vegetable stock
3 oz snow peas, trimmed and
    cut in half
1 tsp cornstarch
1 tbsp cold water
salt

1 Put the bean curd sticks in a bowl. Cover with hot water and let soak for 1 hour. If using fresh lotus root, peel it and slice it; if using dried lotus root, place it in a bowl of hot water and let soak for 1 hour.

2 Prepare the wood ears and dried Chinese mushrooms by soaking them in separate bowls of hot water for 15 minutes. Drain the wood ears, trim off and discard the hard base from each and cut the rest into bite-size pieces. Drain the Chinese mushrooms, trim off and discard the stems and chop the caps roughly.

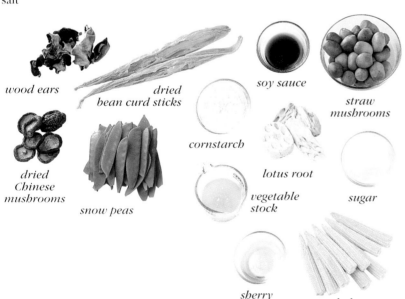

wood ears

dried bean curd sticks

soy sauce

straw mushrooms

dried Chinese mushrooms

snow peas

cornstarch

lotus root

vegetable stock

sugar

sherry

baby corn

3 Drain the bean curd sticks. Cut them into 2-inch-long pieces, discarding any hard pieces. If using dried lotus root, drain well.

4 Heat the oil in a nonstick frying pan or wok. Stir-fry the wood ears, Chinese mushrooms and lotus root for about 30 seconds.

COOK'S TIP

The flavor of this tasty vegetable mix improves on keeping, so any leftovers would taste even better the next day.

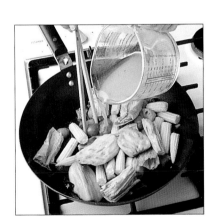

5 Add the pieces of bean curd sticks, straw mushrooms, baby corn, soy sauce, sherry, sugar and stock. Bring to a boil, then cover the pan or wok, lower the heat and simmer for about 20 minutes.

6 Stir in the snow peas with salt to taste and cook, uncovered, for 2 minutes more. Mix the cornstarch to a paste with the water. Add the mixture to the pan or wok. Cook, stirring, until the sauce thickens. Serve at once.

Deep-fried Root Vegetables with Spiced Salt

All kinds of root vegetables may be finely sliced and deep-fried to make "chips". Serve as an accompaniment to an oriental-style meal or simply by themselves as a snack.

Serves 4-6

INGREDIENTS
1 carrot
2 parsnips
2 raw beets
1 sweet potato
peanut oil, for deep frying
¼ tsp cayenne pepper
1 tsp sea salt flakes

cayenne pepper

sweet potato

peanut oil

beet

carrot

parsnips

1 Peel all the vegetables, then slice the carrot and parsnips into long, thin ribbons, and the beets and sweet potato into thin rounds. Pat dry all the vegetables on paper towels.

COOK'S TIP
To save time, you can slice the vegetables using a mandoline or a blender or food processor with a thin slicing disc attached.

2 Half-fill a wok with oil and heat to 350°F. Add the vegetable slices in batches and deep-fry for 2–3 minutes, until golden and crisp. Remove and drain on paper towels.

3 Place the cayenne pepper and sea salt in a mortar and grind together to a coarse powder.

4 Pile up the vegetable "chips" on a serving plate and sprinkle over the spiced salt.

Stir-fried Parsnips

Serve these sweet and piquant parsnips as an accompaniment to other stir-fried dishes or with a selection of vegetable dishes.

Serves 4 as an accompaniment

INGREDIENTS
2 large cloves garlic
12 oz parsnips
1 tbsp vegetable oil
1 in piece ginger root, peeled
  and grated
zest of 1 lime, grated
3 tbsp honey
salt and freshly ground black pepper

lime

ginger root

garlic

parsnip

1 Peel and cut the garlic into slices.

2 Peel and cut the parsnips into long, thin strands.

3 Heat the wok, then swirl in the oil. When the oil is hot, stir-fry the parsnips for 2 minutes.

4 Sprinkle the ginger, lime zest, salt and pepper and honey over the parsnips. Stir to coat the vegetables and serve.

Mixed Mushroom Ragu

These mushrooms are delicious served hot or cold
and can be made up to two days in advance.

Serves 4

INGREDIENTS
1 small onion, finely chopped
1 garlic clove, crushed
1 tsp cilantro seeds, crushed
2 tbsp red wine vinegar
1 tbsp soy sauce
1 tbsp dry sherry
2 tsp tomato paste
2 tsp light brown sugar
⅔ cup vegetable stock
4 oz baby white mushrooms
4 oz cremini mushrooms, quartered
4 oz oyster mushrooms, sliced
salt and freshly ground black pepper
sprig of fresh cilantro, to garnish

oyster mushrooms

sherry

cremini mushrooms

soy sauce

vinegar

cilantro seeds

tomato paste

garlic

cilantro

white mushrooms

onion

1 Put the first nine ingredients into a large saucepan. Bring to a boil and reduce the heat. Cover and simmer for 5 minutes.

2 Uncover the saucepan and simmer for 5 more minutes, or until the liquid has reduced by half.

3 Add the baby white and cremini mushrooms and simmer for 3 minutes. Stir in the oyster mushrooms and cook for a further 2 minutes.

4 Remove the mushrooms with a slotted spoon and transfer them to a serving dish.

5 Boil the juices for about 5 minutes, or until reduced to about 5 tbsp. Season well with salt and pepper.

6 Allow to cool for 2-3 minutes, then pour over the mushrooms. Serve hot or well chilled, garnished with fresh cilantro.

Stir-fried Tofu and Bean Sprouts with Noodles

This is a satisfying dish, which is both tasty and easy to make.

Serves 4

INGREDIENTS
8 oz firm tofu
peanut oil, for deep frying
6 oz medium egg noodles
1 tbsp sesame oil
1 tsp cornstarch
2 tsp dark soy sauce
1 tbsp Chinese rice wine
1 tsp sugar
6–8 scallions, cut diagonally into
   1-in lengths
3 garlic cloves, sliced
1 fresh green chili, seeded
   and sliced
4 oz Chinese cabbage leaves,
   coarsely shredded
2 oz bean sprouts
2 oz cashew nuts, toasted

scallions

garlic

sesame oil

Chinese cabbage

tofu

noodles

bean sprouts

dark soy sauce

Chinese rice wine   *green chili*

1 Drain the tofu and pat dry with paper towels. Cut the tofu into 1-in cubes. Half-fill a wok with peanut oil and heat to 350°F. Deep-fry the tofu in batches for 1–2 minutes, until golden and crisp. Drain on paper towels. Carefully pour all but 2 tbsp of the oil from the wok.

2 Cook the noodles. Rinse them thoroughly under cold water and drain well. Toss in 2 tsp of the sesame oil and set aside. In a bowl, blend together the cornstarch, soy sauce, rice wine, sugar and remaining sesame oil.

3 Reheat the 2 tbsp of peanut oil and, when hot enough, add the lengths of scallion, sliced garlic, sliced chili, shredded Chinese cabbage and bean sprouts. Stir-fry for 1–2 minutes.

4 Add the tofu with the noodles and sauce. Cook, stirring, for about 1 minute, until well mixed. Sprinkle over the cashew nuts. Serve immediately.

Stir-fried Spinach with Garlic and Sesame Seeds

The sesame seeds add a crunchy texture which contrasts well with the wilted spinach in this easy vegetable dish.

Serves 2

INGREDIENTS
8 oz fresh spinach, washed
1½ tbsp sesame seeds
2 tbsp peanut oil
¼ tsp sea salt flakes
2–3 garlic cloves, sliced

spinach

peanut oil

garlic

sesame seeds

1 Shake the spinach to get rid of any excess water, then remove the stalks and discard any yellow or damaged leaves. Lay several spinach leaves one on top of another, roll up tightly and cut crossways into wide strips. Repeat with the remaining leaves.

2 Heat a wok to medium heat, add the sesame seeds and dry-fry, stirring, for 1–2 minutes, until golden brown. Transfer to a small bowl and set aside.

3 Add the oil to the wok and swirl it around. When hot, add the salt, spinach and garlic and stir-fry for 2 minutes until the spinach just wilts and the leaves are coated with the oil.

4 Sprinkle over the sesame seeds and toss well. Serve immediately.

COOK'S TIP
Take care when adding the spinach to the hot oil, as it will spit furiously.

Black Bean and Vegetable Stir-fry

The secret of a quick stir-fry is to prepare all the ingredients first. This colorful vegetable mixture is coated in a classic Chinese sauce.

Serves 4

INGREDIENTS
8 scallions
2 cups white mushrooms
1 red bell pepper
1 green bell pepper
2 large carrots
4 tbsp sesame oil
2 garlic cloves, crushed
4 tbsp black bean sauce
6 tbsp warm water
8 oz bean sprouts
salt and freshly ground black pepper

1. Thinly slice the scallions and white mushrooms. Set them to one side in separate bowls.

scallions

black bean sauce

sesame oil

white mushrooms

red bell pepper

bean sprouts

carrots

garlic cloves

onion

green bell pepper

2. Cut both the bell peppers in half. Remove the seeds, and slice the flesh into thin strips.

3. Cut the carrots in half. Cut each half into thin strips lengthwise. Stack the slices, and cut through them to make very fine strips.

4. Heat the oil in a large wok or frying pan until very hot. Add the scallions and garlic, and stir-fry for 30 seconds.

5. Add the mushrooms, bell peppers and carrots. Stir-fry for 5–6 minutes over a high heat until the vegetables are just beginning to soften.

6 Mix the black bean sauce with the water. Add to the wok or pan, and cook for 3–4 minutes. Stir in the bean sprouts, and stir-fry for 1 minute more, until all the vegetables are coated in the sauce. Season to taste. Serve immediately.

COOK'S TIP
For best results the oil in the wok must be very hot before adding the vegetables.

Spiced Coconut Mushrooms

Here is a simple and delicious way to cook mushrooms. They may be served with almost any Asian meal as well as with broiled or roasted meats and poultry.

Serves 3-4

INGREDIENTS
2 tbsp peanut oil
2 garlic cloves, finely chopped
2 fresh red chilies, seeded and
    sliced into rings
3 shallots, finely chopped
8 oz crimini or white mushrooms,
    thickly sliced
⅔ cup coconut milk
2 tbsp fresh cilantro,
    finely chopped
salt and ground black pepper

red chilies   *coconut milk*

mushrooms

peanut oil

cilantro

garlic

VARIATION
Use chopped fresh chives instead of cilantro if you wish.

1 Heat a wok until hot, add the oil and swirl it around. Add the garlic and chilies, then stir-fry for a few seconds.

2 Add the shallots and stir-fry for 2–3 minutes, until softened. Add the mushrooms and stir-fry for 3 minutes.

3 Pour in the coconut milk and bring to a boil. Boil rapidly over high heat until the liquid is reduced by half and coats the mushrooms. Taste and adjust the seasoning, if necessary.

4 Sprinkle over the cilantro and toss gently to mix. Serve at once.

Stir-fried Bean Sprouts

This fresh, crunchy vegetable, which is almost synonymous with Chinese restaurants, tastes much better when stir-fried at home.

Serves 4

INGREDIENTS

1 tbsp vegetable oil
1 garlic clove, finely chopped
1 tsp grated fresh ginger root
1 small carrot, cut into fine matchsticks
½ cup drained, canned bamboo shoots, cut into fine matchsticks
1 lb (8 cups) bean sprouts
½ tsp salt
large pinch of ground white pepper
1 tbsp dry sherry
1 tbsp light soy sauce
½ tsp sesame oil

bamboo shoots

bean sprouts

carrot

sesame oil

ginger root

garlic

soy sauce

sherry

1 Heat the vegetable oil in a nonstick frying pan or wok. Add the chopped garlic and grated ginger and stir-fry for a few minutes.

2 Add the carrot and bamboo shoot matchsticks to the pan or wok and stir-fry for a few minutes.

COOK'S TIP

Bean sprouts keep best when stored in the refrigerator or other cool place in a bowl of cold water, but you must remember to change the water daily.

3 Add the bean sprouts to the pan or wok with the salt and pepper. Drizzle with the sherry and toss the bean sprouts over the heat for 3 minutes, until hot.

4 Sprinkle with the soy sauce and sesame oil, toss to mix thoroughly, then serve immediately.

Balti Potatoes with Eggplant

Using new potatoes adds to the attractiveness of this dish. Choose the smaller variety of eggplant too, as they are far tastier than the large ones, which contain a lot of water and little flavor. Small eggplant are readily available from Asian markets.

Serves 4

INGREDIENTS
10–12 new potatoes
6 small eggplants
1 medium red bell pepper
1 tbsp corn oil
2 medium onions, sliced
4–6 curry leaves
½ tsp onion seeds
1 tsp crushed coriander seeds
1 tsp cumin seeds
1 tsp ginger pulp
1 tsp garlic pulp
1 tsp crushed dried red chilies
1 tbsp chopped fresh fenugreek
   or celery leaves
1 tsp chopped cilantro
1 tbsp plain low-fat yogurt
cilantro leaves, to garnish

red bell pepper   *onions*   *potatoes*

eggplants   *cilantro*   *garlic pulp*

cumin seeds   *curry leaves*   *fenugreek*   *red chilies*

ginger pulp   *onion seeds*   *yogurt*   *coriander seeds*

1 Cook the unpeeled potatoes in boiling water until just soft. Set aside.

2 Cut the eggplant into quarters.

3 Cut the pepper in half, remove the seeds, then slice the flesh into strips.

4 Heat the oil in a nonstick wok or frying pan and stir-fry the onions, curry leaves, onion seeds, crushed coriander seeds and cumin seeds until the onions are a soft golden brown.

5 Add the ginger, garlic, crushed chilies and fenugreek, followed by the eggplant and potatoes. Stir everything together and cover with a lid. Lower the heat and cook for 5–7 minutes.

COOK'S TIP
To prevent curdling it is always best to whisk the yogurt before adding to a hot dish.

6 Remove the lid, add the cilantro followed by the yogurt and stir well. Serve garnished with cilantro leaves.

Lentil Stir-fry

Mushrooms, artichokes, sugar snap peas and lentils make a satisfying stir-fry supper.

Serves 2–3

INGREDIENTS
4 oz sugar snap peas
1 oz butter
1 small onion, chopped
4 oz cup or white mushrooms,
  sliced
14 oz can artichoke hearts,
  drained and halved
14 oz can green lentils, drained
4 tbsp light cream
¼ cup shaved almonds, toasted
salt and freshly ground black pepper
French bread, to serve

light cream

green lentils

cup mushrooms

sugar snap peas

shaved almonds

artichoke hearts

onion

1 Bring a pan of salted water to a boil. Add the sugar snap peas, and cook for about 4 minutes until just tender. Drain, and refresh under cold running water. Then drain again. Pat dry the peas with paper towels, and set aside.

2 Melt the butter in a frying pan. Add the chopped onion and cook for 2–3 minutes, stirring occasionally.

3 Add the sliced mushrooms to the onion. Stir until combined. Then cook for 2–3 minutes until just tender. Add the artichokes, sugar snap peas and lentils to the pan. Stir-fry for 2 minutes.

4 Stir in the cream and almonds, and cook for 1 minute. Season to taste. Serve at once, with chunks of French bread.

COOK'S TIP
Use strained, plain yogurt instead of the cream, if you like.

Potato, Broccoli and Red Bell Pepper Stir-fry

A hot and hearty stir-fry of vegetables with just a hint of fresh ginger.

Serves 2

INGREDIENTS
1 lb potatoes
3 tbsp peanut oil
¼ cup butter
1 small onion, chopped
1 red bell pepper, seeded and
  chopped
8 oz broccoli, broken into florets
1 in piece of fresh ginger root,
  peeled and grated
salt and freshly ground black pepper

red bell pepper   butter

broccoli

onion

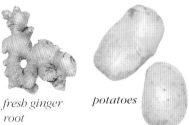

fresh ginger
root   potatoes

COOK'S TIP

Although a wok is the preferred pan for stir-frying, for this recipe, a flat frying pan is best to cook the potatoes quickly.

1 Peel the potatoes, and cut them into ½ in dice.

2 Heat the oil in a large frying pan, and add the potatoes. Cook for 8 minutes over a high heat, stirring and tossing occasionally, until the potatoes are browned and just tender.

3 Drain off the oil. Add the butter to the potatoes in the pan. As soon as it melts, add the onion and red bell pepper. Stir-fry for 2 minutes.

4 Add the broccoli florets and ginger to the pan. Stir-fry for 2–3 minutes more, taking care not to break up the potatoes. Add salt and pepper to taste, and serve immediately.

Braised Tofu with Mushrooms

The mushrooms flavor the bean curd beautifully to make this the perfect vegetarian main course.

Serves 4

INGREDIENTS

12 oz tofu
½ tsp sesame oil
2 tsp light soy sauce
1 tbsp vegetable oil
2 garlic cloves, finely chopped
½ tsp grated fresh ginger root
4 oz (1 cup) fresh shiitake
  mushrooms, stalks removed
6 oz (1½ cups) fresh oyster
  mushrooms
1 cup drained canned straw
  mushrooms
4 oz (1 cup) white mushrooms,
  cut in half
1 tbsp dry sherry
1 tbsp dark soy sauce
6 tbsp vegetable stock
1 tsp cornstarch
1 tbsp cold water
salt and ground white pepper
2 scallions, shredded

1 Put the tofu in a dish and sprinkle with the sesame oil, light soy sauce and a large pinch of pepper. Allow to marinate for 10 minutes, then drain and cut into 1 x ½-inch pieces.

2 Heat the vegetable oil in a nonstick frying pan or wok. When it is very hot, fry the garlic and ginger for a few seconds. Add all the mushrooms and stir-fry for 2 minutes.

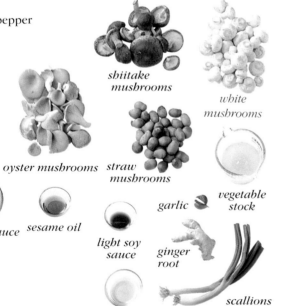

bean curd *oyster mushrooms* *straw mushrooms* *shiitake mushrooms* *white mushrooms* *vegetable stock* *garlic* *cornstarch* *dark soy sauce* *sesame oil* *light soy sauce* *ginger root* *scallions* *sherry*

3 Stir in the sherry, soy sauce and stock, with salt, if needed, and pepper. Simmer for 4 minutes.

4 Mix the cornstarch to a paste with the water. Stir the mixture into the pan or wok and cook, stirring, until thickened.

COOK'S TIP

If fresh shiitake mushrooms are
not available, use dried Chinese
mushrooms soaked in hot water.
Use the soaking liquid instead of
vegetable stock for a more
intense flavor.

5 Carefully add the pieces of tofu, toss
gently to coat thoroughly and simmer for
2 minutes.

6 Scatter the shredded scallions over
the top of the mixture, transfer to a
serving dish and serve immediately.

Broccoli with Soy Sauce

A wonderfully simple dish that you will want to make again and again. The broccoli cooks in next to no time, so don't start cooking until you are almost ready to eat.

Serves 4

INGREDIENTS
1 lb broccoli
1 tbsp vegetable oil
2 garlic cloves, crushed
2 tbsp light soy sauce
salt
fried garlic slices, to garnish

broccoli

garlic

vegetable oil

soy sauce

1 Trim the thick stems of the broccoli; cut the head into large florets.

2 Bring a saucepan of lightly salted water to a boil. Add the broccoli and cook for 3–4 minutes, until crisp-tender.

VARIATION
Most leafy vegetables taste delicious prepared this way. Try blanched romaine lettuce and you may be surprised at how crisp and clean the taste is.

3 Drain the broccoli thoroughly and arrange in a heated serving dish.

4 Heat the oil in a small saucepan. Fry the garlic for 2 minutes to release the flavor, then remove it with a slotted spoon. Pour the oil over the broccoli, taking care, as it will splatter. Drizzle the soy sauce over the broccoli, scatter the fried garlic on top and serve.

Stir-fried Chinese Cabbage

This simple way of cooking Chinese cabbage preserves its delicate flavor.

Serves 4

INGREDIENTS

1½ lb Chinese cabbage
1 tbsp vegetable oil
2 garlic cloves, finely chopped
1-in piece of fresh ginger root,
    finely chopped
½ tsp salt
1 tbsp oyster sauce
4 scallions, cut into 1-in lengths

Chinese cabbage

ginger root

garlic

oyster sauce

scallions

1 Stack the Chinese cabbage leaves and cut them into 1-inch slices.

2 Heat the oil in a wok or large deep saucepan. Stir-fry the garlic and ginger for 1 minute.

3 Add the Chinese cabbage to the wok or saucepan and stir-fry for 2 minutes. Sprinkle with the salt and drizzle with the oyster sauce. Toss the cabbage over the heat for 2 minutes more.

4 Stir in the scallions. Toss the mixture well, transfer it to a heated serving plate and serve.

COOK'S TIP

For guests who are vegetarians, substitute 1 tablespoon light soy sauce and 1 teaspoon sugar for the oyster sauce.

NOODLE DISHES

There are numerous varieties of noodle products throughout Asia, and the diverse methods of preparing them make them incredibly versatile. They are an excellent accompaniment to almost any dish, so depending on the complexity of each recipe, they may be served as a complete meal or simply as a side dish.

Stir-fried Noodles with Bean Sprouts

A classic Chinese noodle dish that makes a marvelous accompaniment.

Serves 4

INGREDIENTS

6 oz (1½ cups) dried thin Chinese
   egg noodles
1 tbsp vegetable oil
1 garlic clove, finely chopped
1 small onion, halved and sliced
8 oz (4 cups) bean sprouts
1 small red bell pepper, seeded and
   cut into strips
1 small green bell pepper, seeded
   and cut into strips
½ tsp salt
¼ tsp ground white pepper
2 tbsp light soy sauce

*dried
egg noodles*

onion

*soy
sauce*

garlic

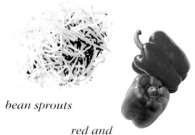

bean sprouts

*red and
green bell peppers*

1 Bring a saucepan of water to the boil. Cook the noodles for 4 minutes, until just tender, or according to the instructions on the package. Drain, refresh under cold water and drain again.

2 Heat the oil in a nonstick frying pan or wok. When the oil is very hot, add the garlic, stir briefly, then add the onion slices. Cook, stirring, for 1 minute, then add the bean sprouts and peppers. Stir-fry for 2–3 minutes.

3 Stir in the cooked noodles and toss over the heat, using two spatulas or wooden spoons, for 2–3 minutes, or until the ingredients are well mixed and have heated through.

4 Add the salt, pepper and soy sauce and stir thoroughly before serving the noodle mixture in heated bowls.

Singapore Rice Noodles

Simple and speedily prepared, this lightly curried rice noodle dish is a full meal in a bowl.

Serves 4

INGREDIENTS

8 oz (2 cups) dried thin
   rice noodles
1 tbsp vegetable oil
1 egg, lightly beaten
2 garlic cloves, finely chopped
1 large fresh red or green chili,
   seeded and finely chopped
1 tbsp medium curry powder
1 red bell pepper, seeded and
   thinly sliced
1 green bell pepper, seeded and
   thinly sliced
1 carrot, cut into matchsticks
¼ tsp salt
¼ cup vegetable stock
4 oz cooked shelled shrimp,
   thawed if frozen
3 oz lean ham, cut into ½-in cubes
1 tbsp light soy sauce

vegetable stock

ham *garlic* *red and green bell peppers*

soy sauce *curry powder* *shrimp*

egg *carrot* *chili*

dried rice noodles

Soak the rice noodles in a bowl of boiling water for 4 minutes, or according to the instructions on the package, then drain thoroughly and set aside.

Heat 1 teaspoon of the oil in a nonstick frying pan or wok. Add the egg and scramble until set. Remove with a slotted spoon and set aside.

Heat the remaining oil in the clean pan. Stir-fry the garlic and chili for a few seconds, then stir in the curry powder. Cook for 1 minute, stirring, then stir in the peppers, carrot sticks, salt and stock.

Bring to a boil. Add the shrimp, ham, scrambled egg, rice noodles and soy sauce. Mix well. Cook, stirring, until all the liquid has been absorbed and the mixture is hot. Serve at once.

Sesame Noodle Salad with Hot Peanuts

An orient-inspired salad with crunchy vegetables and a light soy dressing. The hot peanuts make a surprisingly successful union with the cold noodles.

Serves 4

INGREDIENTS
12 oz egg noodles
2 carrots, peeled and cut into fine
    julienne strips
½ cucumber, peeled and cut into
    ½ in cubes
4 oz celeriac, peeled and cut into fine
    julienne strips
6 scallions, finely sliced
8 canned water chestnuts, drained
    and finely sliced
6 oz bean sprouts
1 small fresh green chili, seeded
    and finely chopped
2 tbsp sesame seeds, to serve
1 cup peanuts, to serve

FOR THE DRESSING
1 tbsp dark soy sauce
1 tbsp light soy sauce
1 tbsp honey
1 tbsp rice wine or dry sherry
1 tbsp sesame oil

2 Drain the noodles, refresh in cold water, then drain again.

3 Mix the noodles with all of the prepared vegetables.

1 Preheat the oven to 400°F. Cook the egg noodles in boiling water, following the instructions on the side of the package.

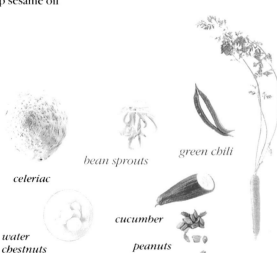

celeriac

bean sprouts

green chili

scallion

sesame seeds

water chestnuts

cucumber

peanuts

carrot

noodles

4 Combine the dressing ingredients in a small bowl, then toss into the noodle and vegetable mixture. Divide the salad between 4 plates.

5 Place the sesame seeds and peanuts on separate cookie sheets and place in the oven. Take the sesame seeds out after 5 minutes and continue to cook the peanuts for a further 5 minutes until evenly browned.

6 Sprinkle the sesame seeds and peanuts evenly over each portion and serve immediately.

Chinese Mushrooms with Cellophane Noodles

Red fermented bean curd adds extra flavor to this hearty vegetarian dish. It is brick red in color, with a very strong, cheesy flavor.

Serves 3–4

INGREDIENTS

4 oz dried Chinese mushrooms
1 oz dried wood ears
4 oz dried bean curd
2 tbsp oil
2 garlic cloves, finely chopped
2 slices fresh ginger root, finely chopped
10 Szechuan peppercorns, crushed
1 tbsp red fermented bean curd
½ star anise
pinch of sugar
1–2 tbsp dark soy sauce
2 oz cellophane noodles, soaked in hot water until soft
salt

dried Chinese mushrooms

dried wood ears

fresh ginger root

Szechuan peppercorns

star anise

dark soy sauce

cellophane noodles

1 Soak the Chinese mushrooms and wood ears separately in bowls of hot water for 30 minutes. Break the dried bean curd into pieces and soak in water according to the package instructions.

2 Strain the mushrooms, squeezing as much liquid from them as possible. Strain and reserve the liquid. Discard the stems and cut the caps in half if large. Drain the wood ears, rinse and drain again. Cut off any gritty parts, then cut each wood ear into two or three pieces.

3 Heat the oil in a heavy pan and sauté the garlic, ginger and Szechuan peppercorns for a few seconds. Add the mushrooms and red fermented bean curd, mix lightly and cook for 5 minutes.

4 Add the reserved mushroom liquid to the pan, with sufficient water to completely cover the mushrooms. Add the star anise, sugar and soy sauce, then cover and simmer for 30 seconds. Add the chopped wood ears and reconstituted bean curd pieces to the pan. Cover and cook for about 10 minutes.

5 Drain the cellophane noodles, add them to the mixture and cook for another 10 minutes, until tender, adding more liquid if necessary. Add salt to taste and serve.

Vegetable Chow Mein with Cashew Nuts

Chow mein is a popular dish that can be served with almost any type of Chinese vegetarian, meat or fish dish.

Serves 3–4

INGREDIENTS
2 tbsp oil
½ cup cashew nuts
2 carrots, cut into thin strips
3 celery ribs, cut into thin strips
1 green bell pepper, seeded and cut
   into thin strips
1 cup bean sprouts
8 oz dried medium or thin
   egg noodles
2 tbsp toasted sesame seeds,
   to garnish

FOR THE LEMON SAUCE
2 tbsp light soy sauce
1 tbsp dry sherry
⅔ cup vegetable stock
2 lemons
1 tbsp sugar
2 tsp cornstarch

cashew nuts

carrots

green bell pepper

bean sprouts

dried egg noodles

toasted sesame seeds

light soy sauce

lemon

1 Stir all the ingredients for the lemon sauce together in a measuring cup. Bring a large saucepan of salted water to a boil.

2 Heat the oil in a wok or large, heavy frying pan. Add the cashew nuts, toss quickly over high heat until golden, then remove with a slotted spoon.

3 Add the carrots and celery to the pan and stir-fry for 4–5 minutes. Add the pepper and bean sprouts and stir-fry for 2–3 minutes more. At the same time, cook the noodles in the pan of boiling water for 3 minutes, or according to the instructions on the package. Drain well and place in a warmed serving dish.

4 Remove the vegetables from the pan with a slotted spoon. Pour in the lemon sauce and cook for 2 minutes, stirring until thick. Return the vegetables to the pan, add the cashew nuts and stir quickly to coat in the sauce.

5 Spoon the vegetables and sauce over the noodles. Sprinkle with sesame seeds and serve.

Egg Noodle Stir-fry

The thick egg noodles and potatoes, along with the vegetables, make this a satisfying and healthy main dish. If possible, use fresh egg noodles, which are available at most large supermarkets.

Serves 4

INGREDIENTS

2 eggs
1 tsp chili powder
1 tsp ground turmeric
¼ cup oil
1 large onion, finely sliced
2 red chilies, seeded and finely sliced
1 tbsp light soy sauce
2 large cooked potatoes, cut into small cubes
6 pieces fried bean curd, sliced
1 cup bean sprouts
4 oz green beans, blanched
12 oz fresh thick egg noodles
salt and freshly ground black pepper
sliced scallions, to garnish

eggs

chili powder

ground turmeric

onion

red chilies

light soy sauce

potatoes

fried bean curd

bean sprouts

green beans

fresh thick egg noodles

scallions

1 Beat the eggs lightly, then strain them into a bowl. Heat a lightly greased omelet pan. Pour in half of the beaten egg just to cover the bottom of the pan. When the egg is set, carefully turn the omelet over and briefly cook the other side.

2 Slide the omelet onto a plate, blot with paper towels, roll up and cut into narrow strips. Make a second omelet in the same way and slice. Set the omelet strips aside for the garnish.

3 In a cup, mix together the chili powder and turmeric. Form a paste by stirring in a little water. Heat the oil in a wok or large frying pan. Sauté the onion until soft. Reduce the heat and add the chili paste, sliced chilies and soy sauce Cook for 2–3 minutes.

4 Add the potatoes and cook for about 2 minutes, mixing well with the chilies. Add the bean curd, then the bean sprouts, green beans and noodles.

5 Gently stir-fry until the noodles are evenly coated and heated through. Take care not to break up the potatoes or the bean curd. Season with salt and pepper. Serve hot, garnished with the omelet strips and scallion slices.

Five-spice Vegetable Noodles

Vary this vegetable stir-fry by substituting mushrooms, bamboo shoots, bean sprouts, snow peas or water chestnuts for some or all of the vegetables suggested below.

Serves 3–4

INGREDIENTS

8 oz dried thin or medium egg
    noodles
2 tbsp sesame oil
2 carrots
1 celery rib
1 small fennel bulb
2 zucchini, halved and sliced
1 red chili, seeded and chopped
1-in piece fresh ginger root, grated
1 garlic clove, crushed
1½ tsp Chinese five-spice
    powder
½ tsp ground cinnamon
4 scallions, sliced
sliced red chili, to garnish (optional)

1 Bring a large pan of salted water to a boil. Add the noodles and cook for 2–3 minutes, until just tender. Drain the noodles, return them to the pan and toss with a little of the sesame oil. Set aside.

celery rib

egg
noodles

carrots

fennel
bulb

red chili

zucchini

five-spice
powder

fresh ginger
root

cinnamon

garlic

scallions

2 Cut the carrot and celery into julienne strips. Cut the fennel bulb in half and cut away the hard core. Cut into slices, then cut the slices into thin strips.

3 Heat the remaining sesame oil in a wok until very hot. Add all the vegetables, including the chopped chili, and stir-fry for 7–8 minutes. Add the ginger and garlic and stir-fry for 2 minutes, then add the spices. Cook for 1 minute.

4 Add the scallions, stir-fry for 1 minute, then stir in ½ cup warm water and cook for 1 minute. Stir in the noodles and toss well together. Serve sprinkled with sliced red chili, if you like.

Fried Noodles with Bean Sprouts and Baby Asparagus

This dish is simplicity itself, with a wonderful contrast of textures and flavors. Use young asparagus, which is beautifully tender and cooks in minutes.

Serves 2

INGREDIENTS

4 oz dried thin or medium egg
   noodles
4 tbsp oil
1 small onion, chopped
1-in piece fresh ginger root, grated
2 garlic cloves, crushed
6 oz young asparagus, trimmed
½ cup bean sprouts
4 scallions, sliced
3 tbsp light soy sauce
salt and freshly ground black pepper

egg noodles

onion

garlic

fresh ginger
root

bean sprouts

scallions   light soy
sauce

asparagus

1 Bring a pan of salted water to a boil. Add the noodles and cook for 2–3 minutes, until just tender. Drain and toss in 2 tablespoons of the oil.

2 Heat the remaining oil in a wok or frying pan until very hot. Add the onion, ginger and garlic and stir-fry for 2–3 minutes. Add the asparagus and stir-fry for another 2–3 minutes.

3 Add the noodles and bean sprouts and stir-fry for 2 minutes.

4 Stir in the scallions and soy sauce. Season to taste, adding salt sparingly, because the soy sauce will add quite a salty flavor. Stir-fry for 1 minute and serve at once.

Spicy Fried Rice Sticks with Shrimp

This recipe is based on the classic Thai noodle dish called *Pad Thai*. Popular all over Thailand, it is enjoyed morning, noon and night.

VARIATION
For a vegetarian dish omit the dried shrimp and replace the jumbo shrimp with cubes of deep-fried tofu.

Serves 4

INGREDIENTS
½ oz dried shrimp
1 tbsp tamarind pulp
3 tbsp Thai fish sauce
  (*nam pla*)
1 tbsp sugar
2 garlic cloves, chopped
2 fresh red chilies, seeded and
  chopped
3 tbsp peanut oil
2 eggs, beaten
8 oz dried rice sticks, soaked in
  warm water for 30 minutes,
  refreshed under cold running
  water and drained
8 oz cooked shelled
  jumbo shrimp
3 scallions, cut into
  1-in lengths
3 oz bean sprouts
2 tbsp coarsely chopped
  roasted unsalted peanuts
2 tbsp fresh cilantro,
  finely chopped
lime slices, to garnish

1 Put the dried shrimp in a small bowl and pour over enough warm water to cover. Let soak for 30 minutes until soft, then drain.

2 Put the tamarind pulp in a bowl and add 4 tbsp hot water. Blend together, then press through a sieve to extract 2 tbsp thick tamarind water. Mix the tamarind water with the fish sauce and sugar.

3 Using a mortar and pestle, pound the garlic and chilies to form a paste. Heat a wok over medium heat, add 1 tbsp of the oil, then add the beaten eggs and stir for 1–2 minutes, until the eggs are scrambled. Remove and set aside. Wipe the wok clean.

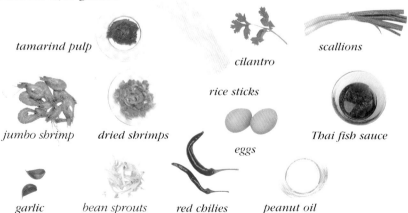

tamarind pulp

cilantro

scallions

rice sticks

jumbo shrimp　　*dried shrimps*

eggs

Thai fish sauce

garlic　　*bean sprouts*　　*red chilies*　　*peanut oil*

4 Reheat the wok until hot, add the remaining oil, then the chili paste and dried shrimp and stir-fry for 1 minute. Add the rice sticks and tamarind mixture and stir-fry for 3–4 minutes.

5 Add the scrambled eggs, shrimp, scallions, bean sprouts, peanuts and cilantro, then stir-fry for 2 minutes, until well mixed. Serve at once, garnishing each portion with lime slices.

Chicken and Shrimp Hot Pot

Made in a portable hot pot, this dish, known as Yosenabe, combines meat, fish, vegetables and noodles to create a warming meal that is cooked at the table.

Serves 4

INGREDIENTS
14 oz chicken thighs or breast
  portions on the bone
8 uncooked tiger shrimp
7 oz dried udon noodles
4 shiitake mushrooms, stems
  removed
½ head bok choy, cut into
  1¼-in slices
3 leeks, sliced diagonally into pieces
  ½ in-thick
6 × 4-in piece bean curd
  (about 5 oz), cut into
  1¼-in cubes
11 oz shirataki noodles, boiled
  for 2 minutes, drained and
  halved

FOR THE YOSENABE STOCK
4 cups kombu and bonito stock
6 tbsp sake or dry white wine
2 tbsp dark soy sauce
4 tsp mirin
2 tsp salt

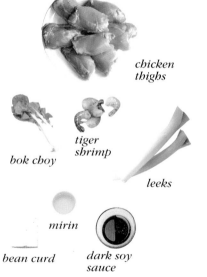

chicken
thighs

tiger
shrimp

shiitake
mushrooms

bok choy

leeks

udon noodles

sake

mirin

kombu and
bonito stock

bean curd

dark soy
sauce

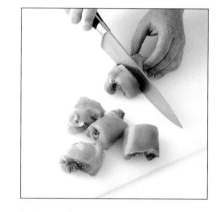

1 Cut the chicken into ½-inch chunks. Remove the black intestinal vein from the shrimp if necessary.

2 Cook the udon noodles for 2 minutes less than the package instructions dictate, drain and rinse thoroughly, then drain again and set aside. Arrange all the remaining ingredients on large plates.

3 Bring all the ingredients for the yosenabe stock to a boil in the hot pot. Add the chicken and simmer for 3 minutes, skimming the broth throughout cooking.

4 Add the remaining ingredients, except the udon noodles and simmer for 5 minutes, or until cooked. Diners serve themselves from the simmering hot pot. Finally, when all the ingredients have been eaten, add the udon noodles to the rest of the soup, heat through and serve in bowls to round off the meal.

Smoked Trout and Noodle Salad

This salad is a wonderful example of how well noodles can combine with a variety of ingredients, such as trout, capers and tomatoes.

Serves 4

INGREDIENTS
8 oz somen noodles
2 smoked trout, skinned and boned
2 hard-cooked eggs, coarsely
    chopped
2 tbsp chopped chives
lime halves, to serve (optional)

FOR THE DRESSING
6 ripe plum tomatoes
2 shallots, finely chopped
2 tbsp tiny capers, rinsed
2 tbsp chopped fresh tarragon
finely grated zest and juice of
    ½ orange
4 tbsp extra virgin olive oil
salt and freshly ground black pepper

somen noodles

smoked trout

chives

hard-cooked eggs

olive oil

orange

plum tomatoes

shallots

fresh tarragon

1 To make the dressing, cut the tomatoes in half, remove the cores and cut the flesh into chunks. Place in a bowl with the shallots, capers, tarragon, orange zest and juice and olive oil. Season with salt and pepper and mix well. Let the dressing marinate for 1–2 hours.

2 Cook the noodles in a large saucepan of boiling water until just tender. Drain and rinse under cold running water. Drain well.

COOK'S TIP
Choose tomatoes that are firm, bright in color and have a smooth surface, avoiding any with blotched or cracked skins.

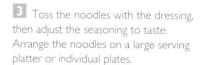

3 Toss the noodles with the dressing, then adjust the seasoning to taste. Arrange the noodles on a large serving platter or individual plates.

4 Flake the smoked trout over the noodles, then sprinkle the coarsely chopped eggs and chopped chives over the top. Serve the lime halves on the side, if you like.

Pork and Noodle Broth with Shrimp

This quick and delicious recipe can also be made with boneless chicken breast portions instead of pork tenderloin.

Serves 4-6

INGREDIENTS

12 oz pork chops or 7 oz pork
   tenderloin
8 oz raw or cooked shrimp
5 oz thin egg noodles
1 tbsp vegetable oil
2 tsp sesame oil
4 shallots, sliced
1 tbsp finely sliced, fresh ginger
   root
1 clove garlic, crushed
1 tsp sugar
6¼ cups chicken stock
2 lime leaves
3 tbsp fish sauce
juice of ½ lime
4 sprigs cilantro, to garnish
chopped green part of 2 scallions, to
   garnish

scallions

pork

noodles

shallots

garlic

shrimp

lime leaves

ginger root

1 If using pork chops, trim away fat and bone completely. Place the meat in the freezer for 30 minutes to firm but not freeze it. Slice the meat thinly and set aside. Shell and devein the shrimp, if raw.

2 Bring a large saucepan of salted water to a boil and simmer the noodles for the time stated on the package. Drain and refresh under cold running water. Set aside.

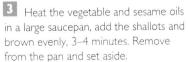

3 Heat the vegetable and sesame oils in a large saucepan, add the shallots and brown evenly, 3–4 minutes. Remove from the pan and set aside.

4 Add the ginger, garlic, sugar and chicken stock and bring to a simmer with the lime leaves. Add the fish sauce and lime juice. Add the pork and simmer for 15 minutes. Add the shrimp and noodles and simmer for 3–4 minutes. Serve in shallow soup bowls and decorate with the cilantro leaves, the green part of the scallions and the browned shallots.

Rice Noodles with Beef and Chili Bean Sauce

This is an excellent combination—tender beef with a chili bean sauce tossed with silky-smooth rice noodles.

Serves 4

INGREDIENTS

1 lb fresh rice noodles
¼ cup oil
1 onion, finely sliced
2 garlic cloves, finely chopped
2 slices fresh ginger root, finely chopped
8 oz mixed bell peppers, seeded and sliced
12 oz sirloin steak, finely sliced against the grain
3 tbsp fermented black beans, rinsed in warm water, drained and chopped
2 tbsp dark soy sauce
2 tbsp oyster sauce
1 tbsp chili bean sauce
1 tbsp cornstarch
½ cup beef stock or water
2 scallions, finely chopped, and 2 red chilies, seeded and finely sliced, to garnish

1 Rinse the noodles under hot water and drain well. Heat half the oil in a wok or frying pan, swirling it around. Add the onion, garlic, ginger and pepper slices.

2 Stir-fry for 3–5 minutes, then remove and keep warm. Add the remaining oil to the wok and swirl to coat the pan. When hot, add the sliced beef and fermented black beans and stir-fry over high heat for 5 minutes, or until they are cooked.

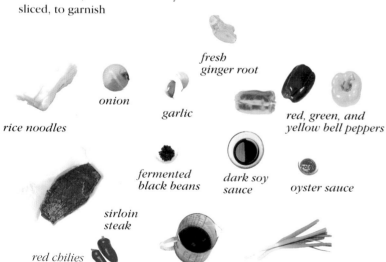

rice noodles

onion

garlic

fresh ginger root

red, green, and yellow bell peppers

fermented black beans

dark soy sauce

oyster sauce

sirloin steak

red chilies

beef stock

scallions

3 In a small bowl, blend the soy sauce, oyster sauce and chili bean sauce with the cornstarch and stock or water and stir until smooth. Add the mixture to the wok, together with the onion and peppers, and cook, stirring, for 1 minute.

4 Add the noodles and mix lightly. Stir over medium heat until the noodles are heated through. Adjust the seasoning if necessary. Serve immediately, garnished with the chopped scallions and finely sliced chilies.

Singapore Noodles

A delicious supper dish with a stunning mix of flavors and textures.

Serves 4

INGREDIENTS
8 oz dried egg noodles
3 tbsp peanut oil
1 onion, chopped
1-in piece fresh ginger root,
   finely chopped
1 garlic clove,
   finely chopped
1 tbsp Madras curry powder
½ tsp salt
4 oz cooked chicken or pork,
   finely shredded
4 oz cooked shelled shrimp
4 oz Chinese cabbage leaves,
   shredded
4 oz bean sprouts
4 tbsp chicken stock
1–2 tbsp dark soy sauce
1–2 fresh red chilies, seeded
   and finely shredded
4 scallions, finely shredded

bean sprouts

Chinese cabbage

noodles

ginger

curry powder

chicken

dark soy sauce

onion

stock

scallions

red chilies

peanut oil

shrimp

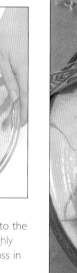

1 Cook the noodles according to the package instructions. Rinse thoroughly under cold water and drain well. Toss in 1 tbsp of the oil and set aside.

2 Heat a wok until hot, add the remaining oil and swirl it around. Add the onion, ginger and garlic and stir-fry for about 2 minutes.

3 Add the curry powder and salt, stir-fry for 30 seconds, then add the egg noodles, chicken or pork and shrimp. Stir-fry for 3–4 minutes.

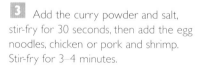

4 Add the Chinese cabbage and bean sprouts and stir-fry for 1–2 minutes. Sprinkle in the stock and soy sauce to taste and toss well until evenly mixed. Serve at once, garnished with the shredded red chilies and scallions.

Peanut Noodles

Add any of your favorite vegetables to this recipe, which is quick to make for a great mid-week supper —and increase the chili, if you can take the heat!

Serves 4

INGREDIENTS
½ lb medium egg noodles
2 tbsp olive oil
2 garlic cloves, crushed
1 large onion, roughly chopped
1 red bell pepper, seeded and
    roughly chopped
1 yellow bell pepper, seeded and
    roughly chopped
¾ lb zucchini, roughly chopped
generous ¾ cup
    roasted unsalted peanuts,
    roughly chopped

FOR THE DRESSING
¼ cup good-quality olive oil
shredded zest and juice of 1 lemon
1 red chili, seeded and
    finely chopped
3 tbsp chopped fresh chives
1–2 tbsp balsamic vinegar
salt and pepper
chopped fresh chives, to garnish

red bell pepper

balsamic vinegar

garlic

red chili *zucchini* *peanuts*

chives *onion* *yellow bell pepper* *egg noodles* *olive oil* *lemon*

1 Soak the noodles according to the package instructions and drain well.

2 Meanwhile, heat the oil in a very large frying pan or wok and cook the garlic and onion for 3 minutes or until beginning to soften. Add the peppers and zucchini and cook for 15 more minutes over medium heat, until beginning to soften and brown. Add the peanuts and cook for 1 more minute.

3 Whisk together the olive oil, grated zest and 3 tablespoons lemon juice, the chili, chives, plenty of seasoning and balsamic vinegar to taste.

4 Toss the noodles into the vegetables and stir-fry to heat through. Add the dressing, stir to coat and serve immediately, garnished with chopped fresh chives.

Birthday Noodles with Hoisin Lamb

In China, the noodles served at birthday celebrations are left long: It is held that cutting them might shorten one's life.

Serves 4

INGREDIENTS

2¼ lb lean boneless lamb shoulder
2 tbsp oil
12 oz thick egg noodles
4 oz haricots verts (French green
  beans), blanched
salt and freshly ground black pepper
2 hard-cooked eggs, halved
2 scallions, finely shredded, to garnish

FOR THE MARINADE

2 garlic cloves, crushed
2 tsp grated fresh ginger root
2 tbsp dark soy sauce
2 tbsp rice wine
1–2 dried red chilies
2 tbsp oil

FOR THE SAUCE

1 tbsp cornstarch
2 tbsp dark soy sauce
2 tbsp rice wine
grated zest and juice of ½ orange
1 tbsp hoisin sauce
1 tbsp wine vinegar
1 tsp light brown sugar

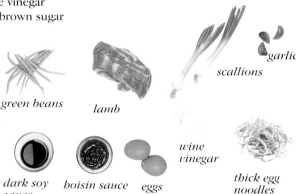

orange *green beans* *lamb* *scallions* *garlic* *fresh ginger root* *dark soy sauce* *hoisin sauce* *eggs* *wine vinegar* *thick egg noodles*

1 Cut the lamb into 2-inch-thick medallions. Mix the ingredients for the marinade in a large, shallow dish. Add the lamb and marinate in the refrigerator for at least 4 hours or overnight. Bring a large saucepan of water to a boil. Add the noodles and cook for 2 minutes only. Drain, rinse under cold water and drain again. Set aside.

2 Heat the oil in a heavy saucepan or flameproof casserole. Sauté the lamb for 5 minutes, until browned. Add just enough water to cover the meat. Bring to a boil, skim, then reduce the heat and simmer for 40 minutes, or until the meat is tender, adding more water as necessary.

3 Make the sauce. Blend the cornstarch with the remaining ingredients in a bowl. Stir into the lamb and mix well without breaking up the meat.

4 Add the noodles with the beans. Simmer gently until both are cooked. Add salt and pepper to taste. Divide the noodle mixture among four large bowls, garnish each portion with half a hard-cooked egg, sprinkle with scallions and serve.

Chiang Mai Noodle Soup

This richly flavored and aromatic noodle soup is a signature dish of the Thai city of Chiang Mai.

Serves 4–6

INGREDIENTS

2½ cups coconut milk
2 tbsp red curry paste
1 tsp ground turmeric
1 lb chicken thighs, boned and cut
    into bite-size chunks
2½ cups chicken stock
¼ cup fish sauce
1 tbsp dark soy sauce
juice of ½–1 lime
1 lb fresh egg noodles, blanched
    briefly in boiling water
salt and freshly ground black pepper

FOR THE GARNISH

3 scallions, chopped
4 red chilies
4 shallots, chopped
¼ cup sliced pickled mustard
    greens, rinsed
2 tbsp fried sliced garlic
cilantro sprigs

coconut
milk

red curry
paste

ground
tumeric

chicken thighs

chicken
stock

fish
sauce

dark soy
sauce

lime

fresh egg
noodles

scallions

red
chilies

cilantro

1 Pour about one-third of the coconut milk into a saucepan and bring to a boil, stirring frequently until it separates.

2 Add the curry paste and ground turmeric, stir to mix completely and cook for a few minutes, until blended.

3 Add the chicken pieces to the saucepan and stir-fry for about 2 minutes. Make sure that all the chunks of meat are coated with the paste.

4 Add the remaining coconut milk, stock, fish sauce, soy sauce and seasoning. Simmer for 7–10 minutes. Remove from the heat and add the lime juice.

Reheat the noodles in boiling water, then drain. Divide the noodles and chicken among the bowls and ladle the hot soup over. Top with the garnishes.

Noodles, Chicken and Shrimp in Coconut Broth

This dish takes a well-flavored broth and adds noodles and a delicious combination of other ingredients to make a satisfying main course.

Serves 8

INGREDIENTS
2 onions, quartered
1-in piece fresh ginger root, sliced
2 garlic cloves
4 macadamia nuts or 8 almonds
1–2 chilies, seeded and sliced
2 lemongrass stems, lower
    2 in sliced
2-in fresh turmeric, peeled and
    sliced, or 1 tsp ground
    turmeric
1 tbsp coriander seeds, dry-fried
1 tsp cumin seeds,
    dry-fried
4 tbsp oil
1⅔ cups coconut milk
6¼ cups chicken stock
13 oz rice noodles, soaked in
    cold water
12 oz cooked tiger shrimp
salt and freshly ground black pepper

FOR THE GARNISH
4 hard-cooked eggs, quartered
8 oz cooked chicken, chopped
1 cup bean sprouts
1 bunch scallions, shredded
deep-fried onions (optional)

1 Place the quartered onions, ginger, garlic and nuts in a food processor with the chilies, sliced lemongrass and turmeric. Process to a paste. Alternatively, pound all the ingredients with a mortar and pestle. Grind the coriander and cumin seeds coarsely and add to the paste.

2 Heat the oil in a pan and fry the spice paste, without coloring, to bring out the flavors. Add the coconut milk, stock and seasoning and simmer for 5–10 minutes.

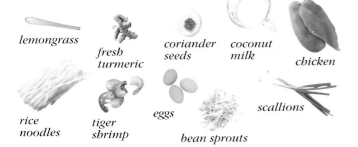

lemongrass

fresh turmeric

coriander seeds

coconut milk

chicken

rice noodles

tiger shrimp

eggs

bean sprouts

scallions

3 Meanwhile, drain the rice noodles and plunge them into a large pan of salted boiling water for 2 minutes. Remove from the heat and drain well. Rinse thoroughly with plenty of cold water, to halt the cooking process.

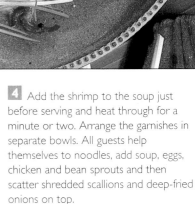

4 Add the shrimp to the soup just before serving and heat through for a minute or two. Arrange the garnishes in separate bowls. All guests help themselves to noodles, add soup, eggs, chicken and bean sprouts and then scatter shredded scallions and deep-fried onions on top.

COOK'S TIP

To dry-fry spices, heat a small, heavy pan over medium heat for 1 minute, add the spices and cook for 2–3 minutes, stirring frequently. Remove from the heat and grind the spices using a mortar and pestle.

Lemongrass Shrimp on Crisp Noodle Cake

For an elegant meal, make four individual noodle cakes instead of one.

Serves 4

INGREDIENTS

11 oz thin egg noodles
¼ cup oil
1¼ lb medium raw jumbo shrimp shelled and deveined
½ tsp ground coriander
1 tbsp ground turmeric
2 garlic cloves, finely chopped
2 slices fresh ginger root, finely chopped
2 lemongrass stalks, finely chopped
2 shallots, finely chopped
1 tbsp tomato paste
1 cup coconut cream
1–2 tbsp fresh lime juice
1–2 tbsp fish sauce
4–6 kaffir lime leaves (optional)
1 cucumber, peeled, seeded and cut into 2-in sticks
1 tomato, seeded and cut into strips
2 red chilies, seeded and finely sliced
salt and freshly ground black pepper
2 scallions, cut into thin strips, and a few cilantro sprigs, to garnish

ground coriander

ground turmeric

garlic

shallots

lemongrass

fresh ginger root

thin egg noodles

raw shrimp

cucumber

tomato

kaffir lime leaves

fish sauce

tomato paste

coconut cream

cilantro

lime

red chilies

scallions

COOK'S TIP
Coconut cream is available in cans at supermarkets and Asian stores. It is richer than coconut milk, but this can be used if coconut cream is unavailable.

1 Cook the egg noodles in a saucepan of boiling water until just tender. Drain, rinse under cold running water and drain well.

2 Heat 1 tablespoon of the oil in a large frying pan. Add the noodles, distributing them evenly, and fry for 4–5 minutes, until crisp and golden. Turn the noodle cake over and fry the other side. Alternatively, make four individual cakes. Keep warm.

3 In a bowl, toss the shrimp with the ground coriander, turmeric, garlic, ginger and lemongrass. Season to taste. Heat the remaining oil in a frying pan. Add the shallots, cook for 1 minute, then add the shrimp and cook for 2 minutes more before removing with a slotted spoon.

4 Stir the tomato paste and coconut cream into the juices in the pan. Stir in lime juice to taste and season with the fish sauce. Bring the sauce to a simmer, add the shrimp, then add the kaffir lime leaves, if using, and the cucumber. Simmer until the shrimp are cooked.

5 Add the tomato, stir until just warmed through, then add the chilies. Serve on top of the crisp noodle cake(s), garnished with strips of scallions and cilantro sprigs.

Cellophane Noodles with Pork

Unlike other types of noodle, cellophane noodles can be successfully reheated.

Serves 3-4

INGREDIENTS
4 oz cellophane noodles
4 dried Chinese black
   mushrooms
8 oz boneless lean pork
2 tbsp dark soy sauce
2 tbsp Chinese rice wine
2 garlic cloves, crushed
1 tbsp fresh ginger
   finely grated
1 tsp chili oil
3 tbsp peanut oil
4-6 scallions, chopped
1 tsp cornstarch blended with
   ¾ cup chicken stock or water
2 tbsp cilantro,
   finely chopped
salt and ground black pepper
cilantro sprigs, to garnish

scallions

noodles

chicken stock   Chinese rice wine

mushrooms

dark soy sauce

pork

chili oil   peanut oil

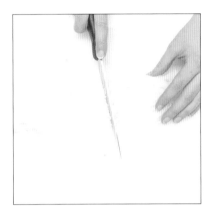

1 Put the noodles and mushrooms in separate bowls and pour over warm water to cover. Let soak for 15–20 minutes until soft; drain well. Cut the noodles into 5 in lengths, using scissors or a knife. Squeeze out any water from the mushrooms, discard the stems and then finely chop the caps.

2 Meanwhile, cut the pork into very small cubes. Put into a bowl with the soy sauce, rice wine, garlic, ginger and chili oil, then let stand for about 15 minutes. Drain, reserving the marinade.

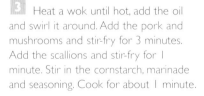

3 Heat a wok until hot, add the oil and swirl it around. Add the pork and mushrooms and stir-fry for 3 minutes. Add the scallions and stir-fry for 1 minute. Stir in the cornstarch, marinade and seasoning. Cook for about 1 minute.

4 Add the noodles and stir-fry for about 2 minutes, until the noodles absorb most of the liquid and the pork is cooked through. Stir in the chopped cilantro. Taste and adjust the seasoning. Serve garnished with cilantro sprigs.

Noodles with Ginger and Cilantro

Here is a simple noodle dish that goes well with most Asian dishes. It can also be served as a snack for 2-3 people.

Serves 4-6

INGREDIENTS
handful of fresh cilantro sprigs
8 oz dried egg noodles
3 tbsp peanut oil
2-in piece fresh ginger root, cut
  into fine shreds
6-8 scallions, cut into shreds
2 tbsp light soy sauce
salt and ground black pepper

scallions

peanut oil

ginger root

cilantro   *noodles*

light soy sauce

COOK'S TIP
Italian noodles are often the easiest to buy. They range in size from very thin to broad. Allow 2 oz per person as a side dish, and up to 4 oz for a main dish.

1 Strip the leaves from the cilantro stalks. Pile them on a chopping board and coarsely chop them, using a cleaver or large sharp knife.

2 Cook the noodles according to the instructions on the package. Rinse under cold water and drain well. Toss in 1 tbsp of the oil.

3 Heat a wok until hot, add the remaining oil and swirl it around. Add the ginger and stir-fry for a few seconds, then add the noodles and scallions. Stir-fry for 3–4 minutes, until hot.

4 Sprinkle over the soy sauce, cilantro and seasoning. Toss well, then serve immediately.

Japanese Noodle Casseroles

Traditionally, these individual casseroles are cooked in earthenware pots. *Nabe* means "pot" and *yaki* means "to heat," providing the Japanese name *nabeyaki udon* for this dish.

Serves 4

INGREDIENTS

4 oz boneless chicken thighs
½ tsp salt
½ tsp sake or dry white wine
½ tsp light soy sauce
1 leek, washed thoroughly
4 oz fresh spinach, trimmed
11 oz dried udon noodles or
   1¼ lb fresh udon noodles
4 shiitake mushrooms, stems
   removed
4 medium eggs
shichimi, or seven-flavor spice, to
   serve (optional)

FOR THE SOUP

6 cups kombu and bonito stock or
   instant dashi
1½ tbsp light soy sauce
1 tsp salt
1 tbsp mirin

light soy sauce
leeks
chicken thighs
sake
spinach
shiitake mushrooms
udon noodles
eggs
kombu and bonito stock
mirin

1 Cut the chicken into small chunks and sprinkle with the salt, sake or wine and soy sauce. Cut the leek diagonally into 1½-inch slices.

2 Boil the spinach for 1–2 minutes, then drain and soak in cold water for 1 minute. Drain, squeeze lightly, then cut into 1½-inch lengths. If using dried udon noodles, boil them according to the package instructions, allowing 3 minutes less than the stated cooking time. Place fresh udon noodles in boiling water, disentangle, then drain.

5 Divide the spinach among the casseroles and simmer, covered, for another minute.

6 Serve immediately, standing the hot casseroles on plates or table mats. Sprinkle seven-flavor spice over the casseroles if you like.

3 For the soup, bring the kombu and bonito stock, soy sauce, salt and mirin to a boil in a saucepan and add the chicken and leek. Skim the broth, then simmer for 5 minutes.

4 Divide the udon noodles among four individual flameproof casseroles. Pour the soup, chicken and leeks into the casseroles. Place over medium heat and add the shiitake mushrooms. Gently break an egg into each casserole. Cover and simmer gently for 2 minutes.

COOK'S TIP

Assorted tempura using vegetables such as sweet potato, carrot and shiitake mushrooms, and fish such as squid and shrimp, could be served in these casseroles instead of chicken and egg.

Tiger Shrimp and Lap Cheong Noodles

Lap cheong is a special air-dried Chinese sausage. It is available at most Chinese markets. If you cannot buy it, substitute with diced ham, chorizo or salami.

Serves 4–6

INGREDIENTS

3 tbsp oil
2 garlic cloves, sliced
1 tsp chopped fresh ginger root
2 red chilies, seeded and chopped
2 lap cheong, about 3 oz, rinsed
  and sliced
1 boneless chicken breast portion,
  thinly sliced
16 uncooked tiger shrimp, shelled,
  tails left intact and deveined
4 oz green beans
1 cup bean sprouts
2 oz Chinese chives
1 lb egg noodles, cooked in boiling
  water until tender
2 tbsp dark soy sauce
1 tbsp oyster sauce
salt and freshly ground black pepper
1 tbsp sesame oil
2 scallions, cut into strips, and
  cilantro leaves, to garnish

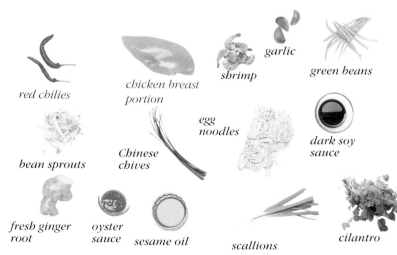

red chilies

chicken breast portion

shrimp

garlic

green beans

bean sprouts

Chinese chives

egg noodles

dark soy sauce

fresh ginger root

oyster sauce

sesame oil

scallions

cilantro

COOK'S TIP

Chinese chives, sometimes called garlic chives, have a delicate garlic/onion flavor. If they are not available, use the green parts of scallions.

1 Heat 1 tablespoon of the oil in a wok or large frying pan and sauté the garlic, ginger and chilies.

2 Add the lap cheong, chicken, shrimp and beans. Stir-fry over high heat for about 2 minutes, or until the chicken and shrimp are cooked. Transfer the mixture to a bowl and set aside.

3 Heat the remaining oil in the wok and add the bean sprouts and Chinese chives. Stir-fry for 1–2 minutes.

4 Add the noodles and toss and stir to mix. Season with soy sauce, oyster sauce, salt and pepper.

5 Return the shrimp mixture to the wok. Reheat and mix well with the noodles. Stir in the sesame oil. Serve garnished with scallions and cilantro leaves.

Five-Flavor Noodles

The Japanese name for this dish is *gomoku yakisoba*, meaning five different ingredients: noodles, pork, cabbage, bean sprouts and peppers.

Serves 4

INGREDIENTS

11 oz dried Chinese thin egg
  noodles or 1¼ lb fresh
  yakisoba noodles
7 oz pork tenderloin, thinly sliced
1½ tbsp oil
½-in piece fresh ginger root, grated
1 garlic clove, crushed
1¼ cups roughly chopped green
  cabbage
½ cup bean sprouts
1 green bell pepper, seeded and cut
  into fine strips
1 red bell pepper, seeded and cut
  into fine strips
salt and freshly ground black pepper
4 tsp ao-nori seaweed, to garnish
  (optional)

FOR THE SEASONING

4 tbsp Worcestershire sauce
1 tbsp light soy sauce
1 tbsp oyster sauce
1 tbsp sugar
white pepper

thin egg noodles
fresh ginger root
garlic
pork tenderloin
bean sprouts
green and red bell peppers
light soy sauce

1 Boil the egg noodles according to the package instructions and drain. Using a sharp chopping knife, carefully cut the pork tenderloin into 1¼–1½-inch strips and season with plenty of salt and pepper. Next, heat 1½ teaspoons of the oil in a large frying pan or wok, stir-fry the pork until just cooked, then transfer to a dish.

2 Wipe the pan with paper towels and heat the remaining oil. Add the ginger, garlic and cabbage and stir-fry for 1 minute.

3 Add the bean sprouts and stir until softened, then add the peppers and stir-fry for 1 minute.

4 Return the pork to the pan and add the noodles. Stir in all the seasoning ingredients together with a little white pepper. Stir-fry for 2–3 minutes. Sprinkle with the ao-nori seaweed, if using.

Beef Noodles with Orange and Ginger

Stir-frying is one of the best ways to cook with the minimum of fat. It's also one of the quickest ways to cook, but you do need to choose tender meat.

Serves 4

INGREDIENTS

1 lb lean beef, e.g. tenderloin or sirloin steak, cut into thin strips
finely grated zest and juice of 1 orange
1 tbsp light soy sauce
1 tsp cornstarch
1-in piece fresh ginger root, finely chopped
6 oz rice noodles
2 tsp sesame oil
1 tbsp sunflower oil
1 large carrot, cut into thin strips
2 scallions, thinly sliced

sirloin steak

orange

light soy sauce

fresh ginger root

carrot

sesame oil

scallions

rice noodles

1 Place the beef in a bowl and sprinkle the orange zest and juice over. If possible, set aside to marinate for at least 30 minutes.

2 Drain the liquid from the meat and set aside, then mix the meat with the soy sauce, cornstarch and ginger. Cook the noodles according to the instructions on the package. Drain well, toss with the sesame oil and keep warm.

3 Heat the sunflower oil in a wok or large frying pan and add the beef. Stir-fry for 1 minute, until lightly colored, then add the carrot and stir-fry for another 2–3 minutes.

4 Stir in the scallions and the reserved liquid from the meat, then cook, stirring, until boiling and thickened. Serve hot with the rice noodles.

Toasted Noodles with Vegetables

Slightly crisp noodle cakes topped with vegetables make a superb dish.

Serves 4

INGREDIENTS

6 oz (1½ cups) dried thin Chinese
   egg noodles
1 tbsp vegetable oil
2 garlic cloves, finely chopped
4 oz (1 cup) baby corn
4 oz (1 cup) fresh shiitake
   mushrooms, halved
3 celery ribs, sliced
1 carrot, diagonally sliced
4 oz (1 cup) snow peas
¾ cup sliced drained canned
    bamboo shoots
1 tbsp cornstarch
1 tbsp cold water
1 tbsp dark soy sauce
1 tsp sugar
1¼ cups vegetable stock
salt and ground white pepper
scallion curls, to garnish

bamboo shoots *baby corn* *carrot* *celery* *shiitake mushrooms* *dried egg noodles*

1 Bring a saucepan of water to a boil. Add the egg noodles and cook according to instructions on the package until just tender. Drain, refresh under cold water, drain again, then dry thoroughly on paper towels.

2 Heat ½ teaspoon oil in a nonstick frying pan or wok. When it starts to smoke, spread half the noodles over the bottom. Fry for 2–3 minutes, until lightly toasted. Carefully turn the noodles over (they stick together like a cake), fry the other side, then slide onto a heated serving plate. Repeat with the remaining noodles to make two cakes. Keep hot.

3 Heat the remaining oil in the clean pan, and cook the garlic for a few seconds. Halve the corn lengthwise, add to the pan with the mushrooms and stir-fry for 3 minutes, adding a little water, if needed, to prevent the mixture from burning. Add the celery, carrot, snow peas and bamboo shoots. Stir-fry for 2 minutes, or until the vegetables are crisp-tender.

4 Mix the cornstarch to a paste with the water. Add the mixture to the pan with the soy sauce, sugar and stock. Cook, stirring, until the sauce thickens. Season with salt and white pepper. Divide the vegetable mixture between the noodle cakes, garnish with the scallion curls and serve immediately. Each noodle cake serves two people.

Deluxe Fried Noodles

This makes a tasty side dish for three to four people or a meal for two people, served with just a separate vegetable or meat dish.

Serves 2–4

INGREDIENTS

1½ oz dried Chinese mushrooms
10 oz fine egg noodles
1 tbsp sesame oil
3 tbsp oil
2 garlic cloves, crushed
1 onion, chopped
2 green chilies, seeded and thinly sliced
1 tbsp curry powder
6 oz green beans
4 oz bok choy, thinly shredded (about 2 cups)
6 scallions, sliced
3 tbsp dark soy sauce
6 oz cooked, shelled shrimp
salt

Chinese mushrooms

fine egg noodles

sesame oil   *garlic* onion

green chilies *curry powder*

green beans *bok choy*

shrimp *dark soy sauce* *scallions*

1 Place the mushrooms in a bowl. Cover with warm water and soak for 30 minutes. Drain, reserving 3 tablespoons of the soaking water, then slice, discarding the stems.

2 Cook the noodles in a pan of lightly salted boiling water according to the directions on the package. Drain, place in a bowl and toss with the sesame oil.

3 Heat a wok, add the oil and stir-fry the garlic, onion and chilies for 3 minutes. Stir in the curry powder and cook for 1 minute, then add the mushrooms, beans, bok choy and scallions. Stir-fry for 3–4 minutes.

4 Add the noodles, soy sauce, reserved mushroom soaking water and shrimp. Toss over the heat for 2–3 minutes, until the noodles and shrimp are heated through, then serve.

Gingered Chicken Noodles

A blend of ginger, spices and coconut milk flavors, this delicious supper dish is made in minutes. If desired, add a little fish sauce to taste, just before serving.

Serves 2–4

INGREDIENTS

12oz skinless, boneless chicken
   breast portions
8oz zucchini
10oz eggplant
about 2 tbsp oil
2-in piece fresh ginger root,
   finely chopped
6 scallions, sliced
2 tsp Thai green curry paste
1⅔ cups coconut milk
2 cups chicken stock
4oz medium egg noodles
3 tbsp chopped cilantro
1 tbsp lemon juice
salt and white pepper
chopped cilantro, to garnish

1 Cut the chicken into bite-size pieces. Halve the zucchini lengthwise and roughly chop them. Cut the eggplant into similar-size pieces.

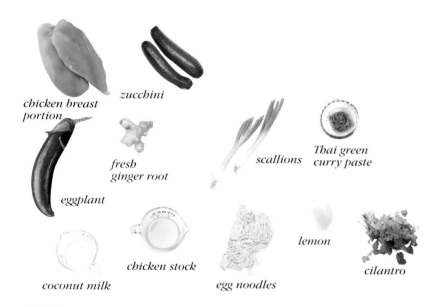

chicken breast portion

zucchini

fresh ginger root

scallions

Thai green curry paste

eggplant

coconut milk

egg noodles

lemon

cilantro

COOK'S TIP

You can use fresh or dried noodles for this dish. If using dried, you will need to soak them in hot water for a few minutes to soften, then use as directed in the recipe.

2 Heat the oil in a large saucepan or wok and cook the chicken until golden, in batches if necessary. Remove the pieces with a slotted spoon and leave to drain on paper towels.

3 Add a little more oil, if necessary, and cook the ginger and scallions for 3 minutes. Add the zucchini and cook for 2–3 minutes. Stir in the curry paste and cook for 1 minute. Add the coconut milk, stock, eggplant and chicken and simmer for 10 minutes.

4 Add the noodles and cook for another 5 minutes, or until the chicken is cooked and the noodles are tender. Stir in the chopped cilantro and lemon juice and adjust the seasoning. Serve garnished with chopped cilantro.

Alfalfa Crab Salad with Crisp Fried Noodles

The crisp noodles make a delicious contrast, both in flavor and texture, with this healthy mixture of crab and vegetables.

Serves 4–6

INGREDIENTS
oil, for deep-frying
2 oz Chinese rice noodles
5 oz frozen lump crabmeat, thawed
½ cup alfalfa sprouts
1 small head iceberg lettuce
4 sprigs cilantro, roughly chopped
1 ripe tomato, peeled, seeded and diced
4 sprigs fresh mint, roughly chopped, plus an extra sprig to garnish

FOR THE SESAME LIME DRESSING
3 tbsp vegetable oil
1 tsp sesame oil
½ small red chili, seeded and finely chopped
1 piece stem ginger in syrup, cut into matchsticks
2 tsp ginger syrup
2 tsp light soy sauce
juice of ½ lime

Chinese rice noodles

crabmeat

alfalfa sprouts

iceberg lettuce

tomato

mint

cilantro

red chili

lime

1 First make the dressing. Combine the vegetable and sesame oils in a bowl. Add the chili, ginger, ginger syrup and soy sauce and stir in the lime juice. Set aside.

2 Heat the oil in a wok or deep-fat fryer to 385°F. Fry the noodles, one handful at a time, until crisp. Lift out and drain on paper towels.

3 Flake the crabmeat into a bowl and toss with the alfalfa sprouts.

4 Finely chop the lettuce and mix with the cilantro, tomato and mint. Place in a bowl, top with the noodles and the crabmeat and alfalfa salad and garnish with a sprig of mint. Serve with the sesame lime dressing.

Noodles with Vegetables

Thin Italian egg pasta is a good alternative to egg noodles, use it fresh or dried.

Serves 6

INGREDIENTS
1¼ lb thin tagliarini
1 red onion
4 oz shiitake mushrooms
3 tbsp sesame oil
3 tbsp dark soy sauce
1 tbsp balsamic vinegar
2 tsp superfine sugar
1 tsp salt
celery leaves, to garnish

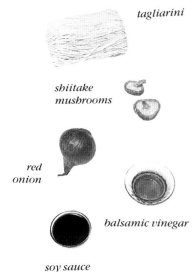

tagliarini

shiitake mushrooms

red onion

balsamic vinegar

soy sauce

1 Boil the tagliarini in a large pan of salted boiling water, following the instructions on the pack.

2 Thinly slice the red onion and the mushrooms, using a sharp knife.

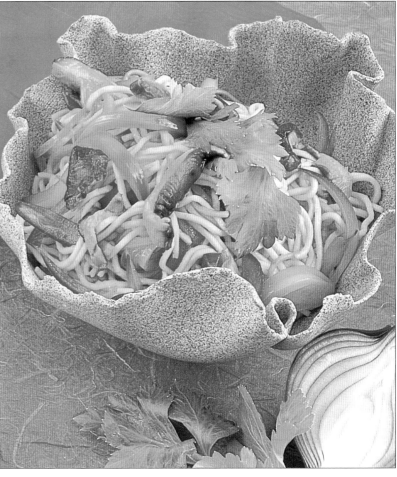

3 Heat the wok, then add 1 tbsp of the sesame oil. When the oil is hot, stir-fry the onion and mushrooms for 2 minutes.

4 Drain the tagliarini, then add to the wok with the soy sauce, balsamic vinegar, sugar and salt. Stir-fry for 1 minute, then add the remaining sesame oil, and serve garnished with celery leaves.

Thai Fried Noodles

A staple of day-to-day Thai life, this dish is often served from the food stalls that line many Thai streets.

Serves 4

INGREDIENTS

6 oz ribbon rice noodles
2 tbsp oil
2 garlic cloves, crushed
4 oz pork tenderloin, finely
   chopped
2 canned anchovy fillets, chopped
2 tbsp lemon juice
3 tbsp fish sauce
1 tbsp sugar
8 oz bean curd
2 eggs, beaten
3 oz cooked shelled shrimp
½ cup bean sprouts
½ cup unsalted roasted peanuts
5 tbsp chopped cilantro
cilantro sprigs, to garnish (optional)
crushed red pepper and fish sauce,
   to serve

garlic

ribbon rice
noodles

lemon

pork
tenderloin

fish sauce

anchovy
fillets

bean curd

eggs

sugar

cilantro

shrimp

bean sprouts

peanuts

crushed red
pepper

1 Soak the noodles in boiling water according to the package instructions; drain well.

2 Heat the oil in a wok or large frying pan and cook the garlic until golden. Add the pork and stir-fry until cooked through and golden.

3 Reduce the heat slightly and stir in the anchovies, lemon juice, fish sauce and sugar. Bring to a gentle simmer.

4 Stir in the bean curd, taking care not to break it up. Fold in the noodles gently, until they are coated in the liquid.

5 Make a gap at the side of the pan and add the beaten eggs. Allow them to scramble slightly and then stir them into the noodles.

6 Stir in the shrimp and most of the bean sprouts, peanuts and cilantro. Cook until piping hot. Serve the noodles topped with the remaining bean sprouts, peanuts and chopped cilantro, sprinkled with crushed red pepper and more fish sauce, to taste. Garnish with fresh cilantro sprigs, if you like.

Mixed Rice Noodles

A delicious noodle dish made extra special by adding avocado and garnishing with shrimp.

Serves 4

INGREDIENTS

1 tbsp sunflower oil
1 in piece ginger root, peeled
    and grated
2 cloves garlic, crushed
3 tbsp dark soy sauce
8 oz peas, thawed if frozen
1 lb rice noodles
1 lb fresh spinach, well washed and
    coarse stalks removed
2 tbsp smooth peanut butter
2 tbsp tahini
2/3 cup milk
1 ripe avocado, peeled and pitted
roasted peanuts and shelled shrimp,
    to garnish

rice noodles

ginger root

peas

peanut butter

spinach

1 Heat the wok, then add the oil. When the oil is fairly hot, stir-fry the ginger and garlic for approximately 30 seconds. Add 1 tbsp of the dark soy sauce and 2/3 cup boiling water.

2 Add the peas and noodles, then cook for 3 minutes. Stir in the spinach. Remove the vegetables and noodles, drain and keep warm.

3 Stir the peanut butter, remaining soy sauce, tahini and milk together in the wok, and simmer for 1 minute.

4 Add the vegetables and noodles, slice in the avocado and toss together. Serve piled on individual plates. Spoon some sauce over each portion and garnish with peanuts and shrimp.

Chicken Fried Noodles

This delicious dish makes a filling meal. Take care when frying vermicelli as it has a tendency to spit when added to hot oil.

Serves 4

INGREDIENTS
½ cup vegetable oil
8 oz rice vermicelli
5 oz green beans, ends removed
    and halved lengthwise
1 onion, finely chopped
2 skinless chicken breast portions,
    about 6 oz each, cut into strips
1 tsp chili powder
8 oz cooked shrimp
3 tbsp dark soy sauce
3 tbsp white wine vinegar
2 tsp superfine sugar
fresh cilantro sprigs, to garnish

rice vermicelli

chicken breast portion

onion

green beans

shrimp

1 Heat the wok, then add 4 tbsp of the oil. Break up the vermicelli into 3 in lengths. When the oil is hot, fry the vermicelli in batches. Remove from the heat and keep warm.

2 Heat the remaining oil in the wok, then add the green beans, onion and chicken and stir-fry for 3 minutes until the chicken is cooked.

3 Sprinkle in the chili powder. Stir in the shrimp, soy sauce, vinegar and sugar, and stir-fry for 2 minutes.

4 Serve the chicken, shrimp and vegetables on the vermicelli, garnished with sprigs of fresh cilantro.

Bamie Goreng

This fried noodle dish from Indonesia is wonderfully accommodating. To the basic recipe you can add other vegetables, such as mushrooms, tiny pieces of zucchini, broccoli, leeks or bean sprouts, if you like.

Serves 6

INGREDIENTS

1 lb dried egg noodles
1 skinless chicken breast portion
4 oz pork tenderloin
4 oz calf's liver (optional)
2 eggs, beaten
6 tbsp oil
2 tbsp butter
2 garlic cloves, crushed
4 oz cooked, shelled shrimp
4 oz spinach or boy choy
2 celery ribs, finely sliced
4 scallions, cut into strips
about ¼ cup chicken stock
dark and light soy sauce
1 onion, thinly sliced
oil, for deep-frying
salt and freshly ground black pepper
celery leaves, to garnish

dried egg noodles   *chicken breast portions*   *pork tenderloin*

garlic   *shrimp*   *spinach*   *celery*

scallions   *dark soy sauce*   *light soy sauce*   *onion*

1 Cook the noodles in salted boiling water for 3–4 minutes. Drain, rinse with cold water and drain again. Set aside until required.

2 Using a small, sharp chopping knife, finely slice the chicken breast, pork tenderloin and calf's liver, if using.

3 Season the eggs. Heat 1 teaspoon of the oil with the butter in a small pan until melted and then stir in the eggs and keep stirring until scrambled. Set aside.

4 Heat the remaining oil in a wok and fry the garlic with the chicken, pork and liver for 2–3 minutes. Add the shrimp, spinach or bok choy, celery and scallions, tossing well. Add the noodles and toss well. Add enough stock to moisten the noodles and dark and light soy sauce to taste.

5 In a separate wok or deep-fat fryer, deep-fry the onion until crisp and golden, turning constantly. Drain well. Stir the scrambled egg into the noodles and serve garnished with the fried onion and celery leaves.

Stir-fried Sweet-and-Sour Chicken

As well as being quick, this Southeast Asian dish is decidedly tasty, and you will find yourself making it again and again.

Serves 3–4

INGREDIENTS
10 oz dried medium egg noodles
2 tbsp oil
3 scallions, chopped
1 garlic clove, crushed
1-in piece fresh ginger root, grated
1 tsp paprika
1 tsp ground coriander
3 boneless chicken breast portions, sliced
8 oz sugar snap peas, trimmed
4 oz baby corn, halved
1 cup bean sprouts
1 tbsp cornstarch
3 tbsp light soy sauce
3 tbsp lemon juice
1 tbsp sugar
3 tbsp chopped cilantro, to garnish

ground coriander

bean sprouts

chicken breast portions

cilantro

egg noodles

garlic

scallions

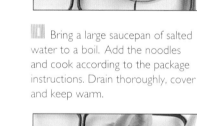

1 Bring a large saucepan of salted water to a boil. Add the noodles and cook according to the package instructions. Drain thoroughly, cover and keep warm.

2 Heat the oil. Add the scallions and cook over gentle heat. Mix in the next five ingredients, then stir-fry for 3–4 minutes. Add the next three ingredients and cook briefly. Add the noodles.

3 Combine the cornstarch, soy sauce, lemon juice and sugar in a small bowl. Add to the wok and simmer briefly to thicken. Serve garnished with chopped cilantro.

COOK'S TIP

Large wok lids are cumbersome and can be difficult to store in a small kitchen. Consider placing a circle of waxed paper against the food surface to keep cooking juices in.

Fried Singapore Noodles

Thai fish cakes vary in their size, and their hotness. You can buy them from Oriental supermarkets, but, if you cannot get hold of them, simply omit them from the recipe.

Serves 4

INGREDIENTS
6 oz rice noodles
4 tbsp vegetable oil
½ tsp salt
3 oz cooked shrimp
6 oz cooked pork, cut into
  matchsticks
1 green bell pepper, seeded and
  chopped into matchsticks
½ tsp sugar
2 tsp curry powder
3 oz Thai fish cakes
2 tsp dark soy sauce

rice noodles

pork

bell pepper

shrimp

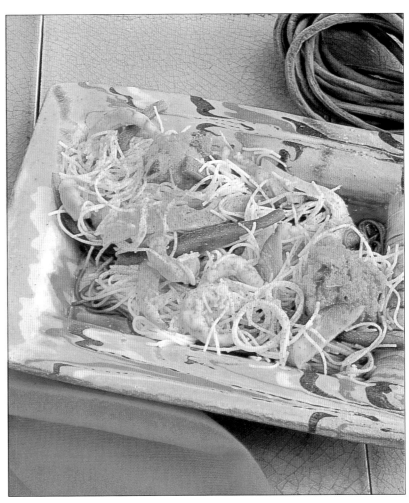

1 Soak the rice noodles in water for about 10 minutes, drain well, then pat dry with paper towels.

2 Heat the wok, then add half the oil. When the oil is hot, add the noodles and salt and stir-fry for 2 minutes. Transfer to a heated serving dish to keep warm.

3 Heat the remaining oil and add the shrimp, pork, pepper, sugar, curry powder and remaining salt. Stir-fry the ingredients for 1 minute.

4 Return the noodles to the pan and stir-fry with the Thai fish cakes for 2 minutes. Stir in the soy sauce and serve.

Noodles with Lemongrass, Chilies and Herbs

Traditional Thai ingredients provide a colorful contrast to a tasty noodle stew.

Serves 6

INGREDIENTS
2 tbsp sunflower oil
1 onion, thickly sliced
1 lemongrass stem, finely chopped
1 tbsp Thai red curry paste
3 zucchini, thickly sliced
1 cup Savoy cabbage, thickly sliced
2 carrots, thickly sliced
5 oz broccoli, stem sliced thickly and head separated into florets
2 × 14-oz cans unsweetened coconut milk
2 cups vegetable stock
5 oz egg noodles
1 tbsp Thai fish sauce
2 tbsp soy sauce
4 tbsp chopped fresh cilantro

FOR THE GARNISH
2 lemongrass stems
1 bunch cilantro
8–10 small red chilies

1 Heat the oil in a large saucepan or wok. Add the onion, lemongrass and Thai red curry paste. Stirring occasionally, cook for 5–10 minutes until the onion has softened.

2 Add the zucchini, cabbage, carrots and broccoli stem. Using two spoons, toss all the vegetables with the onion mixture and cook gently for about 5 minutes more.

3 Stir in the coconut milk and vegetable stock and bring to a boil. Add the noodles and the broccoli florets, lower the heat and simmer gently for 20 minutes.

4 Meanwhile, make the garnish. Split the lemongrass lengthwise through the root. Gather the cilantro into a small bouquet and lay it on a platter, following the curve of the rim.

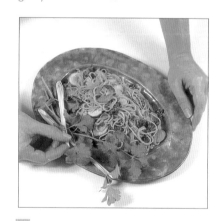

5 Tuck the lemongrass halves into the bouquet and add the chilies to resemble flowers. Stir the fish sauce, soy sauce and chopped cilantro into the noodle mixture. Spoon onto the platter, taking care not to disturb the herb bouquet.

egg noodles

carrots

lemon-grass

broccoli

Savoy cabbage

soy sauce

cilantro

zucchini

coconut milk

Thai red curry paste

onion

Thai fish sauce

red chilies

Crisp Noodles with Mixed Vegetables

In this dish, rice vermicelli noodles are deep-fried until crisp, then tossed into a colorful selection of stir-fried vegetables.

Serves 3-4

INGREDIENTS
2 large carrots
2 zucchini
4 scallions
4 oz Chinese long beans or
   green beans
4 oz dried vermicelli rice noodles
   or cellophane noodles
peanut oil, for deep frying
1-in piece fresh ginger root,
   cut into shreds
1 fresh red chili, sliced
4 oz fresh shiitake or
   white mushrooms,
   thickly sliced
few Chinese cabbage leaves,
   coarsely shredded
3 oz bean sprouts
2 tbsp light soy sauce
2 tbsp Chinese rice wine
1 tsp sugar
2 tbsp cilantro leaves,
   coarsely torn

scallions

mushrooms

Chinese long beans

cilantro

bean sprouts

red chilies

carrot

Chinese cabbage

zucchini

ginger root

Chinese rice wine

light soy sauce

COOK'S TIP
If a milder flavor is preferred, remove the seeds from the chili.

1 Cut the carrots and zucchini into fine sticks, and then shred the scallions into similar-size pieces. Trim the beans. If using Chinese long beans, cut them into short lengths.

2 Break the noodles into lengths of about 3 in. Half-fill a wok with oil and heat it to 350°F. Deep-fry the raw noodles, about a handful at a time, for 1–2 minutes, until puffed and crispy. Drain on paper towels. Carefully pour off all but 2 tbsp of the oil.

3 Reheat the oil in the wok. When hot, add the beans and stir-fry for 2–3 minutes. Add the ginger, red chili, mushrooms, carrots and zucchini and stir-fry for 1–2 minutes.

4 Add the Chinese cabbage, bean sprouts and scallions. Stir-for for 1 minute, then add the soy sauce, rice wine and sugar. Cook, stirring, for about 30 seconds.

5 Add the noodles and cilantro and toss to mix, taking care not to crush the noodles too much. Serve immediately, piled up on a plate.

Celebration Thai Noodles

This Thai speciality, called *mee krob*, is a crisp tangle of fried rice vermicelli tossed in a piquant sauce. It is served at weddings and other special occasions.

Serves 4

INGREDIENTS

oil, for deep-frying
6 oz rice vermicelli
1 tbsp chopped garlic
4–6 dried chilies, seeded and
    chopped
2 tbsp chopped shallot
1 tbsp dried shrimp, rinsed
4 oz ground pork
4 oz uncooked, shelled shrimp,
    chopped
2 tbsp brown bean sauce
2 tbsp rice wine vinegar
3 tbsp fish sauce
3 tbsp palm sugar or
    brown sugar
2 tbsp tamarind or lime juice
½ cup bean sprouts

FOR THE GARNISH
2 scallions, cut into thin strips
cilantro leaves
2-egg omelet, rolled and sliced
2 red chilies, seeded and chopped
2 heads pickled garlic (optional)

rice vermicelli noodles
garlic
chilies
dried shrimp
ground pork
uncooked shrimp
bean sprouts
scallions

1 Heat the oil in a wok. Break the rice vermicelli apart into small handfuls about 3 inches long. Deep-fry in the hot oil until they puff up. Remove and drain on paper towels.

2 Carefully pour off all but 2 tablespoons of the hot oil from the wok. Add the garlic, chilies, shallots and dried shrimp. Cook until fragrant, then add the ground pork and stir-fry for 3–4 minutes, until it is no longer pink. Add the shrimp and stir-fry for another 2 minutes. Transfer the mixture to a plate and set aside.

3 Stir the brown bean sauce, vinegar, fish sauce and palm or brown sugar into the wok. Bring to a gentle boil, stir to dissolve the sugar and cook until thick and syrupy. Add the tamarind or lime juice and adjust the seasoning. It should be sweet, sour and salty.

4 Reduce the heat. Add the pork and shrimp mixture and the bean sprouts to the sauce, stir to mix and then add the rice noodles, tossing gently to coat them with the sauce. Transfer the noodles to a platter. Garnish with scallions, cilantro leaves, omelet strips, red chilies and pickled garlic, if you like.

Chicken Curry with Rice Vermicelli

Lemongrass gives this Southeast Asian curry a wonderful, lemony flavor and fragrance.

Serves 4

INGREDIENTS
1 chicken, 3–3½ lb
8 oz sweet potatoes
¼ cup oil
1 onion, finely sliced
3 garlic cloves, crushed
2–3 tbsp Thai curry powder
salt
1 tsp sugar
2 tsp fish sauce
2½ cups coconut milk
1 lemongrass stalk, cut in half
12 oz rice vermicelli, soaked in hot water until soft

FOR THE GARNISH
½ cup bean sprouts
2 scallions, finely sliced diagonally
2 red chilies, seeded and finely sliced
8–10 mint leaves

chicken

Thai curry powder

coconut milk

rice vermicelli noodles

lemongrass

bean sprouts

mint leaves

red chilies

scallions

1 Skin the chicken. Cut the flesh into small pieces. Peel the sweet potatoes and cut them into large chunks, about the size of the chicken pieces.

2 Heat half the oil in a large, heavy saucepan. Add the onion and garlic and cook until the onion softens. Add the chicken pieces and stir-fry until they change color. Stir in the curry powder. Season with salt and sugar and mix thoroughly, then add the fish sauce, coconut milk and lemongrass. Cook over low heat for 15 minutes.

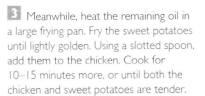

3 Meanwhile, heat the remaining oil in a large frying pan. Fry the sweet potatoes until lightly golden. Using a slotted spoon, add them to the chicken. Cook for 10–15 minutes more, or until both the chicken and sweet potatoes are tender.

4 Drain the rice vermicelli and cook them in a saucepan of boiling water for 3–5 minutes. Drain well. Place in shallow bowls, with the chicken curry. Garnish with bean sprouts, scallions, chilies and mint leaves, and serve.

RICE DISHES

Rice is a staple food throughout most of Asia and is often served in a separate bowl to which other dishes are added. Select from recipes including Egg Fried Rice, Sticky Rice Balls filled with Chicken, Red Fried Rice and Chinese Jeweled Rice.

Chinese Jeweled Rice

This rice dish, with its many different, interesting ingredients, can make a meal in itself.

Serves 4

INGREDIENTS

12 oz long grain rice
3 tbsp vegetable oil
1 onion, roughly chopped
4 oz cooked ham, diced
6 oz canned white crabmeat
3 oz canned water chestnuts, drained
   and cut into cubes
4 dried black Chinese mushrooms,
   soaked, drained and cut into dice
4 oz peas, thawed if frozen
2 tbsp oyster sauce
1 tsp sugar

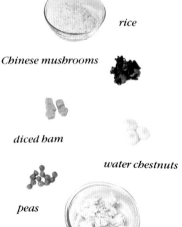

rice

Chinese mushrooms

diced ham

water chestnuts

peas

crabmeat

1 Rinse the rice, then cook for about 10–12 minutes in 2½–3 cups water in a saucepan with a tight-fitting lid. When cooked, refresh under cold water. Heat the wok, then add half the oil. When the oil is hot, stir-fry the rice for 3 minutes, then remove and set aside.

2 Add the remaining oil to the wok. When the oil is hot, cook the onion until softened but not colored.

3 Add all the remaining ingredients and stir-fry for 2 minutes.

4 Return the rice to the wok and stir-fry for 3 minutes, then serve.

Egg Fried Rice

The best rice for this is long-grain rice or fragrant rice from Thailand. Allow ⅓ cup raw rice per person.

Serves 4

INGREDIENTS
1⅓ cups rice
1 cup cold water
1 tsp salt
½ tsp vegetable oil
3 eggs
pinch of salt
2 scallions, finely chopped
2–3 tbsp vegetable oil
4 oz green peas

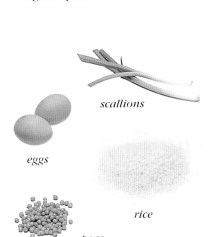

scallions

eggs

rice

peas

1 Wash and rinse the rice until the water runs clear. Place the rice in a saucepan and add the water. There should be no more than ¾ inch of water above the surface of the rice.

2 Bring to a boil, add the salt and oil, then stir to prevent the rice from sticking to the bottom of the pan. Reduce the heat to very, very low and cook, covered, for 15–20 minutes. Remove from the heat and let stand for about 10 minutes.

3 In a bowl, lightly beat the eggs with a pinch of the salt and a few pieces of the scallions.

4 Heat the oil in a preheated wok and lightly scramble the eggs. Add the rice and stir to make sure that each grain of rice is separated. Add the remaining salt, scallions and peas. Blend well and serve.

Sticky Rice Balls Filled with Chicken

These rice balls can be either steamed or deep-fried. The fried versions are crunchy and are excellent for serving at cocktail parties.

Makes about 30

INGREDIENTS

1 lb ground chicken
1 egg
1 tbsp tapioca flour
4 scallions, finely chopped
2 tbsp chopped cilantro
2 tbsp fish sauce
pinch of sugar
⅓ cup glutinous (sticky) rice, cooked
banana leaves
oil for brushing
freshly ground black pepper
sweet chili sauce, to serve

FOR THE GARNISH
1 small carrot, shredded
1 red bell pepper, cut into strips
chopped chives

scallions

glutinous rice

tapioca flour

oil

ground chicken

egg

sugar

cilantro

banana leaves

chives

sweet chili sauce

red bell pepper

fish sauce

carrot

COOK'S TIP

Try to find banana leaves for this recipe, as they impart their own subtle flavor of fine tea. The leaves are used in Thai cooking for wrapping foods as well as lining steamers.

1 In a mixing bowl, combine the ground chicken, egg, tapioca flour, scallions and cilantro. Mix well and season with fish sauce, sugar and freshly ground black pepper.

2 Using chopsticks, spread the cooked sticky rice on a plate or baking sheet.

3 Place teaspoonfuls of some of the chicken mixture on the bed of rice, placing them evenly spaced apart. With damp hands, roll and shape this mixture in the rice to make balls about the size of a walnut. Repeat with the rest of the chicken mixture.

4 Line a bamboo steamer with banana leaves and lightly brush them with oil. Place the chicken balls on the leaves, spacing well apart to prevent them from sticking together. Steam over high heat for about 10 minutes, or until cooked. Remove and arrange on serving plates. Garnish with shredded carrot, red pepper and chives. Serve with sweet chili sauce as a dip.

Thai Fried Rice

This hot and spicy dish is easy to prepare and makes a meal in itself.

VARIATION
Add 2 oz frozen peas to the chicken in step 3, if you wish.

Serves 4

INGREDIENTS
8 oz Thai jasmine rice
3 tbsp vegetable oil
1 onion, chopped
1 small red bell pepper, seeded
   and cut into ¾-in cubes
12 oz skinless and boneless
   chicken breast portions, cut
   into ¾-in cubes
1 garlic clove, crushed
1 tbsp mild curry paste
½ tsp paprika
½ tsp ground turmeric
2 tbsp Thai fish sauce
   (*nam pla*)
2 eggs, beaten
salt and ground black pepper
fried basil leaves, to garnish

rice

Thai fish sauce

chicken

curry paste

onion

egg

red bell
pepper

paprika

turmeric

vegetable oil

1 Put the rice in a sieve and wash thoroughly under cold running water. Then put the rice in a heavy pan and add 6¼ cups boiling water. Return to a boil, then simmer, leaving the pan uncovered, for 8–10 minutes; drain well. Spread out the grains on a tray and set aside to cool.

2 Heat a wok until hot, add 2 tbsp of the oil and swirl it around. Add the onion and red bell pepper and stir-fry for 1 minute.

3 Add the chicken, garlic, curry paste and spices and stir-fry for 2–3 minutes.

4 Reduce the heat to medium, add the cooled rice, fish sauce and seasoning. Stir-fry for 2–3 minutes, until the rice is very hot.

5 Make a well in the center of the rice and add the remaining oil. When hot, add the beaten eggs, allow to cook for about 2 minutes until lightly set, then stir into the rice.

6 Sprinkle over the fried basil leaves and serve immediately.

Nutty Rice and Mushroom Stir-fry

This delicious and substantial supper dish can be eaten hot or cold with salads.

Serves 4–6

INGREDIENTS
12 oz long grain rice
3 tbsp sunflower oil
1 small onion, roughly chopped
8 oz portabello mushrooms, sliced
½ cup hazelnuts, roughly chopped
½ cup pecans, roughly chopped
½ cup almonds, roughly chopped
4 tbsp fresh parsley, chopped
salt and freshly ground black pepper

rice

almonds

portabello mushroom

hazelnuts

pecans

1 Rinse the rice, then cook for about 10–12 minutes in 2½–3 cups water in a saucepan with a tight-fitting lid. When cooked, refresh under cold water. Heat the wok, then add half the oil. When the oil is hot, stir-fry the rice for 2–3 minutes. Remove and set aside.

2 Add the remaining oil and stir-fry the onion for 2 minutes until softened.

3 Mix in the portabello mushrooms and stir-fry for 2 minutes.

4 Add all the nuts and stir-fry for 1 minute. Return the rice to the wok and stir-fry for 3 minutes. Season with salt and pepper. Stir in the parsley and serve.

Special Fried Rice

Special Fried Rice is a very popular rice recipe in China. Because it contains shrimp and ham, it can almost make a meal in itself.

Serves 4

INGREDIENTS

2 oz cooked shrimp, shelled
2 oz cooked ham
3 eggs
1 tsp salt
2 scallions, finely chopped, plus
   extra to garnish
4 tbsp oil
1 cup peas, thawed if frozen
1 tbsp light soy sauce
1 tbsp Chinese rice wine or
   dry sherry
scant 1 cup long-grain rice, cooked

shrimp

ham

eggs

scallions

*long-grain
rice*

peas

soy sauce

oil

salt

sherry

1 Pat the cooked shrimp dry with paper towels, making sure no moisture remains. Cut the ham into small dice about the same size as the peas.

2 In a bowl, lightly beat the eggs with a pinch of the salt and a few pieces of the chopped scallions, using chopsticks or a fork.

COOK'S TIP
Chinese rice wine can be found in large supermarkets and Asian food stores.

3 Heat the wok, add about half of the oil and when it is hot, stir-fry the peas, shrimp and ham for about 1 minute. Add the soy sauce and rice wine or sherry. Transfer the mixture to a dish and keep hot.

4 Heat the remaining oil in the wok and scramble the eggs lightly. Add the rice and stir to separate the grains. Add the remaining salt and scallions and the shrimp mixture. Stir well and heat until the rice is piping hot. Garnish with chopped scallions.

Rice, Shrimp and Egg Strips

This dish can easily be adapted by adding any cooked ingredients you have to hand. Crispy shrimp crackers or shrimp toasts make ideal accompaniments for serving.

Serves 4

INGREDIENTS
8 oz long grain rice
2 large eggs
2 tbsp vegetable oil
1 green chili
2 scallions, roughly chopped
2 cloves garlic, crushed
8 oz cooked chicken
8 oz cooked shrimp
3 tbsp dark soy sauce
shrimp crackers, to serve

rice

soy sauce

egg

chili

shrimp

1 Rinse the rice and then cook for 10–12 minutes in 2 cups water in a saucepan with a tight-fitting lid. When cooked, refresh under cold water.

2 Lightly beat the eggs. Heat 1 tbsp of oil in a small frying pan and swirl in the beaten egg. When cooked on one side, flip over and cook on the other side, remove from the pan and leave to cool. Cut the omelet into strips.

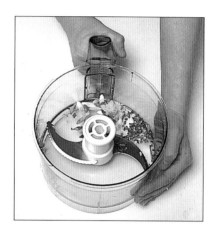

3 Carefully remove the seeds from the chili and chop finely, wearing rubber gloves to protect your hands if necessary. Place the scallions, chili and garlic in a food processor and blend to a paste.

4 Heat the wok, and then add the remaining oil. When the oil is hot, add the paste and stir-fry for 1 minute.

5 Add the chicken and shrimp.

6 Add the rice and stir-fry for 3–4 minutes. Stir in the soy sauce and serve with shrimp crackers.

Asian Fried Rice

This is a great way to use leftover cooked rice. Make sure the rice is very cold before attempting to fry it, as warm rice will become soggy. Some supermarkets sell frozen cooked rice.

Serves 4-6

INGREDIENTS

5 tbsp oil
4 oz shallots, halved and
thinly sliced
3 garlic cloves, crushed
1 red chili, seeded and finely
chopped
6 scallions, finely chopped
1 red bell pepper, seeded and finely
chopped
8 oz white cabbage, finely shredded
6 oz cucumber, finely chopped
1/2 cup peas, thawed if frozen
3 eggs, beaten
1 tsp tomato paste
2 tbsp lime juice
1/4 tsp Tabasco sauce
1 1/4 cups long-grain rice, cooked
and cooled
1 cup cashew nuts, roughly chopped
about 2 tbsp chopped cilantro,
plus extra to garnish
salt and freshly ground black pepper

1 Heat half the oil in a large nonstick frying pan or wok and cook the shallots until very crisp and golden. Remove with a slotted spoon and drain well on paper towels.

2 Add the rest of the oil to the pan. Cook the garlic and chili for 1 minute. Add the scallions and pepper and cook for another 3–4 minutes.

3 Add the cabbage, cucumber and peas and cook for 2 minutes more.

red bell pepper

white cabbage

chili

scallions *cilantro*

garlic

Tabasco sauce

oil

shallots

cucumber

eggs

lime juice

peas

cashew nuts

long-grain rice

tomato paste

4 Make a gap in the pan and add the beaten eggs. Scramble the eggs, stirring occasionally, and then stir them into the vegetables.

5 Add the tomato paste, lime juice and Tabasco and stir to combine.

6 Increase the heat and add the rice, cashew nuts and cilantro with plenty of seasoning. Stir-fry for 3–4 minutes, until piping hot. Serve garnished with the crisp shallots and extra cilantro.

Indonesian Fried Rice

This fried rice dish makes an ideal supper on its own or even as an accompaniment. It is a very quick meal to prepare, as the rice is already cooked.

Serves 4

INGREDIENTS

4 shallots, roughly chopped
1 red chili, seeded and chopped
1 garlic clove, chopped
thin sliver of dried shrimp paste
3 tbsp oil
8 oz boneless lean pork, cut into fine strips
1 cup long-grain rice, boiled and cooled
3 or 4 scallions, thinly sliced
4 oz cooked shelled shrimp
2 tbsp sweet soy sauce
chopped cilantro and fine cucumber shreds, to garnish

scallions   shrimp

oil   pork

chili

long-grain rice

shallots   soy sauce

dried shrimp paste

garlic

1 In a mortar, pound the shallots, chili, garlic and shrimp paste with a pestle until they form a paste.

2 Heat a wok until hot, add 2 tablespoons of the oil and swirl it around. Add the pork and stir-fry for 2–3 minutes. Remove the pork from the wok, set aside and keep hot.

3 Add the remaining oil to the wok. When hot, add the spiced shallot paste and stir-fry for about 30 seconds.

4 Reduce the heat. Add the rice, scallions and shrimp. Stir-fry for 2–3 minutes. Add the pork and sprinkle with the soy sauce. Stir-fry until piping hot. Serve garnished with the chopped cilantro and cucumber shreds.

Chinese Cabbage and Black Rice Stir-Fry

The slightly nutty, chewy black glutinous rice contrasts beautifully with the Chinese cabbage.

Serves 4

INGREDIENTS

8 oz (1⅓ cups) black glutinous rice
  or brown rice
3¼ cups vegetable stock
1 tbsp vegetable oil
8 oz Chinese cabbage, cut into
  ½-in strips
4 scallions, thinly sliced
salt and ground white pepper
½ tsp sesame oil

black rice

vegetable oil

sesame oil

Chinese cabbage

scallions

vegetable stock

1 Rinse the rice until the water runs clear, then drain and pour into a saucepan. Add the stock and bring to a boil. Lower the heat, cover the pan and cook gently for 30 minutes. Remove from the heat and let stand for 15 minutes without lifting the pan lid.

2 Heat the vegetable oil in a nonstick frying pan or wok. Stir-fry the Chinese cabbage for 2 minutes, adding a little water to prevent it from burning.

3 Drain the rice, stir it into the pan and cook for 4 minutes, using two spatulas or spoons to toss it with the Chinese cabbage over the heat.

4 Add the scallions, with the salt and pepper and sesame oil. Cook for 1 minute more. Serve immediately.

Rice with Mushrooms and Shrimp

Although mushrooms are not a very common vegetable in India, this dish provides a perfect combination of flavors.

Serves 4

INGREDIENTS
5 oz basmati rice
1 tbsp corn oil
1 medium onion, chopped
4 black peppercorns
1-in piece cinnamon stick
1 bay leaf
¼ tsp black cumin seeds
2 cardamom pods
1 tsp garlic pulp
1 tsp ginger pulp
1 tsp garam masala
1 tsp chili powder
1½ tsp salt
4 oz frozen cooked, shelled
   shrimp, thawed
4 oz mushrooms, cut into
   large pieces
2 tbsp chopped cilantro
½ cup plain low-fat yogurt
1 tbsp lemon juice
2 oz frozen peas
1 cup water
1 red chili, seeded and sliced,
   to garnish

1 Wash the rice well and let it soak in water.

2 Heat the oil in a nonstick wok or frying pan and add the onion, peppercorns, cinnamon, bay leaf, cumin seeds, cardamom, garlic pulp, ginger pulp, garam masala, chili powder and salt. Lower the heat and stir-fry for about 2 minutes.

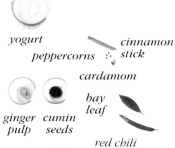

basmati rice
mushrooms
shrimp
chili powder
garam masala
onion
salt
yogurt
peppercorns
cinnamon stick
cardamom
ginger pulp
cumin seeds
bay leaf
garlic pulp
lemon juice
peas
red chili
cilantro

3 Add the shrimp and cook for 2 minutes, before adding the mushrooms.

4 Add the cilantro and the yogurt, followed by the lemon juice and peas.

5 Drain the rice and add it to the shrimp mixture. Pour in the water, cover the pan and cook over medium heat for about 15 minutes, checking once.

6 Remove from the heat and let stand, still covered, for about 5 minutes. Transfer to a serving dish and serve garnished with the sliced red chili.

Red Fried Rice

This vibrant rice dish owes its appeal as much to the bright colors of red onion, red bell pepper and tomatoes as it does to their flavors.

Serves 2

INGREDIENTS
¾ cup basmati rice
2 tbsp peanut oil
1 small red onion, chopped
1 red bell pepper, seeded and
  chopped
8 oz cherry tomatoes, halved
2 eggs, beaten
salt and freshly ground black pepper

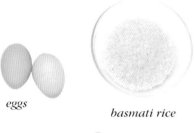

eggs

basmati rice

cherry tomatoes

red onion

red bell pepper

1 Wash the rice several times under cold running water. Drain well. Bring a large pan of water to a boil. Add the rice, and cook for 10–12 minutes.

2 Meanwhile, heat the oil in a wok until very hot. Add the onion and red pepper, and stir-fry for 2–3 minutes. Add the cherry tomatoes, and stir-fry for 2 minutes more.

3 Pour in the beaten eggs all at once. Cook for 30 seconds without stirring, then stir to break up the egg as it sets.

4 Drain the cooked rice thoroughly. Add to the wok, and toss it over the heat with the vegetable and egg mixture for 3 minutes. Season the fried rice with salt and pepper to taste.

Rice and Vegetable Stir-Fry

If you have some leftover cooked rice and a few vegetables to spare, then you've got the basis for this quick and tasty side dish.

Serves 4

INGREDIENTS

$\frac{1}{2}$ cucumber
1 small red or yellow bell pepper
2 carrots
3 tbsp sunflower or peanut oil
2 scallions, sliced
1 garlic clove, crushed
$\frac{1}{4}$ small green cabbage, shredded
scant $\frac{1}{2}$ cup cup long-grain rice,
    cooked
2 tbsp light soy sauce
1 tbsp sesame oil
fresh parsley or cilantro, chopped
    (optional)
1 cup unsalted cashew nuts, almonds
    or peanuts
salt and freshly ground black pepper

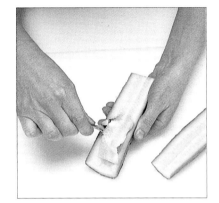

1 Halve the cucumber lengthwise and scoop out the seeds with a teaspoon. Slice the flesh diagonally. Set aside.

2 Cut the red or yellow pepper in half and remove the core and seeds. Slice the pepper thinly.

cucumber

scallions

carrots

garlic *bell pepper*

green cabbage

soy sauce

long-grain rice *sunflower oil* *parsley* *sesame oil* *cashew nuts*

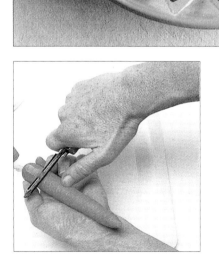

3 Peel the carrots and cut into thin slices. Heat the oil in a wok or large frying pan and stir-fry the sliced scallions, garlic, carrots and pepper for 3 minutes, until the vegetables are crisp but still tender.

4 Add the cabbage and cucumber and cook for another minute or two, until the leaves begin to wilt. Mix in the rice, soy sauce, sesame oil and seasoning. Reheat the mixture thoroughly, stirring and tossing all the time. Add the herbs, if using, and nuts. Check the seasoning and adjust if necessary. Serve piping hot.

Sticky Rice Parcels

This is a superb dish, packed with flavor. The parcels look pretty and are a pleasure to eat.

Serves 4

INGREDIENTS

1 lb (2⅔ cups) glutinous rice
4 tsp vegetable oil
1 tbsp dark soy sauce
¼ tsp five-spice powder
1 tbsp dry sherry
4 skinless and boneless chicken thighs, each cut into 4 pieces
8 dried Chinese mushrooms, soaked in hot water until soft
1 oz dried shrimp, soaked in hot water until soft
½ cup sliced drained canned bamboo shoots
1¼ cups chicken stock
2 tsp cornstarch
1 tbsp cold water
4 lotus leaves, soaked in warm water until soft
salt and ground white pepper

1 Rinse the glutinous rice until the water runs clear, then let soak in water for 2 hours. Drain and stir in 1 teaspoon of the oil and ½ teaspoon salt. Line a large steamer with a piece of clean cheesecloth. Transfer the rice into this. Cover and steam over boiling water for 45 minutes, stirring the rice from time to time and adding water if needed.

2 Mix the soy sauce, five-spice powder and sherry. Put the chicken pieces in a bowl, add the marinade, stir to coat, then cover and let marinate for 20 minutes.

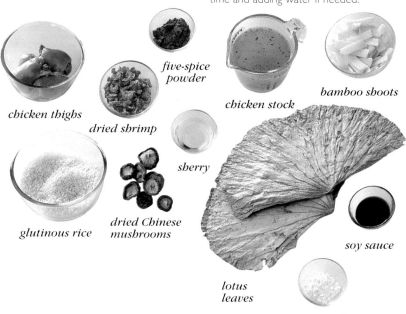

chicken thighs

dried shrimp

five-spice powder

chicken stock

bamboo shoots

glutinous rice

dried Chinese mushrooms

sherry

lotus leaves

soy sauce

cornstarch

3 Drain the Chinese mushrooms, cut out and discard the stems, then chop the caps roughly. Drain the dried shrimp. Heat the remaining oil in a nonstick frying pan or wok. Stir-fry the chicken for 2 minutes, then add the mushrooms, shrimp, bamboo shoots and stock. Simmer for 10 minutes.

4 Mix the cornstarch to a paste with the cold water. Add the mixture to the pan and cook, stirring, until the sauce has thickened. Add salt and white pepper to taste. Lift the cooked rice out of the steamer and let it cool slightly.

COOK'S TIP
The sticky rice parcels can be made several days in advance and simply resteamed before serving. If you do this, allow an extra 20 minutes' cooking time to ensure that the filling is hot.

5 With lightly dampened hands, divide the rice into four equal portions. Put half of one portion in the center of a lotus leaf. Spread it into a round and place a quarter of the chicken mixture on top. Cover with the remaining half portion of rice. Fold the leaf around the filling to make a neat rectangular parcel. Make three more parcels in the same way.

6 Prepare a steamer. Put the rice parcels, seam side down, in the steamer. Cover and steam over high heat for about 30 minutes. Serve the parcels on individual heated plates, inviting each diner to unwrap his or her own.

Fragrant Rice

A lovely, soft, fluffy rice dish, perfumed with fresh lemongrass.

Serves 4

INGREDIENTS
1 piece of lemongrass
2 limes
1 cup brown basmati rice
1 tbsp olive oil
1 onion, chopped
1 in piece of fresh ginger root, peeled and finely chopped
1½ tsp coriander seeds
1½ tsp cumin seeds
3 cups fresh vegetable stock or water
4 tbsp chopped fresh cilantro
lime wedges, to serve

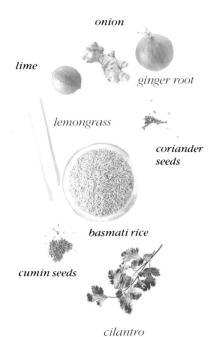

onion

lime

ginger root

lemongrass

coriander seeds

basmati rice

cumin seeds

cilantro

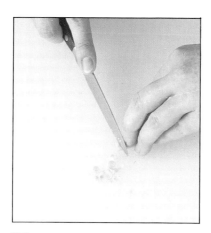

1 Finely chop the lemongrass.

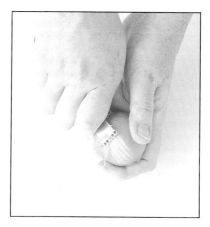

2 Remove the zest from the limes using a zester or fine grater.

3 Rinse the rice in plenty of cold water until the water runs clear. Drain through a sieve.

4 Heat the oil in a large pan and add the onion and spices, lemongrass and lime zest and cook gently for 2–3 minutes.

COOK'S TIP

Other varieties of rice, such as white basmati or long grain, can be used for this dish but you will need to adjust the cooking times accordingly.

5 Add the rice and cook for another minute, then add the stock and bring to a boil. Reduce the heat to very low and cover the pan. Cook gently for 30 minutes then check the rice. If it is still crunchy, cover the pan again and leave for a further 3–5 minutes. Remove from the heat.

6 Stir in the fresh cilantro, fluff up the grains, cover and leave for 10 minutes. Serve with lime wedges.

Fried Rice with Mushrooms

A tasty rice dish that is almost a meal in itself. Sesame oil adds a hint of nutty flavor.

Serves 4

INGREDIENTS
8 oz (1¼ cups) long-grain rice
1 tbsp vegetable oil
1 egg, lightly beaten
2 garlic cloves, crushed
6 oz (1¼ cups) white mushrooms, sliced
1 tbsp light soy sauce
¼ tsp salt
½ tsp sesame oil
cucumber matchsticks, to garnish

egg

garlic

long-grain rice

soy sauce

sesame oil

white mushrooms

1 Rinse the rice until the water runs clear, then drain thoroughly. Place it in a saucepan. Measure the depth of the rice against your index finger, then bring the finger up to just above the surface of the rice and add cold water to the same depth as the rice.

2 Bring the water to a boil. Stir, boil for a few minutes, then cover the pan. Lower the heat to a simmer and cook the rice gently for 5–8 minutes, until all the water has been absorbed. Remove the pan from the heat and, without lifting the lid, let sit for another 10 minutes before stirring or forking up the rice.

3 Heat 1 teaspoon of the vegetable oil in a nonstick frying pan or wok. Add the egg and cook, stirring with a chopstick or wooden spoon, until scrambled. Remove and set aside.

4 Heat the remaining vegetable oil in the pan or wok. Stir-fry the garlic for a few seconds, then add the mushrooms and stir-fry for 2 minutes, adding a little water, if needed, to prevent burning.

5 Stir in the cooked rice and cook for about 4 minutes, or until the rice is hot, stirring from time to time.

COOK'S TIP

When you cook rice this way, you may find there is a crust at the bottom of the pan. Don't worry; simply soak the crust in water for a couple of minutes to break it up, then drain it and fry it with the rest of the rice.

6 Add the scrambled egg, soy sauce, salt and sesame oil. Cook for 1 minute to heat through. Serve immediately, garnished with cucumber matchsticks.

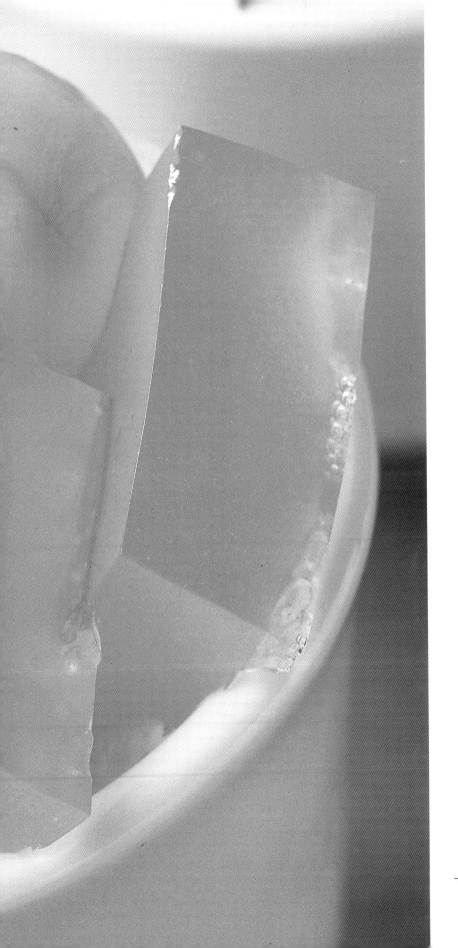

DESSERTS

Asian desserts are generally quite sweet—typical dishes include Pears with Ginger and Star Anise and Golden Steamed Sponge Cake. Most of the recipes in this section make the perfect finish to a well-balanced meal.

Pears with Ginger and Star Anise

Star anise and ginger give a refreshing twist to these poached pears. Serve them chilled.

Serves 4

INGREDIENTS
6 tbsp sugar
1¼ cups white dessert wine
thinly pared zest and juice of
    1 lemon
3-in piece of fresh ginger root,
    bruised
5 star anise
10 cloves
2½ cups cold water
6 slightly unripe pears
3 tbsp drained stem ginger
    in syrup, sliced
plain yogurt, to serve

stem ginger *white wine*

star anise *cloves*

lemon

ginger root

pears

sugar

1 Place the sugar, dessert wine, lemon zest and juice, fresh ginger root, star anise, cloves and water in a saucepan just large enough to hold the pears snugly in an upright position. Bring to a boil.

2 Meanwhile, peel the pears, leaving the stems intact. Add them to the wine mixture, making sure that they are totally immersed in the liquid.

3 Return the wine mixture to a boil, lower the heat, cover and simmer for 15–20 minutes, or until the pears are tender. Lift out the pears with a slotted spoon and place them in a heatproof dish. Boil the wine syrup rapidly until it is reduced by about half, then pour over the pears. Allow them to cool, then chill.

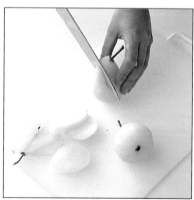

4 Cut the pears into thick slices and arrange the slices on four serving plates. Remove the ginger and whole spices from the wine sauce, stir in the stem ginger and spoon the sauce over the sliced pears. Serve with plain yogurt.

Golden Steamed Sponge Cake

Cakes are not traditionally served for dessert in China, but this light sponge is very popular with dim sum at lunchtime.

Serves 8

INGREDIENTS
1½ cups all-purpose flour
1 tsp baking powder
¼ tsp baking soda
3 large eggs
⅔ cup light brown sugar
3 tbsp walnut oil
2 tbsp golden or light corn syrup
1 tsp vanilla extract

brown sugar *eggs*

light corn syrup *walnut oil*

vanilla extract

all-purpose flour

baking powder

baking soda

1 Sift the flour, baking powder and baking soda into a bowl. Line a 7-inch-diameter bamboo steamer or cake pan with baking parchment.

2 In a mixing bowl, beat the eggs with the sugar until thick and frothy. Beat in the oil and syrup, then let the mixture stand for about 30 minutes.

3 Add the dry ingredients to the egg mixture with the vanilla extract, beating rapidly to form a thick batter.

4 Pour the batter into the parchment-lined steamer or pan. Cover and steam over boiling water for 30 minutes, or until the sponge springs back when gently pressed with a finger. Allow to cool for a few minutes before serving.

Mango and Coconut Stir-fry

Choose a ripe mango for this recipe. If you buy one that is a little under-ripe, leave it in a warm place for a day or two before using.

Serves 4

INGREDIENTS
¼ coconut
1 large, ripe mango
juice of 2 limes
zest of 2 limes, finely grated
1 tbsp sunflower oil
1 tbsp butter
1½ tbsp honey
sour cream or yogurt, to serve

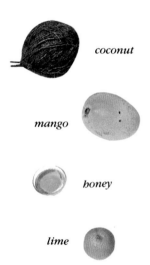

coconut

mango

honey

lime

COOK'S TIP

Because of the delicate taste of desserts, always make sure your wok has been scrupulously cleaned so there is no transference of flavors— a garlicky mango isn't quite the effect you want to achieve!

1 Prepare the coconut shreds by draining the milk from the coconut and shredding the flesh with a peeler.

2 Peel the mango. Cut the pit out of the middle of the fruit. Cut each half of the mango into slices.

3 Place the mango slices in a bowl and pour over the lime juice and zest, to marinate them.

4 Meanwhile, heat the wok, then add 2 tsp of the oil. When the oil is hot, add the butter. When the butter has melted, stir in the coconut shreds and stir-fry for 1–2 minutes until the coconut is golden brown. Remove and drain on paper towels. Wipe out the wok. Strain the mango slices, reserving the juice.

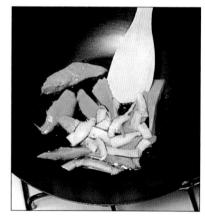

5 Heat the wok and add the remaining oil. When the oil is hot, add the mango and stir-fry for 1–2 minutes, then add the juice and allow to bubble and reduce for 1 minute. Then stir in the honey, sprinkle on the coconut and serve with sour cream or yogurt.

Watermelon, Ginger and Grapefruit Salad

This pretty, pink combination is very light and refreshing for any summer meal.

Serves 4

INGREDIENTS
1 lb/2 cups diced watermelon flesh
2 ruby or pink grapefruit
2 pieces stem ginger in syrup
2 tbsp stem ginger syrup

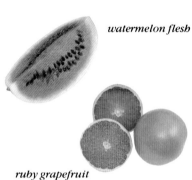

watermelon flesh

ruby grapefruit

stem ginger in syrup

COOK'S TIP

Toss the fruits gently—grapefruit segments will break up easily and the appearance of the dish will be spoiled.

1 Remove any seeds from the watermelon and cut into bite-sized chunks.

2 Using a small sharp knife, cut away all the peel and white pith from the grapefruits and carefully lift out the segments, catching any juice in a bowl.

3 Finely chop the ginger and place in a serving bowl with the melon cubes and grapefruit segments, adding the reserved juice.

4 Spoon over the ginger syrup and toss the fruits lightly to mix evenly. Chill before serving.

Mandarins in Orange-flower Syrup

Mandarins, tangerines, clementines, mineolas: any of these lovely citrus fruits are suitable for this recipe.

Serves 4

INGREDIENTS
10 mandarins
1 tbsp confectioners' sugar
2 tsp orange-flower water
1 tbsp chopped pistachio nuts

orange-flower water

pistachio nuts

mandarins

confectioners' sugar

COOK'S TIP

The mandarins look very attractive if you leave them whole, especially if there is a large quantity for a special occasion, but you may prefer to separate the segments.

1 Thinly pare a little of the colored zest from one mandarin and cut it into fine shreds for decoration. Squeeze the juice from two mandarins and reserve it.

2 Peel the remaining fruit, removing as much of the white pith as possible. Arrange the whole fruit in a wide dish.

3 Mix the reserved juice, sugar and orange-flower water and pour it over the fruit. Cover the dish and chill for at least an hour.

4 Blanch the shreds of zest in boiling water for 30 seconds. Drain, leave to cool and sprinkle them over the mandarins, with the pistachio nuts, to serve.

Caramelized Apples

A sweet, sticky dessert which is very quickly made,
and usually very quickly eaten!

Serves 4

INGREDIENTS
1½ lb sweet apples
½ cup sweet butter
1 oz fresh white bread crumbs
½ cup ground almonds
zest of 2 lemons, finely grated
4 tbsp corn syrup
4 tbsp thick strained yogurt,
   to serve

lemon

corn syrup

ground almonds

apple

1 Peel and core the apples.

2 Carefully cut the apples into ½ in-thick rings.

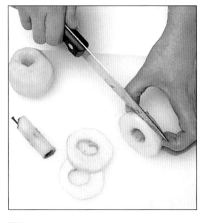

3 Heat the wok, then add the butter. When the butter has melted, add the apple rings and stir-fry for 4 minutes until golden and tender. Remove from the wok, reserving the butter. Add the bread crumbs to the hot butter and stir-fry for 1 minute.

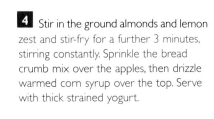

4 Stir in the ground almonds and lemon zest and stir-fry for a further 3 minutes, stirring constantly. Sprinkle the bread crumb mix over the apples, then drizzle warmed corn syrup over the top. Serve with thick strained yogurt.

Heavenly Jellies with Fruit

Delicate vanilla-flavored jelly, set with ribbons of egg white inside it, makes a delightful dessert served with fresh fruit.

Serves 6

INGREDIENTS
¼ oz agar-agar
3¾ cups boiling water
½ cup sugar
1 tsp vanilla extract
1 egg white, lightly beaten
8 oz (1½ cups) strawberries
1 lb fresh lychees, or 19-oz can
   lychees, drained

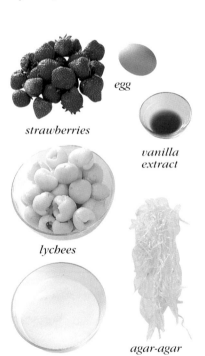

strawberries

egg

vanilla extract

lychees

agar-agar

sugar

1 Put the agar-agar in a saucepan. Add the boiling water, return to a boil and then lower the heat. Simmer the mixture for 10–15 minutes, stirring occasionally, until the agar-agar has dissolved completely.

2 Stir in the sugar. As soon as it has dissolved, strain the syrup through a fine sieve placed over a bowl. Return the mixture to the saucepan.

3 Immediately stir in the vanilla extract, then gently pour in the egg white in a steady stream; the heat will cook the egg. Stir once to distribute the threads of cooked egg white.

4 Pour the mixture into a shallow 11 x 7-inch baking pan and allow to cool. The jelly will set at room temperature, but will set faster and taste better if it is transferred to the refrigerator as soon as it has cooled completely.

5 Cut the strawberries in halves or quarters. If using fresh lychees, peel them and remove the pits. Divide the fruit among six small serving dishes or cups.

VARIATION
The jelly can be made with equal amounts of coconut milk and water and served with mangoes for a more tropical taste.

6 Turn the jelly out of the pan and cut it into diamond shapes to serve with the strawberries and lychees.

Sticky Rice with Tropical Fruit Topping

A popular dessert. Mangoes, with their delicate fragrance, sweet and sour flavor and velvety flesh, blend especially well with coconut sticky rice. You need to start preparing this dish the day before.

Serves 4

INGREDIENTS
²/₃ cup glutinous (sticky) rice
¾ cup thick coconut milk
3 tbsp sugar
pinch of salt
2 ripe mangoes
strips of lime zest, to decorate

glutinous rice

coconut milk

sugar

mangoes

lime

1 Rinse the glutinous rice thoroughly in several changes of cold water, then let soak overnight in a bowl of fresh, cold water. Drain and spread the rice in an even layer in a steamer lined with cheesecloth. Cover and steam for about 20 minutes, or until the grains of rice are tender.

2 Meanwhile, reserve 3 tablespoons of the top of the coconut milk and combine the rest with the sugar and salt in a saucepan. Bring to a boil, stirring until the sugar dissolves, then pour into a bowl and let cool a little. Turn the rice out into a bowl and pour the coconut mixture over it. Stir, then set aside for 10–15 minutes.

3 Peel the mangoes and cut the flesh into slices. Place on top of the rice and drizzle with the reserved coconut milk. Decorate with strips of lime zest.

VARIATION

If mangoes are not available, top the sticky rice pudding with a compote made by poaching dried apricots in water to cover for about 15 minutes.

Crisp Cinnamon Toasts

This recipe is very simple to prepare. You can use fancy cutters to create a pretty dessert or, if you do not have cutters, simply cut the crusts off the bread and cut it into little fingers.

Serves 4

INGREDIENTS
2 oz raisins
3 tbsp Grand Marnier
4 medium slices white bread
3 eggs, beaten
1 tbsp ground cinnamon
2 large oranges
1½ tbsp sunflower oil
2 tbsp sweet butter
1 tbsp raw sugar
thick strained yogurt, to serve

orange

raisins

egg

raw sugar

bread

1 Soak the raisins in the Grand Marnier for 10 minutes.

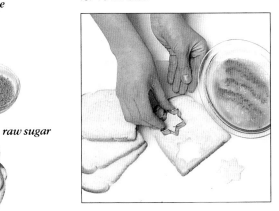

2 Cut the bread into shapes with a cutter. Place the shapes in a bowl with the eggs and cinnamon to soak.

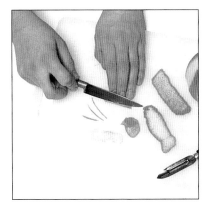

3 Peel the oranges. Remove any excess pith from the peel, then cut it into fine strips and blanch. Refresh it in cold water, then drain.

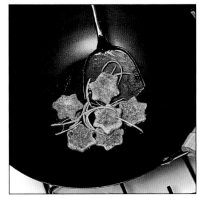

4 Strain the raisins. Heat the wok, then add the oil. When the oil is hot, stir in the butter until melted, then add the bread and fry, turning once, until golden brown. Stir in the raisins and orange zest, and sprinkle with sugar. Serve warm with thick strained yogurt.

Crêpes with Red Bean Paste

Sweetened red beans are often used in desserts because the color is associated with good luck.

Serves 4

INGREDIENTS
2½ cups cold water
6 oz (1 scant cup) adzuki beans,
    soaked overnight in cold water
1 cup all-purpose flour
1 large egg, lightly beaten
1¼ cups low-fat milk
1 tsp vegetable oil
6 tbsp sugar
½ tsp vanilla extract
plain yogurt, to serve (optional)

adzuki beans

egg

vegetable oil

vanilla extract

all-purpose flour

low-fat milk

sugar

COOK'S TIP
Both the crêpes and the bean paste can be made well in advance and kept frozen, ready for thawing, reheating and assembling when needed.

1 Bring the water to a boil in a saucepan. Drain the beans, add them to the pan and boil rapidly for 10 minutes. Skim off any scum from the surface of the liquid, then lower the heat, cover the pan and simmer, stirring occasionally, for 40 minutes, or until the beans are soft.

2 Meanwhile, make the crêpes. Sift the flour into a bowl and make a well in the center. Pour in the egg and half the milk. Beat, gradually drawing in the flour until it has all been incorporated. Beat in the remaining milk to make a smooth batter. Cover; set aside for 30 minutes.

3 Heat an 8-inch nonstick omelet pan and brush lightly with the vegetable oil. When the oil is hot, pour in a little of the batter, swirling the pan to cover the bottom thinly.

4 Cook the crêpe for 2 minutes, until the bottom has browned lightly. Flip the crêpe over and cook the second side for about 1 minute, then slide it onto a plate. Make seven more crêpes in the same way. Cover the crêpes with foil and keep hot.

5 When the beans are soft and all the water has been absorbed, tip them into a food processor and process until almost smooth. Add the sugar and vanilla extract and process briefly until the sugar has dissolved.

6 Spread a little of the bean paste on the center of each crêpe and fold them into flat parcels. Place on a baking sheet and cook under a hot broiler for a few minutes, until crisp and lightly toasted on each side. Serve immediately, on their own or with a little plain yogurt.

Mango and Ginger Clouds

The sweet, perfumed flavor of ripe mango combines beautifully with ginger, and this low-fat dessert makes the very most of them both.

Serves 6

INGREDIENTS
3 ripe mangoes
3 pieces stem ginger
3 tbsp stem ginger syrup
½ cup silken tofu
3 egg whites
6 pistachio nuts, chopped

tofu

mangoes

pistachio nuts

eggs

stem ginger in syrup

1 Cut the mangoes in half, remove the pits and peel them. Coarsely chop the flesh.

2 Put the mango flesh in a food processor bowl, with the ginger, syrup and tofu. Process until smooth. Spoon into a bowl.

VARIATIONS

This dessert can be served lightly frozen. If you prefer not to use ginger, omit the ginger pieces and syrup and use 3 tbsp honey instead.

3 Put the egg whites in a bowl and whisk them until they form soft peaks. Fold them lightly into the mango mixture.

4 Spoon the mixture into wide dishes or glasses and chill before serving, sprinkled with the chopped pistachios.

Pineapple Wedges with Allspice and Lime

Fresh pineapple is easy to prepare and always looks very festive, so this dish is perfect for easy entertaining.

Serves 4

INGREDIENTS
1 medium-size, ripe pineapple
1 lime
1 tbsp dark brown sugar
1 tsp ground allspice

ground allspice   *pineapple*

brown sugar

lime

VARIATION

For a quick hot dish, place the pineapple slices on a baking sheet, sprinkle them with the lime juice, sugar and allspice and place them under a hot broiler for 3–4 minutes, or until golden and bubbling. Sprinkle with shreds of lime zest and serve.

1 Cut the pineapple lengthwise into quarters and remove the core.

2 Loosen the flesh, by sliding a knife between the flesh and the skin. Cut the flesh into slices, leaving it on the skin.

3 Remove a few shreds of zest from the lime and then squeeze out the juice.

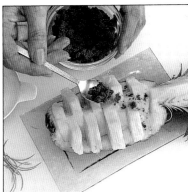

4 Sprinkle the pineapple with the lime juice and zest, sugar and allspice. Serve immediately, or chill for up to an hour.

Apples and Raspberries in Rose Pouchong Syrup

Inspiration for this dessert stems from the fact that the apple and the raspberry belong to the rose family. The subtle flavors are shared here in an infusion of rose-scented tea.

Serves 4

INGREDIENTS
1 tsp rose pouchong tea
1 tsp rose water (optional)
¼ cup sugar
1 tsp lemon juice
5 dessert apples
1½ cups fresh raspberries

tea

apples

sugar

raspberries

COOK'S TIP
If fresh raspberries are out of season, use the same weight of frozen fruit or a 14 oz can of well drained fruit.

1 Warm a large tea pot. Add the rose pouchong tea and 3¾ cups of boiling water together with the rose water, if using. Allow the tea to stand and steep for 4 minutes.

2 Measure the sugar and lemon juice into a stainless steel saucepan. Strain in the tea and stir to dissolve the sugar.

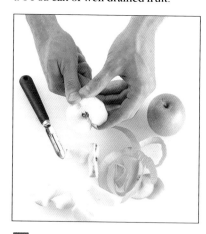

3 Peel and core the apples, then cut into quarters.

4 Poach the apples in the syrup for about 5 minutes.

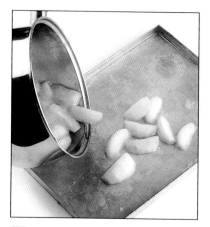

5 Transfer the apples and syrup to a large metal tray and leave to cool to room temperature.

6 Pour the cooled apples and syrup into a bowl, add the raspberries and mix to combine. Spoon into individual glass dishes or bowls and serve warm.

Tapioca and Taro Pudding

Usually served warm, this is a light and refreshing "soup," popular with children and adults alike.

Serves 4–6

INGREDIENTS
⅔ cup tapioca
6 cups cold water
8 oz taro
8 oz (⅔ cup) rock sugar
1¼ cups coconut milk

taro

rock sugar

coconut milk

tapioca

COOK'S TIP
Taro is a starchy tuber that tastes rather like a potato. If it is difficult to obtain, use sweet potato instead.

1 Rinse the tapioca, drain well, then put in a bowl with fresh water to cover. Let soak for 30 minutes.

2 Drain the tapioca and put it in a saucepan with 3¾ cups water. Bring to a boil, lower the heat and simmer for about 6 minutes, or until the tapioca is transparent. Drain, refresh under cold water, and drain again.

3 Peel the taro and cut it into diamond-shaped slices, about ½ inch thick. Pour the remaining water into a saucepan and bring it to a boil. Add the taro and cook for 10–15 minutes, or until it is just tender.

4 Using a slotted spoon, lift out half of the taro slices and set them aside. Continue to cook the remaining taro until it is very soft. Pour the taro and cooking liquid into a food processor and process until smooth.

5 Return the taro "soup" to the clean pan; stir in the sugar and simmer, stirring occasionally, until the sugar has dissolved.

6 Stir in the tapioca, reserved taro and coconut milk. Cook for a few minutes. Serve immediately in heated bowls or let cool and then chill before serving.

Mango Ice Cream with Exotic Fruit Salad

Exotic fruits are now widely available: choose your fruits with care, taking color, shape and taste into account, then use them to create your own still life next to a great mango and ginger ice cream.

Serves 6–8

INGREDIENTS
2 large ripe mangoes, peeled and coarsely chopped
2 pieces of stem ginger, plus 2 tablespoons ginger syrup
1 cup heavy cream

FOR THE DECORATION
1 star fruit, thickly sliced
1 mango, peeled and cut into wedges
1 cantaloupe melon, cut into wedges
6 strawberries, cut in half
1 small bunch frosted grapes

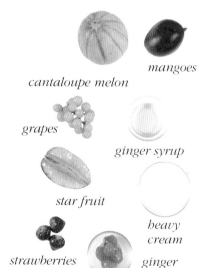

cantaloupe melon   *mangoes*

grapes

ginger syrup

star fruit

heavy cream

strawberries   *ginger*

1 Purée the mangoes in a food processor or blender with the ginger and ginger syrup, until smooth.

2 Whip the cream in a large bowl until it forms fairly firm peaks. Fold in the mango purée.

3 Transfer to a freezer container. Freeze for 2 hours, then beat with an electric mixer until smooth. Return the ice cream to the freezer and freeze for at least 8 hours. Alternatively, freeze in an ice cream maker according to the manufacturer's instructions.

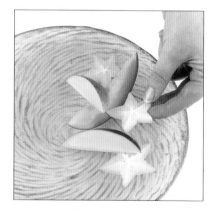

4 About 30 minutes before serving, transfer the ice cream to the refrigerator to soften slightly. Arrange the prepared fruit on individual plates and add two scoops of ice cream to each one.

Caramel Rice

Indulge in this version of the classic sweet rice dish, which is particularly delicious when served with fresh fruit.

Serves 4

INGREDIENTS

¹/₃ cup short-grain rice
5 tbsp raw or brown sugar
pinch of salt
14-oz can evaporated milk
   with enough water added
   to make 2½ cups
pat of butter
1 small fresh pineapple
2 crisp eating apples
2 tsp lemon juice

short-grain
rice

pineapple

lemon

eating
apples

evaporated
milk

raw sugar

butter

1 Preheat the oven to 300°F. Put the rice in a sieve and wash under cold running water. Drain well and put into a lightly greased soufflé dish. Add 2 tablespoons of the sugar and the salt to the dish. Pour in the diluted evaporated milk and stir gently. Dot the surface of the rice with butter. Bake for 2 hours, then set aside to cool for about 30 minutes.

COOK'S TIP

Rice pudding is a popular dessert in many different countries, so the possibilities for making different variations are endless. You can try sprinkling grated nutmeg on top instead of sugar, or decorate it with chopped almonds, pistachio nuts and ground cinnamon. Rice pudding is also delicious chilled.

2 Meanwhile, peel, core and slice the pineapple and apples, then cut the pineapple into chunks. Toss the fruit in the lemon juice and set aside.

3 Preheat the broiler and sprinkle the remaining sugar over the rice pudding. Broil for 5 minutes, until the sugar has caramelized. Let the rice stand for 5 minutes to allow the caramel to harden, then serve with the fresh fruit.

Blushing Pears

Pears poached in rosé wine and sweet spices absorb all the subtle flavors and turn a soft pink color.

Serves 6

INGREDIENTS
6 firm pears
1¼ cups rosé wine
⅔ cup cranberry or clear apple
   juice
strip of thinly pared orange zest
1 cinnamon stick
4 whole cloves
1 bay leaf
5 tbsp superfine sugar
small bay leaves, to decorate

wine

pears   *cranberry juice*

cinnamon

sugar

orange

1 Thinly peel the pears with a sharp knife or vegetable peeler, leaving the stems attached.

2 Pour the wine and cranberry or apple juice into a large heavy pan. Add the orange zest, cinnamon stick, cloves, bay leaf and sugar.

3 Heat gently, stirring all the time until the sugar has dissolved. Add the pears and stand them upright in the pan. Pour in enough cold water to barely cover them. Cover and cook very gently for 20–30 minutes, or until just tender, turning and basting occasionally.

4 Using a slotted spoon, gently lift the pears out of the syrup and transfer to a serving dish.

5 Bring the syrup to a boil and boil rapidly for 10–15 minutes, or until it has reduced by half.

COOK'S TIP

Check the pears by piercing with a skewer or sharp knife towards the end of the poaching time because some may cook more quickly than others.

6 Strain the syrup and pour over the pears. Serve hot or well-chilled, decorated with bay leaves.

Tropical Fruit Phyllo Clusters

These fruity phyllo clusters are ideal for a family treat or a dinner party dessert. They are delicious served either hot or cold.

Makes 8

INGREDIENTS

1 banana, sliced
1 small mango, peeled, pitted
  and diced
lemon juice, to sprinkle
1 small cooking apple,
  coarsely grated
6 fresh or dried dates, pitted
  and chopped
2 oz dried pineapple, chopped
¼ cup golden raisins
¼ cup light brown sugar
1 tsp ground mixed spice
8 sheets phyllo pastry
2 tbsp sunflower oil
confectioners' sugar, to serve

mango   *banana*   *lemon juice*

cooking apple   *dried dates*   *dried pineapple*

golden raisins   *light brown sugar*   *ground mixed spice*

sunflower oil

phyllo pastry

1 Preheat the oven to 400°F. Line a baking sheet with wax paper. Toss the banana and mango with lemon juice to prevent discoloration.

2 Add the apple, dates, pineapple, raisins, sugar and spice and mix well.

3 To make each fruit cluster: cut each sheet of phyllo pastry in half crosswise to make 2 squares/rectangles (16 squares in total). Lightly brush two squares of pastry with oil and place one on top of the other at a 45° angle.

4 Spoon some fruit filling into the center, gather the pastry up over the filling and secure with string. Place the cluster on the prepared baking sheet and lightly brush all over with oil.

5 Repeat with the remaining pastry squares and filling to make a total of 8 fruit clusters. Bake for 25–30 minutes, until golden brown and crisp.

6 Carefully snip and remove the string from each cluster and serve hot or cold, dusted with sifted confectioners' sugar.

Mango and Lime Sorbet in Lime Shells

This tartly flavored sorbet looks pretty served in the lime shells, but is also good served in scoops for a more traditional presentation.

Serves 4

INGREDIENTS
4 large limes
1 medium-size ripe mango
½ tbsp powdered gelatin
2 egg whites
1 tbsp granulated artificial sweetener
lime zest strips, to decorate

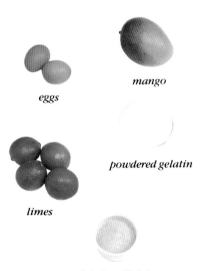

mango

eggs

powdered gelatin

limes

granulated artificial sweetener

COOK'S TIP

If you have lime juice left over from this recipe, it will freeze well for future use. Pour it into a small freezer container, seal it and freeze for up to six months. Or freeze it in useful measured amounts; pour 1 tbsp into each compartment of an ice-cube tray and freeze the tray.

1 Cut a thick slice from the top of each of the limes, and then cut a thin slice from the bottom end so that the limes will stand upright. Squeeze out the juice from the limes. Use a small knife to remove all the membrane from the center.

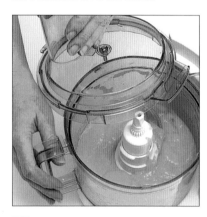

2 Halve, pit, peel and chop the mango and purée the flesh in a food processor with 2 tbsp of the lime juice. Dissolve the gelatin in 3 tbsp of lime juice and stir it into the mango mixture.

3 Whisk the egg whites until they hold soft peaks. Whisk in the sweetener. Fold the egg white mixture quickly into the mango mixture. Spoon the sorbet into the lime shells. Any leftover sorbet that will not fit into the lime shells can be frozen in small ramekins.

4 Place the filled shells in the freezer until the sorbet is firm. Cover the shells with plastic wrap. Before serving, allow the shells to stand at room temperature for about 10 minutes; decorate them with strips of lime zest.

Thai-style Dessert

Black glutinous rice, also known as black sticky rice, makes a tasty pudding. It tastes nutty, rather like wild rice.

Serves 4-6

INGREDIENTS
scant 1 cup black glutinous (sticky) rice
2 tbsp light brown sugar
2 cups coconut milk
3 eggs
2 tbsp sugar

light brown sugar

coconut milk

eggs

black glutinous rice

sugar

1 Combine the glutinous rice, brown sugar, half the coconut milk and 1 cup of water in a saucepan. Bring to a boil, then simmer, stirring from time to time, for 15–20 minutes, or until the rice has absorbed most of the liquid. Preheat the oven to 300°F.

3 Place the dish or ramekins in a baking pan. Pour in enough boiling water to come halfway up the sides of the dish or ramekins. Cover with foil and bake for 35 minutes to 1 hour, or until the custard is set. Serve warm or cold, whichever you prefer.

VARIATION

Black glutinous rice is popular in South-east Asia for sweet dishes. Its character contributes to the delicious flavor of this dessert. Use white glutinous rice if the black grain is difficult to find.

2 Transfer the rice to one large ovenproof dish or divide it among individual ramekins. Mix the eggs, remaining coconut milk and sugar in a bowl. Strain and pour the mixture evenly over the rice mixture.

COOK'S TIP

A pan of water in which dishes of delicate food are cooked is known as a bain-marie.

Toffee Apples

All the flavor and texture of this classic Chinese dessert without the fuss and fat of deep-frying.

Serves 6

INGREDIENTS
2 tbsp butter
6 tbsp cold water
6 tbsp all-purpose flour
1 egg
1 eating apple
1 tsp vegetable oil
¾ cup sugar
1 tsp sesame seeds

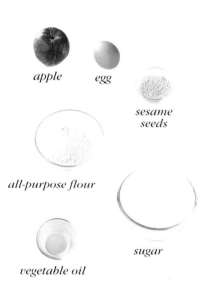

apple   *egg*

sesame seeds

all-purpose flour

sugar

vegetable oil

1 Preheat the oven to 400°F. Put the butter and water in a small saucepan and bring to a boil. Remove from the heat and add the flour all at once. Stir vigorously until the mixture forms a smooth paste that leaves the sides of the pan clean.

2 Cool the choux paste for 5 minutes, then beat in the egg, mixing thoroughly until the mixture is smooth and glossy.

3 Peel and core the apple and cut it into ½-inch chunks.

4 Stir the apple into the choux paste and place teaspoonfuls on a dampened nonstick baking sheet. Bake for 20–25 minutes, until brown and crisp on the outside but still soft inside.

5 When the pastries are cooked, heat the oil in a saucepan over low heat and add the sugar. Cook, without stirring, until the sugar has melted and turned golden brown, then sprinkle in the sesame seeds. Remove the pan from the heat.

COOK'S TIP
A slightly unripe banana can be used instead of an apple.

6 Have ready a bowl of ice water. Add the pastries, a few at a time, to the caramel and toss to coat them all over. Remove with a slotted spoon and quickly dip in the ice water to set the caramel; drain well. Serve immediately. If the caramel becomes too thick before all the pastries have been coated, reheat it gently until it liquefies before continuing.

INDEX

ACKNOWLEDGEMENTS

The publishers would like to thank the following for their contributions to this book:

RECIPES

Janet Brinkworth, Matthew Drennan, Sarah Edmonds, Christine France, Silvana Franco, Shirley Gill, Shehzad Husain, Kathy Man, Annie Nichols, Anne Sheasby, Steven Wheeler, Elizabeth Wolf-Cohen

PHOTOGRAPHERS

William Adams-Lingwood, Karl Adamson, James Duncan, Michelle Garrett, David Jordan, Amanda Heywood, Ferguson Hill, Don Last, Thomas Odulate

STYLISTS

Madeleine Brehaut, Clare Hunt, Kay McGlone, Fiona Tillett, Judy Williams

HOME ECONOMISTS

Kit Chan, Sarah Edmonds, Lucy McElvie, Stephen Wheeler